CLAUDIA HELLMANN · CLAUDINE WEBER-HOF

ON LOCATION

CITIES OF THE WORLD IN FILM

WITH A FOREWORD BY WIM WENDERS

CONTENTS

Wim Wenders: The Urban Landscape 4
The Magic of Movie Locations 6

1. BEIJING
The Last Emperor 8

2. BERLIN
CITY OF CONTRASTS 12
One, Two, Three 16
Wings of Desire 18
Run Lola Run 20

3. CHICAGO
GANGSTERS AND THE BLUES 22
The Blues Brothers 26
The Untouchables 28

4. FLORENCE
PICTURE PERFECT IN TUSCANY 30
A Room with a View 34
Much Ado About Nothing 36

5. HAVANA
FLAIR OF THE CARIBBEAN 38
Strawberry and Chocolate 42
Buena Vista Social Club 44

6. HONG KONG
MOVIE CAPITAL OF THE FAR EAST 46
Enter the Dragon 50
Chungking Express 52
Chinese Box 54

7. LAS VEGAS
SIN CITY IN THE DESERT 56
Ocean's Eleven 60
Casino 62
Fear and Loathing in Las Vegas 64

8. LONDON
SEX, SPIES AND HIGH SOCIETY 66
A Clockwork Orange 70
Notting Hill 72
Shakespeare in Love 74
Bridget Jones's Diary 76
Harry Potter and the Sorcerer's Stone 78

9. LOS ANGELES
MOVIE CAPITAL OF THE WORLD 80
Rebel Without a Cause 84
The Graduate 86
Chinatown 88
Blade Runner 90
L.A. Story 92
L.A. Confidential 94
Mulholland Drive 96

10. NEW YORK

THE ULTIMATE URBAN BACKDROP 98
Breakfast at Tiffany's 102
The French Connection 104
Taxi Driver 106
Manhattan 108
When Harry Met Sally 110
25th Hour 112

11. PARIS

CITY OF LOVE, CITY OF FILM 114
Breathless 118
The Lovers on the Bridge 120
Dangerous Liaisons 122
The Fabulous Destiny of Amélie Poulain 124

12. PRAGUE

OLD-WORLD CHARM IN CENTRAL EUROPE 126
Amadeus 130
Mission: Impossible 132

13. ROME

ALL ROADS LEAD TO CINECITTÀ 134
Roman Holiday 138
La Dolce Vita 140
The Talented Mr. Ripley 142

14. SAN FRANCISCO

ALLURE AND INTRIGUE BY THE BAY 144
Vertigo 148
Bullitt 150
Dirty Harry 152
Mrs. Doubtfire 154
The Rock 156

15. SYDNEY

HOLLYWOOD DOWN UNDER 158
Muriel's Wedding 162
The Matrix 164

16. TOKYO

WHERE QUIET MEETS CHAOS 166
Godzilla 170
Lost in Translation 172

17. VENICE

UNDER THE SPELL OF A SINKING CITY 174
Summertime 178
Death in Venice 180
Don't Look Now 182
The Wings of the Dove 184
Bread and Tulips 186

18. VIENNA

The Third Man 188

Index and Credits 190

THE URBAN LANDSCAPE

By Wim Wenders

I am neither an architect nor a city planner. If I have any qualification to discuss "landscape from a point of view of images" as a filmmaker, then it is because I am a traveler, because I have lived and worked in different cities in the world, because I have put up my camera in front of many landscapes, urban landscapes mostly, but also deserts.

Film is a city art. It has come into existence and it has blossomed together with the great cities of the world since the end of the nineteenth century. Movies have witnessed their development from the quiet places they were at the turn of the century to the bursting and hectic megacities of today. Movies have witnessed their destruction during the wars, they have seen the skyscrapers go up, they have seen the ghettos, they have seen the rich get richer and the poor poorer. The cinema is the mirror of the twentieth-century city and twentieth-century mankind. Like no other art, films are the historic documents of our time. The seventh art, as it is called, is able to get to the essence of things, to capture the climate and the currents of their time, to express the hopes and the fears, and the desires as a popular mass language like nothing else. Movies are also entertainment, and entertainment is the city's need par excellence. The cities just had to create cinema, cinema belongs in the city, and it reflects the city. (...)

A street, or a house front, or a mountain, or a bridge, or a river, or whatever, is not just "background." Each also has a history, a "personality," an identity that deserves to be tak-

en seriously. All influence the human characters in the front of the frame, they create a mood, a sense of time, a certain emotion. They can be ugly or beautiful, old or young. But they are certainly "present," and even for an actor that's all that counts. They deserve to be taken seriously. I worked in Australia over the last few years and I was fortunate to get to know the Aboriginal people a little bit. I was amazed to learn that for them every landscape formation embodies some figure from a mythical past. Every hill, every rock carries a "story" that is related to their "dreamtime." And that reminded me that as a child I had similar beliefs. A tree was not just a tree, but also a ghost, and the shapes of houses were like the shapes of faces. There were serious houses, and sinister houses, and friendly houses. A river could be frightening, but also soothing. Streets had personalities. There were some that I rather avoided and others that were good company. Mountains and shapes of the horizon were like definitions of certain longings or nostalgia, and I vividly remember my fear of a big rock in a forest called the "sitting woman." For a child, landscapes and cityscapes evoke emotions, associations, ideas, stories. We tend to forget

that when we grow old. Basically, I think, we just learn to protect ourselves from the knowledge of our childhood, when we lived so much more out of our eyes, and when what we saw defined our sense of "self" and of "home."

Talking about that rock, another rock comes to mind. I lived in New York for a while, in an apartment facing Central Park. When I walked out of the building I faced a big black piece of rock that stood there just at the edge of the park. It had different colors depending on the weather. It was the sort of granite rock that the whole city was built on. And each time I looked at it, it gave me a feeling of orientation. It was so much older than the whole city around. It was solid. In a strange way it gave me confidence because I felt connected. I remember that I once smiled at it, as if it were a friend. It gave me some form of rest, it made me calmer. The city that I now live in is entirely built on sand, very white sand, and every now and then you can see a piece of it, even if it is only on a construction site. But that sand, too, gives me a feeling of connectedness, even of security. It tells me where I am. Of course, the buildings do that, too, but in a different way.

Berlin is a very peculiar city because it was so terribly damaged during the war, and because the division of the city continued this destruction. Berlin has a lot of empty spaces. You see houses that are completely blank on one side, because the neighboring house was destroyed and is still missing. These bleak walls are called *Brandmauern* ("fire-walls") and you don't see them much in other cities. These empty spaces feel like wounds, and I like the city for its wounds. They show its history better than any history book or document. When I shot *Wings of Desire* I realized that I was always looking for these empty spaces, these no man's lands. I felt the city defined itself much better where it was empty than where it was full. (...)

Cities do not tell stories. But they can tell history. Cities can show and carry their *history*; they can make it visible, or they can hide it. They can open your eyes, like movies, or they can close them. They can leave you abused, or they can nourish your imagination.

Top: **An angel's view: Cassiel (Otto Sander) sits on the shoulder of the winged goddess atop the Column of Victory in Berlin, a scene from *Wings of Desire* by director Wim Wenders.**

LET FAMOUS FILMS BE YOUR TRAVEL GUIDE

Of cinema's various delights, film locations may be the most charming. An address, a certain city square, or even a particular park bench can close the gap between the dream world of movies and everyday life, and the effect is pure magic.

Try it out. Peer into the shop window on the spot where Audrey Hepburn stood in *Breakfast at Tiffany's.* If *The Third Man's* postwar milieu thrills you, ride the Vienna Ferris wheel where Holly Martins confronted Harry Lime, or descend into the sewer system for a subterranean tour. Hit the Italian nightclub where Matt Damon and Jude Law partied Americano-style in *The Talented Mr. Ripley,* or see Rome through the eyes of the original Paparazzo in Fellini's new-wave epic *La Dolce Vita.* Hoping for a ticket on the Hogwarts Express? We've got the London coordinates for the barrier you'll have to pass through to climb aboard for a *Harry Potter* adventure.

From nostalgic classics to contemporary box-office hits, certain movies successfully marry plot to place in a way that is singularly memorable. This volume, with its mix of movie stills and striking contemporary photos, offers a lighthearted, round-the-world tour so you, too, can go "on location." Once you visit a few famous film locations, you'll experience a thrilling sense of déjà vu: the feeling of having "been there before" in the movies. If this is your first time, you'll be surprised how powerful this can be. Traveling to film locations is an adventure that allows you to live powerful cinematic experiences all over again – even if it's just from the comfort of your sofa.

Think of Griffith Observatory in the Hollywood Hills and feel the tension of James Dean's knife fight in *Rebel Without a Cause.* Remember how Bill Murray hoped for "More Than This" at a karaoke bar in Tokyo's neon-lit Shinjuku district. Nowhere else in the world would he – or you, the viewer – have felt quite so

Lost in Translation. Each time you stroll across a much-filmed city square or sit down to dine in a café that you know well from the movies, the thrill of discovery is new. No one will ever be able to eat at Katz's Deli again without reliving *When Harry Met Sally,* as permanent a New York landmark as the riverside view of Queensboro Bridge from Woody Allen's *Manhattan.*

The magic of places and unforgettable locations in film provided the inspiration for *On Location – Cities of the World in Film.* First we selected movies that were box office hits or critical successes that also did a good job of capturing the atmosphere of a big city. Then we went to work tracking down film locations throughout Europe, North America, Australia, and the Far East over the course of several years, researching and photographing the best and most famous with the help of colleagues from the film and tourism industries. With a bit of detective work we were able to uncover a world of information on film locations that we think readers would enjoy visiting in person. To us, compiling this volume is proof of the addictive nature of film location travel.

As with any project worth doing, it is only as good as the people who helped shape it. We had the best. The authors would like to thank Gerhard Grubbe of Grubbe Media, whose courage and creativity helped see this book through to completion; China expert and San Francisco resident Daniela Yew, for her chapters on Hong Kong and the Bay City; designers Marion Sauer and Johannes Reiner of the Vor-Zeichen agency in Munich, for making *On Location* the visual celebration it is; Peter Mere-

dith, a good friend and talented editor with an exacting eye for detail who improved our manuscript and caught our mistakes; Julia Fuchshuber, photo editor and friend who accompanied us on so many trips; Dr. Andreas Lindner, whose belief in sticking with worthwhile projects has been an inspiration to us. His library of travel guides and periodicals at his publishing house and web portal, WorldGuide (www.wgpremium.com), has brought us a wealth of ideas and information over the last few years.

This book lives through its photographs. To David Weber we owe our thanks for most of the original photography; he was extremely generous in devoting his time and resources to making this project a success. We would also like to thank the seasoned photographers Volkmar Janicke and Hans Engels, who contributed beautiful shots of cities in the Far East and Cuba, respectively. Martin Bunzendahl did a great job of photographing the Chicago locations. Sally Trussler of Brunel University near London was kind enough to send us photos of the locations from *A Clockwork Orange.*

Our correspondents around the world were a great source of support and information gathering. They include Luke Brighty of Sydney Movie Tours and author of *Sydney Movie Locations* and the upcoming book *A Film Location Guide to Australia,* who offered great advice as well as location tips and photos of his hometown; Dr. Brigitte Timmermann, author of *The Third Man: In the Footsteps of a Movie Classic,* who leads Orson Welles fans on the adventuresome Vienna Walks & Talks; Arthur Duncan of Arthur Duncan Journey, whose sojourns to Beijing cleared

The authors on the trail of famous movie locations in Paris.

up many details for our chapter on the Forbidden City; Karina Shima and Ami Endo of the Park Hyatt in Tokyo; Jürgen Biefang of Small Fish Productions in Munich, who offered advice and mentorship; Kara Alaimo of the Mayor's Office of Film, Theatre and Broadcasting in New York City who helped us to track down film locations in the Big Apple; Chris Lopata and Deb Seager in New York City; Arnie Bernstein, author of *Hollywood on Lake Michigan* and Chicago film aficionado; Rusty and Margit Loudermilk in Los Angeles, whose help during a photo trip was invaluable; and Valentina Lori and Francesca Breetzke of Wim Wenders's firm Reverse Angle Pictures, Berlin, for their assistance with film stills and locations in the German capital.

Whether you're bound for New York, Paris, or Hong Kong, traveling can be so much more fun if you follow your cinematic fancy. Bon voyage!

Claudia Hellmann and Claudine Weber-Hof

THE LAST EMPEROR

Director Bernardo Bertolucci

Starring John Lone, Joan Chen, Peter O'Toole, Ruocheng Ying, Victor Wong, Dennis Dun, Ryuichi Sakamoto, Maggie Han

France/Italy/UK, 1987

A poet of the Tang dynasty once wrote, "Unless you have witnessed the magnificence of the royal palace, you can never sense the dignity of the emperor." Director Bernardo Bertolucci was very much in agreement with this philosophy. To tell the story of China's last emperor, Bertolucci knew he would have to film from within the Forbidden City itself. In an unprecedented move, the Chinese government granted the world-renowned Italian filmmaker full access to the centuries-old complex, home to the Ming and Qing emperors from the 15th century until 1924 and known as the Imperial Palace Museum ever since. The result: a cinematic masterpiece.

The first feature film shot in the **Forbidden City** is as breathtaking as it is heartbreaking. The epic story of the life of the last Qing Dynasty emperor, Aisin-Gioro Pu-Yi (1906-67), swept the Oscars, taking nine awards, including Best Picture, Best Director, Best Cinematography, and Best Screenplay Based on Material from Another Medium. Bertolucci, best known for *The Conformist* (1970) and his sultry *Last Tango in Paris* (1972), looked to primary sources for inspiration and information. Using two books – Pu-Yi's autobiography *From Emperor to Citizen* and imperial tutor Reginald Johnston's *Twilight in the Forbidden City* – he was able to recreate the excess and eccentricity of a dying form of governance. As co-author of the screenplay, he paced the whole film, even the opening scenes, to reflect the lockstep nature of court life.

Above: **Peter O'Toole as Reginald Johnston with his imperial student.**
Left: **A view over the Forbidden City in the heart of Beijing.**

Born into the royal family in 1906, Aisin-Gioro Pu-Yi (played as an adult by John Lone) is selected by the fearsome, dying empress dowager, Tzu-Hsi, to ascend the Dragon Throne. Protocol required the toddler's removal from his biological mother into the hands of a nanny. Mother and child pass through the imposing **Meridian Gate** of the fortress-like Forbidden City, and young beauty Ar Mo (Jade Go) is charged with the responsibil-

The spectacular coronation before the Hall of Supreme Harmony. The child king is proclaimed "Lord of Ten Thousand Years" in an elaborate ceremony.

ities of the royal surrogate: to raise the next "Son of Heaven." But nothing could prepare the child for the demanding traditional formalities about to take place.

The Qing dynasty was almost three centuries old in 1908, but the spectacular coronation of Pu-Yi as the "Lord of Ten Thousand Years" takes on an unexpectedly light-hearted air. Flaunting convention, the child-king stands bolt upright on the gilt throne of the **Hall of Supreme Harmony** and flaps his royal yellow shirtsleeves. Priests cluck at his impertinence, his father wags a disapproving finger, but nothing can be done. To the consternation of all officialdom, the giggling three-year-old bounds down from his holy seat and runs to the door to lift a fluttering curtain over his head. Suddenly the scope of his power is revealed: Armies of eunuchs, monks, and servants kneel before him in the sprawling court between the **Gate of Supreme Harmony and the Hall of Supreme Harmony,** the highest and most important structure of the entire Forbidden City. The prince dashes amid the ranks of kowtowing subjects, searching for the source of a mysterious sound. A kindly soldier presents him with an unexpected gift: a singing cricket in a box.

Tradition held that the Chinese emperor was the mediator between heaven and earth, but in the early 20th century, times

were changing. Outside walls up to 50 feet (15 meters) thick reputedly guarding 800 buildings comprising 9,999 treasure-filled rooms, trouble was afoot. In 1912 China was declared a republic, and the new government forced Pu-Yi, known also as Emperor Hsuan T'ung, to abdicate. He was permitted to stay within the Forbidden City, ostensibly for his own protection, a fact that Pu-Yi learned by accident during a state visit from his mother and his brother, Pu Chieh. The entourage arrives at his **private quarters** to the **east of the Hall of Supreme Harmony,** an area marked with imperial yellow embellishments. His only ally until then had been his nanny, Ar Mo, but after he is spied nuzzling her in the **Garden of Harmonious Pleasures** at the **Summer Palace** on the edge of town, she is banned from his presence.

Perhaps the happiest development of his last years in the Forbidden City is the arrival of his British tutor, Reginald Johnston (Peter O'Toole).

The Summer Palace on Kunming Lake.

A golden lion stands watch in the Imperial Palace.

Breaking with tradition, Johnston makes sure the emperor gets badly needed eyeglasses, and even a bike. Pu-Yi recognizes that his status is growing even more precarious when he decides one day to attempt to leave the Forbidden City. He races from his imperial quarters and crosses the bridged courtyard before the **Gate of Supreme Harmony,** the largest open space in the sprawling complex. He tries to make it out of the **Meridian Gate,** and yet his own guard rushes forward to block his exit. Despite vociferous threats, the turbaned soldiers forbid him to leave.

Convinced he can somehow escape by alliance, he weds Wan Jung, nicknamed Elizabeth (Joan Chen), at the **Hall of Celestial and Terrestrial Union,** a square building between the main Harmony group and the northern wall. The real bridal chamber would have been in the **Hall of Earthly Peace,** also the empress's quarters, a room not used for filming. Pu-Yi does not leave his royal prison, however, until 1924. He, his wife, and First Concubine Wen Hsiu (Vivian Wu) are playing tennis in the courtyard east of the Hall of Middle Harmony when soldiers rush onto the terrace of the **Hall of Preserving Harmony.** The heavily armed delegation announces that he will finally be granted his dearest wish: to exit the Forbidden City by way of the Meridian Gate, to depart in style in a convoy of the latest-model motorcars. Free at last. Or so the young royal thinks.

Pu-Yi and his skeleton court flee to the northeastern Chinese city of Tientsin to live a life of luxury. At a great party, filmed at the Palace of Congress of the spa town of Salsomaggiore Terme near Parma, the northern Italian birthplace of Bertolucci, "Henry" Pu-Yi croons "Am I Blue" and makes plans with Elizabeth to see the West, maybe Monte Carlo, perhaps Paris. When the radio announces that Chiang Kai-Shek has taken Shanghai, the guests applaud loudly. Henry's deposers have themselves been deposed, and a shady Japanese fellow in a tuxedo suggests they hurry to his embassy. In a poor choice of alliances, Pu-Yi agrees to become the emperor of Manchukuo, Japanese-held Manchuria. Once dethroned, he was imprisoned in Russia for several years, then returned to China where he spent another decade in jail. Finally, in 1959, he was released into the population at large, a simple gardener and citizen of the People's Republic of China, a different man than he was born to be.

The year is 1967, the last of Pu-Yi's life. He approaches the Forbidden City, buys a ticket and passes through the **Meridian Gate** to the **Hall of Supreme Harmony** where he was made emperor all those years ago. He steps over the heavy ropes cordoning off the building, and ascends a grand stair. He even takes a few tentative steps up the white marble slab resplendent in imperial dragons, a privilege of the emperor himself. As he approaches the gilded throne between two golden pillars and flanked by green urns and bronze storks, the watchman's tiny son hails him, saying that it is not allowed to climb the steps to the throne. Pu-Yi's argument is short and sweet, and made with a smile: He was once emperor of all China, he explains, and he can even prove it – he left something here as a boy. He searches behind and below the throne cushions, and pulls forth a small box. The boy inspects it, then looks up to find Pu-Yi gone. The boy opens the box carefully, and the magical truth of Pu-Yi's heritage is revealed.

Top: **Pu-Yi can't wait to leave the Forbidden City, the palace complex that has become his prison. Actor John Lone plays the frustrated ruler who finally gets a chance at a life beyond the palace walls during a tennis match, when soldiers rush onto the terrace of the Hall of Preserving Harmony** (bottom).

GUGONG
(Imperial Palace or Forbidden City)

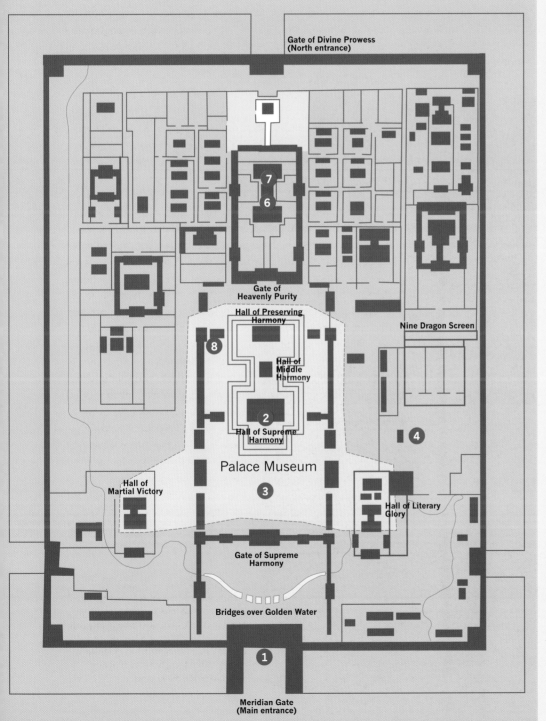

Gate of Divine Prowess
(North entrance)

7

6

Gate of
Heavenly Purity

Hall of Preserving
Harmony

8

Hall of
Middle
Harmony

Nine Dragon Screen

2

Hall of Supreme
Harmony

Palace Museum

Hall of
Martial Victory

3

4

Hall of Literary
Glory

Gate of Supreme
Harmony

Bridges over Golden Water

1

Meridian Gate
(Main entrance)

5

The Last Emperor

1. Meridian Gate
2. Hall of Supreme Harmony
3. Courtyard between the Gate of Supreme Harmony and the Hall of Supreme Harmony
4. Private quarters to the east of the Hall of Supreme Harmony
5. Garden of Harmonious Pleasures at the Summer Palace, northwest of the Forbidden City
6. Hall of Celestial and Terrestrial Union between the main Harmony group and the northern palace wall
7. Hall of Earthly Peace
8. Courtyard east of the Hall of Middle Harmony

Top: **The unforgettable wedding night.**
Bottom: **It's easy to get lost among the countless gates and halls of the Forbidden City.**

Berlin today is a prosperous, flourishing metropolis. Not so in 1946 when Roberto Rossellini filmed *Germania, anno zero* amid the ruins of the city.

CITY OF CONTRASTS

From glamorous imperial city to the heart of the Third Reich; from a *Trümmerstadt,* or city in ruins, to a city divided during the Cold War; and from a modern metropolis to the capital of reunited Germany, Berlin can look back upon an eventful century. The city's numerous metamorphoses between misery and might are reflected in the movies that have been filmed in and around it. Over the decades, these productions have left us a kaleidoscope of personalities and achievements that have made Berlin a major film city.

Germany's movie pioneers may not have achieved the fame of Thomas Edison or the Lumière brothers, but Berlin did nurture several important forerunners in the film business, men such as Ottomar Anschütz and Max Skladanowsky. At the end of the 19th century, early projectors such as the *Anschütz'sche Schnellseher* lured thousands of curious visitors to fairs and carnivals. Oskar Messter, the father of German film, developed and produced everything himself, from cameras and film stock to copying machines and projectors, and was the first to produce films for domestic commercial distribution. In 1896 he opened the first Berlin movie theater

at Unter den Linden 21, a very respectable address. The early "theaters of living pictures" were oddities, but grand, palatial cinemas soon followed.

Army commander Erich Ludendorff is credited with developing the German film industry into a highly organized production process, an area that the more "creative" inventors were slow to explore. Universum-Film-A.G. (Ufa) was founded under his aegis in 1917, and though originally set up to produce propaganda, it churned out countless popular movies after World War I. The vast studio complexes in Babelsberg near Potsdam, close to Berlin, and later also in Berlin's Tempelhof quarter were the largest of their kind in Europe, attracting famous directors such as Fritz Lang and Friedrich Wilhelm Murnau, who made the city into the hub of German filmmaking. Masterpieces such as *The Cabinet of Dr. Caligari* (1919) and *Metropolis* (1927) were filmed here. Even international silent movie stars such as Asta Nielsen and Greta Garbo came to Berlin.

Magnificent palaces such as the Uffizi in Florence and entire streets from cities around the world were rebuilt in painstaking detail in Babelsberg, but it was the real metropolis just outside the studio doors that provided the greatest inspiration. "The dingiest corner of Berlin inspires me a thousand times more than all this expensive cardboard India," wrote critic Alfred Polgar in 1921. Berlin as a set would play an increasingly important role in film. *Berlin – Die Sinfonie der Großstadt* (1927) captured life in the metropolis in a vibrant filmic collage. In the film version of Alfred Döblin's novel *Berlin Alexanderplatz* (1931), the restlessness and traffic of modern city life frightens Franz Biberkopf (Heinrich George), who complains after having been released from prison that he can't find his way anymore.

Time and again filmmakers portray Berlin as a place of great hope that never failed to disappoint. The communist love story *Kuhle Wampe* (1932), co-authored by playwright Bertolt Brecht, showed the impoverished conditions of a worker's family during the Depression. By contrast, Nazi films such as *Zwei in einer großen Stadt* (1941) and *Großstadtmelodie* (1943) present the city in an overly positive light. When the National Socialists came to power, Berlin lost a great many distinguished filmmakers to emigration. Some of them, like Billy Wilder and

Fritz Lang, as well as actors Peter Lorre and Marlene Dietrich, would rise to international stardom in Hollywood.

The idealized myth of Berlin as conjured by Leni Riefenstahl in her films of the Olympics and in *Triumph of the Will* (1935) was all but dead at the end of World War II. Instead, filmmakers were eager to train the cameras on the destroyed city. Roberto Rossellini captured shocking images of emaciated children in rags amidst mountains of debris in *Germany, Year Zero* (*Germania, anno zero,* 1947). Ruins, postwar suffering, and the fate of war returnees were themes central to German films such as *Somewhere in Berlin* (1946) and *... and the Sky Above Us* (1947).

Berlin's original Lola: Marlene Dietrich thrilled audiences as a dancer named Lola long before the film *Run Lola Run* was made.

Even Hollywood filmed among the rubble: The Berlin airlift provided the authentic background for the German-American love story *The Big Lift* (1950) starring Montgomery Clift. Carol Reed, who had already created a dramatic masterpiece in postwar Vienna, tried to repeat the success of *The Third Man* (1949) with his atmospheric spy thriller *The Man Between* (1953), in which the destroyed city serves as the backdrop for a mysterious love story that takes place between the occupied sectors of Berlin.

Zwei unter Millionen (1961), the story of an East Berlin truck driver and his wife who try their luck on the West side of the city, was shot just before the Wall went up. The filming of Billy Wilder's East-West satire *One, Two, Three* (1961) would be interrupted by the building of the Wall, and the absurdities of a divided city would fascinate filmmakers for decades. On both sides of the Wall, directors created films about the pain of separation, such as the GDR production of *The Divided Heaven* (1964) or Wim Wenders's masterful *Wings of Desire* (1987). Despite obvious ideological differences, the parallels of life on both sides of the Wall were impossible to overlook: The wild *Halbstarken* of West Berlin seen in *Teenage Wolfpack* (1956) found their counterpart in East Berlin in the rebellious gangs of *Berlin Ecke Schönhauser* (1957). Berlin's lost youth is remembered most poignantly in *Christiane F. – We Children from Bahnhof Zoo* (1981), a film about a young drug addict, filmed on location in the city.

Kiosks are standard fare in Berlin, and appear in films like *Wings of Desire*.

The reunification of Germany on October 3, 1990, opened another chapter in the history of Berlin while simultaneously sparking a boom in film production. These days the city is focused on a bright future as the re-established German capital, and is no longer so burdened by the weight of its past. In the mid-nineties, Berlin was Europe's biggest building site. While modern skyscrapers shot up at the famous Potsdamer Platz intersection, *Life Is All You Get* (1997) depicted a rather ordinary Berlin with grim concrete apartment blocks and cramped supermarkets. For his box-office hit *Run Lola Run* (1998), Tom Tykwer also ignored the Berlin of glossy tourist brochures and instead captured the fast pace that is the essence of the new city. Enough time has passed for nostalgia to develop for the good old days of the GDR, with comedies like *Sun Alley* (1999) and *Good Bye Lenin!* (2003) taking a wry look at bittersweet memories of life in East Berlin.

Designed by architect Helmut Jahn, the Sony Center on Potsdamer Platz with its dramatically lit tent roof is a symbol of the new Berlin.

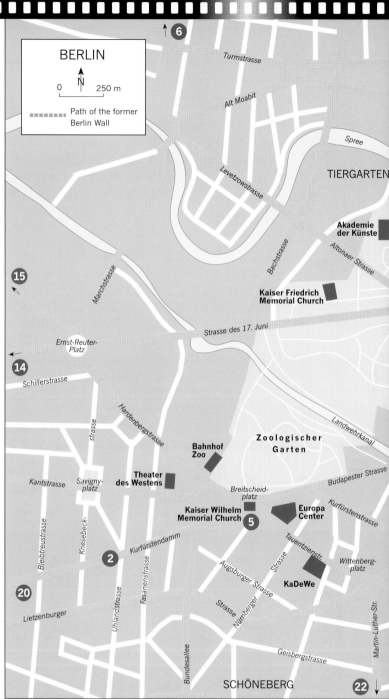

One, Two, Three

1. Former Anhalter Train Station, Askanischer Platz
2. The quarter between the Tiergarten, the Ku'damm, and the Column of Victory
3. Tempelhof Airport
4. Brandenburg Gate

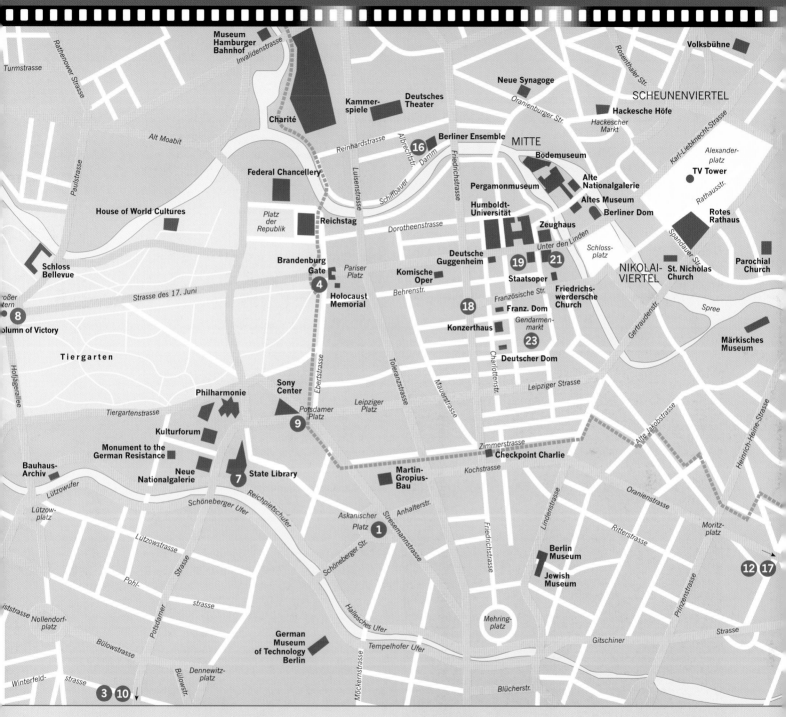

Museum Hamburger Bahnhof

Invalidenstrasse

Turmstrasse

Rathenower Strasse

Kammer-spiele

Deutsches Theater

Charité

Neue Synagoge

Oranienburger Str.

SCHEUNENVIERTEL

Hackesche Höfe

Hackescher Markt

Volksbühne

Rosenthaler Str.

Alt Moabit

Paulstrasse

Reinhardstrasse

Luisenstrasse

Schiffbauer

Albrechtstr.

Damm

16

Berliner Ensemble

MITTE

Bodemuseum

Pergamonmuseum

Alte Nationalgalerie

Altes Museum

Berliner Dom

Karl-Liebknecht-Strasse

Alexander-platz

TV Tower

Rathausstr.

Federal Chancellery

House of World Cultures

Platz der Republik

Reichstag

Dorotheenstrasse

Humboldt-Universität

Zeughaus

Unter den Linden

Schloss-platz

NIKOLAI-VIERTEL

Rotes Rathaus

Spandauer Str.

St. Nicholas Church

Parochial Church

Schloss Bellevue

Großer tern

Strasse des 17. Juni

Brandenburg Gate

Pariser Platz

4

Holocaust Memorial

Deutsche Guggenheim

Komische Oper

Behrenstr.

19

Staatsoper

21

Friedrichs-werdersche Church

Gertraudenstr.

Spree

Märkisches Museum

8

olumn of Victory

Tiergarten

Hofjägerallee

Ebertstrasse

Toleranzstrasse

Leipziger Platz

18

Französische Str.

Franz. Dom

Gendarmen-markt

23

Deutscher Dom

Mauerstrasse

Charlottenstr.

Leipziger Strasse

Philharmonie

Sony Center

Potsdamer Platz

9

Tiergartenstrasse

Kulturforum

Monument to the German Resistance

Neue Nationalgalerie

7

State Library

Konzerthaus

Zimmerstrasse

Checkpoint Charlie

Kochstrasse

Lindenstrasse

Alte Jakobstrasse

Oranienstrasse

Ritterstrasse

Heinrich-Heine-Strasse

Moritz-platz

Bauhaus-Archiv

Lützowufer

Lützow-platz

Reichpietschufer

Schöneberger Ufer

Martin-Gropius-Bau

Askanischer Platz

1

Stresemannstrasse

Anhalterstr.

Friedrichstrasse

Berlin Museum

Jewish Museum

12 **17**

Prinzenstrasse

Lützowstrasse

Strasse

Pohl-strasse

Potsdamer Strasse

Schöneberger Str.

Hallesches Ufer

Tempelhofer Ufer

Möckernstrasse

Mehring-platz

ststrasse

Winterfeld-strasse

Nollendorf-platz

Bülowstrasse

Dennewitz-platz

Bülowstr.

German Museum of Technology Berlin

Blücherstr.

Gitschiner

Strasse

3 **10**

Wings of Desire

5. Kaiser Wilhelm Memorial Church, Breitscheidplatz
6. Tegel Airport
7. State Library, Potsdamer Strasse 33
8. Column of Victory
9. Potsdamer Platz
10. Air-raid bunkers, Pallasstrasse 28-30
11. Former Anhalter Train Station (see point 1)
12. Fragment of the Berlin Wall on Waldemarstrasse
13. Kaisersaal of the former Grand Hotel Esplanade, Bellevuestrasse 1, Potsdamer Platz (see point 9)

Run Lola Run

14. Deutsche Oper subway station
15. Corner of Osnabrücker Strasse and Tauroggener Strasse
16. Lola's house, Albrechtstrasse 13
17. Oberbaumbrücke
18. Französische Strasse subway station
19. Bebelplatz, Behrenstrasse 37
20. Oberfinanzdirektion on Kurfürstenplatz, Kurfürstendamm 193/194
21. Kronprinzenpalais, Unter den Linden 3
22. Schöneberg Town Hall at John-F.-Kennedy-Platz
23. Gendarmenmarkt

ONE, TWO, THREE

Director Billy Wilder

Starring James Cagney, Horst Buchholz,
Pamela Tiffin, Liselotte Pulver, Leon Askin

USA, 1961

Few films have parodied world politics as convincingly as this irreverent East-West satire. Fast-paced and funny, just like the screwball comedies of the thirties but with a hefty pinch of *realpolitik*, *One, Two, Three* is brimming with gags that show mercy to no man: Russians, Germans, Yankees, Southerners, capitalists, communists, and former Nazis – the film pokes fun at one and all. This is the story of C.R. MacNamara (James Cagney), a businessman who runs a Coca-Cola factory in West Berlin and who is asked to look after his Atlanta-based boss's daughter for a few weeks. When spoiled Southern belle Scarlett (Pamela Tiffin) falls in love with the East Berlin communist Otto Ludwig Piffl (Horst Buchholz) and decides to elope with him to Moscow, MacNamara tries everything to break up the unlikely match. Plan B is to transform uncouth Comrade Piffl in record time – one, two, three – into a presentable capitalist while at the same time capturing the soda market on the other side of the Iron Curtain.

Fleeing the Nazis because of his Jewish heritage, Billy Wilder had left Berlin in 1933 and become a world-famous director in Hollywood. He returned as early as 1945 to a bombed-out Berlin as the chief of the movie section of the American Information Control Division, an experience he would recycle in the comedy *A Foreign Affair* (1948), starring Marlene Dietrich. He returned to Berlin once again at the height of the Cold War to film *One, Two, Three*. Several key scenes in the film, including a wild car

A German Marilyn Monroe: Ingeborg (Lilo Pulver), MacNamara's secretary, knows how to turn all the Russians' heads.

MacNamara (James Cagney) senses trouble when he picks up the boss's daughter at Tempelhof Airport, where planes bearing relief supplies for West Berlin landed during the Berlin Airlift of 1948 to 1949.

Racing his motorcycle, Piffl (Horst Buchholz) speeds past the original dividing line between East and West Berlin, the stately Brandenburg Gate.

chase with MacNamara and three Russian functionaries, are set in East Berlin, but were actually filmed on the west side of the city. The filmmaker considered the derelict houses in the run-down district by the bombed-out **Anhalter Train Station** at **Askanischer Platz** to be the perfect stand-in for the city's Soviet sector. In contrast, shots of the newly renovated quarter between the **Tiergarten,** the **Ku'damm,** and the **Column of Victory** (Siegessäule) made the new West Berlin shine. **Tempelhof Airport,** which became famous during the Berlin airlift of 1948-49, also featured in some scenes.

Location shots centered on the neoclassical **Brandenburg Gate,** an important junction between East and West. In mid-July, Wilder declared to a reporter from *The New York Times* that, "Those people over there have no sense of humor. That's their trouble. So now we'll get back at them. Just wait and see what we shoot on the other side." Numerous curious onlookers showed up when Berlin-born Horst "Hotte" Buchholz was filmed speeding a motorcycle up and down the Strasse des 17. Juni between the Column of Victory and the Brandenburg Gate. Unfortunately, the Soviet sector started a few yards in front of the Gate, and attempts to obtain permission to film Buchholz riding under the blocky triumphal arch turned into a battle between Wilder and the East Berlin authorities. Officials had initially granted the permit, but when they spotted a balloon with the words "Russki Go Home" attached to the motorcycle – part of the film's plot, in which MacNamara tries to get the young communist into trouble – they were not amused. East German policemen arrived and watched the filming through binoculars from the other side of the Gate. Wilder scored an early victory when he phoned the Russian commander and explained that such images would give movie-going audiences around the world an unflattering impression of his sector as a cold-hearted police state. The armed *Volkspolizisten* disap-

peared from the scene, but the authorities demanded to see the script. "Nonsense," quipped Wilder. "I wouldn't even show the script to President Kennedy."

The saucy director had no idea what dramatic developments lay in store. On August 13, 1961, he and the rest of the world would watch helplessly as barriers and barbed wire went up around the Gate. The Berlin Wall was being born, and its rise could easily have put an end to the half-finished film. But Wilder moved the rest of the shooting to the Bavaria Studios in Munich, where he had a life-size copy of the Brandenburg Gate built. When *One, Two, Three* opened in the theaters that December, however, the flick's black humor failed to go over well with German audiences. "What breaks our hearts, Billy Wilder finds funny," wrote an outraged reviewer in the *Berliner Zeitung*. It wasn't until after its re-release in the mid-eighties and after the fall of the Berlin Wall a few years later that Wilder's satire about the absurdities of the Cold War achieved its enduring cult status.

Wilder chose the run-down neighborhood near the bombed-out Anhalter Train Station – once Germany's largest railway terminus – as one of the film's backdrops.

WINGS OF DESIRE

Der Himmel über Berlin

Director   Wim Wenders

Starring   Bruno Ganz, Otto Sander, Solveig Dommartin, Peter Falk, Curt Bois

Germany/France, 1987

The angel Damiel takes in the city from the Column of Victory. Mere mortals can also view Berlin from a platform by the winged goddess's feet.

Wim Wenders's hauntingly beautiful portrait of Berlin is the story of an angel who has had enough of observing life on earth and yearns to experience it for himself. It was filmed in various Berlin neighborhoods during the late eighties, a time when the city was still divided into East and West. Wenders asserted later in an interview that no other metropolis had ever worked so well for him as a symbol and as a place of history and of survival.

The film approaches Berlin from the heavens, a dramatic aerial descent in stark black and white. The angel Damiel (Bruno Ganz) is atop the famous bombed-out bell tower of the **Kaiser Wilhelm Memorial Church** (Kaiser-Wilhelm-Gedächtnis-kirche) on **Breitscheidplatz** observing the traffic chaos below. He listens in on snippets of human conversation from his eyrie high above the city, a cacophony of voices that provides aural accompaniment to the camera's dramatic sweep as it follows the path of an airplane descending through the clouds to **Tegel Airport.** Once past the old television tower, cinematographer Henri Alekan takes the audience on an eavesdropping tour of the housing blocks of **Charlottenburg,** peeking into apartments and listening to the thoughts of their inhabitants. Single thoughts swell to a mighty chorus as angels wander invisibly amongst visitors reading at the **State Library** (Berliner Staatsbibliothek) at **Potsdamer Strasse 33,** close to Potsdam Platz. Only when seated on the shoulder of the winged goddess atop the **Column of Victory** (Siegessäule) some 230 feet (70 meters) above it all do the angels take an occasional break from the city's bustle.

During his sojourns in the Berlin streets, the angel Damiel is entranced at the sight of a pretty French trapeze artist named Marion (Solveig Dommartin), soaring as though winged through the heights of a circus tent on an abandoned lot on Friedrich-strasse. In the meantime, the angel Cassiel (Otto Sander) accompanies an aged Berlin poet named Homer (Curt Bois) on his quest for Potsdamer Platz. The once lively square that the old man finds is now nothing more than a barren wasteland, devoid of the shops and cafés he knew in happier days. History has since made these touching scenes at the no man's land of **Potsdamer Platz** impossible to repeat. After the fall of the Berlin Wall in 1989, the historic urban crossroads became the focus of ambitious developers and architects whose glass-and-steel skyscrapers now form a major business and entertainment complex anchored by the tent-roofed Sony Center. Visitors flock to shop and enjoy the sidewalk cafés in this popular quarter.

The more Damiel sees of the city, the stronger his resolve becomes to trade in his ethereal existence for a shot at being human. An encounter with an American actor and former angel (Peter Falk) proves to be a turning point. Falk is in the midst of making a film about Berlin during the Third Reich at the old **air-raid bunkers** at **Pallasstrasse 28-30.** To underscore the visual connection between then and now, Wenders intersperses his narrative with images of the bombed-out city in the aftermath of World War II. At a street vendor's stand on the down-at-heel site of the **Anhalter Train Station,** a once important railway hub whose postwar ruins were demolished in 1960, Falk begins to tell Damiel about the small pleasures of being human, from drinking coffee to rubbing his hands together to warm them.

Damiel is convinced that he must become human, and at the **Berlin Wall**'s notorious "death strip," where many would-be escapees were shot as they attempted to cross over to the West, the "fallen angel" awakens as a man. Here Wenders switches the film from black and white to color so that the audience, like Damiel, suddenly sees the world in an entirely new way. "Wall artist" Thierry Noir famously painted a long row of faces on this fragment of the Wall on **Waldemarstrasse** in Kreuzberg, a section of the concrete barrier that was unfortunately demolished during the reconstruction of Berlin. However, various artists have brightly decorated a 0.8-mile (1.3-kilometer) stretch of the Berlin Wall known as the East Side Gallery on the former East-West border between the Oberbaumbrücke and Ostbahnhof, a bizarre showplace along the River Spree that claims – somewhat credibly – to be the largest open-air gallery in the world.

At the Berlin Wall, Damiel experiences what it is to be human for the first time.

Above: **Wenders filmed on a vacant lot behind the Anhalter Train Station.**
Below: **Damiel and Marion fall in love in the Kaisersaal.**

The circus has since moved on, and yet intuitively Damiel knows where to find the trapeze artist Marion. At a bar adjacent to the **Kaisersaal** of the former **Grand Hotel Esplanade** at **Bellevue-strasse 1,** Damiel and Marion look into one another's eyes for the very first time. The renowned hotel on **Potsdamer Platz** was beloved of high society in the twenties and thirties but was almost completely destroyed during World War II. Miraculously, some of the hotel's opulent rooms, such as the stuccoed Kaisersaal, or Emperor's Hall, escaped devastation, and hosted parties and concerts after the war. When the Sony Center rose on this site in the mid-1990s, engineers hydraulically lifted the 1,400-ton, two-story Kaisersaal on air cushions and shifted it some 250 feet (75 meters) to the west. Today it has been transformed into a restaurant encased in glass at the edge of the futuristic Sony Center, forming a bridge between the past and the present.

The lovers make a final appearance at the Kaisersaal in the closing sequences of the film. Damiel is now fully human and holds a cable as Marion swings weightlessly through the air. The former angel's declaration after just one day as a member of mankind is an homage to life and love, and the discoveries he made in Berlin: "She took me home last night and I found my home. I know now what no angel knows."

RUN LOLA RUN

Lola rennt

Director	Tom Tykwer
Starring	Franka Potente, Moritz Bleibtreu, Herbert Knaup, Nina Petri, Armin Rohde, Joachim Król

Germany, 1998

Girl power, Berlin-style: Lola's sprint through the city earned returns at the box office worldwide.

A woman with flaming red hair sprints for a full eighty minutes through the streets of Berlin – it's not every day that a film creates such a memorable image. Director Tom Tykwer shot Germany's biggest surprise hit and major film export of 1998 on a budget of only $1.8 million, using pulsating techno music, dizzying camera angles, and visual stunts such as animated sequences to create a cinematic computer-game effect. The heroine, Lola (Franka Potente, also known from *The Bourne Identity,* 2002), must master an urban obstacle course at lightning speed, a sheer impossibility for fans who take to the streets of Berlin only to discover that her zigzagging, cross-town journey is a miracle of creative editing.

The movie opens under high pressure: Lola has twenty minutes to raise an outrageous sum of money to save her boyfriend Manni (Moritz Bleibtreu). The hapless wannabe gangster is a cash courier for an organized car theft ring, but he's not very good at it. He forgot a shopping bag stuffed with the cash on a train at the **Deutsche Oper subway station** shortly before the handover. In desperation he calls Lola, using a phone booth specially erected for the film at the **corner of Osna-**

Manni (Moritz Bleibtreu) is counting on Lola to get him out of a jam.

brücker Strasse and Tauroggener Strasse. If anybody can help him, he figures, she can. The audience is left to wonder how. A thousand cartoon thoughts race through Lola's head – and all at once she begins to run. She rushes out of the apartment, down the stairwell, and out of the house at **Albrechtstrasse 13** north of Schifferbaudamm on the River Spree.

Lola dashes through the brick arcades of the **Oberbaumbrücke,** a bridge that connects the East and West sides of the city. She races further west on Friedrichstrasse and past the **Französische Strasse subway station** before turning left onto Behrenstrasse. Lola's destination and only hope is the Deutsche Transfer Bank on **Bebelplatz,** where her father is the manager. Financial institutions generally like to avoid even the appearance of being connected with robbery at all costs, so here the director had to improvise. The facade of the historic building at **Behrenstrasse 37** at the south end of **Bebelplatz** stood in as the fictitious bank in the film. Ironically, its history is intimately connected with finance. The late 19th-century building that was part of Frederick the Great's "Forum Fridericianum" was home to the Dresdner Bank until 1945, when it became the Central

Bank of the German Democratic Republic. Now the location is home to the new Grand Hotel de Rome, part of the deluxe Rocco Forte group.

For interior shots of the bank, part of the regional tax authority, the **Oberfinanzdirektion on Kurfürstenplatz** at **Kurfürstendamm 193/194,** was transformed into a counter area. Lola begs her father to give her the money to no avail. Manni's nerves are increasingly on edge back at the phone booth. Finally, instead of heeding Lola's plea not to budge until she gets there, he pulls out a pistol and attempts to rob the Bolle supermarket across the street, a grocery store that in reality is a

The turrets and arcades of the Oberbaum Bridge (left) and Lola's house on Albrechtstrasse.

branch of the well-known Spar chain. Lola finally arrives at the meeting point empty-handed. But if it seems like the movie will end after this fast-paced twenty-five-minute segment, think again. Before the shocking conclusion has a chance to sink in, director Tykwer reaches into his bag of tricks and sends his heroine back to square one. The red telephone rings, and like an updated version of *Groundhog Day* (1993), Lola starts the dash to save Manni's life again.

Here's where the games really begin: Even though Lola takes practically the same route through Berlin, everything is just slightly different, with tiny details and coincidences that transform the big picture as Dinah Washington's 1950s ballad "What a Difference a Day Makes" swells in the background. When Tykwer rolls the dice for a third and final time, fate sends Lola running across Karl-Marx-Allee and Unter den Linden to a casino. The exterior is the neoclassical **Kronprinzenpalais** at **Unter den Linden 3,** the former residence of Crown Prince Frederick II across from the Deutsches Historisches Museum. The scenes where Lola bets all her money on one card were shot at the **Schöneberg Town Hall** at **John-F.-Kennedy-Platz.** Simultaneously, Manni manages to turn his original mistake around completely, and Tykwer gets to surprise the audience with a happy ending after all.

Shortly after the film's release, Tykwer claimed that *Run Lola Run* could easily have been set in a different city — New York, perhaps, or Beijing. And yet you could argue that no city was changing quite as rapidly just then as Berlin, renowned in the late nineties as "Europe's biggest building site." Tykwer deliberately avoided shooting tourist landmarks such as the Kaiser Wilhelm Memorial Church on Breitscheidplatz, known locally as the Gedächtniskirche, or the iconic Brandenburg Gate. Not even the famous **Gendarmenmarkt,** which the camera captures from above as Lola crosses, is recognizable until the film's third sequence. Tykwer presented Berlin as a nondescript modern metropolis, but the city is unmistakable as the vibrant German capital for those who know and love it.

Stately Schöneberg Town Hall was transformed into a casino during filming.

The whole crazy affair kicks off at the Deutsche Oper subway station.

CHICAGO

GANGSTERS AND THE BLUES

While countless directors have filmed on location in Chicago, most have served up the city as a side order rather than the main dish. *The Blues Brothers* and *The Untouchables* are two blockbuster exceptions, films that bring "sweet home Chicago" to life using two of the city's most enduring topics, the blues and the mob. Filmmakers' favorite cityscapes for creating an authentic, Windy City effect have long included the ever-shrinking musical mecca at the Maxwell Street Market and gangster hangouts near upscale South La Salle Street.

Charlie Chaplin made movies in Chicago before heading out to Hollywood.

But what about all those other famous flicks that boast a Chicago connection? Scenes from Alfred Hitchcock's *North by Northwest* (1959) were filmed at Chicago's Ambassador East Hotel and La Salle Street Station, but the most memorable sequences were shot in rural Bakersfield, California, and New York City. *The Sting* (1973), a classic gangster tale starring Paul Newman and Robert Redford, was filmed primarily on Universal Studios' famous Main Street back lot, an outdoor set made up to look like the Chicago Loop. Eighties' brat-pack movies such as *Risky Business* (1983), *Sixteen Candles* (1984), and *The Breakfast Club* (1985) all have a Chicago angle, but their settings are so suburban that with one exception, *Ferris Bueller's Day Off* (1986), the choice of city seems incidental. The same is true of Macaulay Culkin as Kevin McCallister, the cute kid who is left disastrously *Home Alone* (1990) in Winnetka, a bedroom community north of the city.

Not so with *Hoop Dreams* (1994), Steve James and Frederick Marx's critically acclaimed documentary about two inner-city Chicago athletes who dream of making it big in pro basketball. P. J. Hogan sends Julia Roberts to swank hotels and restaurants in downtown Chi-town in *My Best Friend's Wedding* (1997), his directorial follow-up to a much better party in Sydney at *Muriel's Wedding* (1994). Robbie Coltrane and Paul Newman look on with mixed feelings as Kevin Costner and Robin Wright Penn fall in love between the newsroom of the *Chicago Tribune* and North Carolina's Outer Banks, all because of a *Message in a Bottle* (1999).

Chicago had a close connection with film long before its popularity as a location in the nineties. Most filmmakers joined the cinematic gold rush around 1909 when the first studios opened in L.A., but the "City of Big Shoulders" didn't shrug off its interest in the movies. The Midwestern railway hub dubbed "the hog butcher to the world" for its meatpacking industry had been remaking itself as a stylish metropolis since before the turn of the century, when the great fire of 1871 laid waste to much of the city. As Arnie Bernstein details in his book *Hollywood on Lake Michigan*, Thomas Edison may not have been ready to introduce his newly invented peep-show machine – a forerunner to the modern projector – at the World's Columbian Exposition in 1893, but early movie mania still hit Chicago hard.

Renowned as the blues capital of the world, Chicago is home to some of the genre's best clubs.

In *The Blues Brothers* as in real life, Pilgrim Baptist Church on Chicago's South Side is a magnet for fans of gospel music.

The mastermind of the World's Columbian Exposition, architect Daniel Burnham, was an unwitting accomplice in making Chicago an attractive film location. Burnham and partner John W. Root pioneered the steel-frame high-rise, a technological coup that would change the city and the world. Suddenly architects could build higher than ever before. Skyscrapers started shooting up along the shores of Lake Michigan, with Burnham's road map for urban development providing a clear vision for parks, boulevards, and beautiful buildings. Highlights include the *Chicago Tribune* headquarters, Union Station, and art déco towers like the Chicago Board of Trade. As marble lobbies, gilt columns, and mosaicked board rooms soared into the clouds, so did Chicago's expectations of keeping its place as the "Second City" after New York. As if on cue, the 1960s delivered a sleek, new generation of skyscrapers, thanks to German-American design guru Mies van der Rohe and his ideological scions at the Illinois Institute of Technology. The trend caught on with American corporations and their architects, forever altering the city's look. The Richard J. Daley Center, the Sears Tower, and the John Hancock Center round out an inspired skyline that attracts Hollywood and hometown directors alike to film romance, comedy, and murder mysteries in the Midwestern metropolis.

Pretty backdrops were one thing, but actual moviemaking was quite another, and Chicago's role as a studio town was a brief but colorful endeavor. Charlie Chaplin failed to see Chicago's longstanding allure, and his first thought after completing *His New Job* (1915) with the Essanay Film Manufacturing Company was how to get out of town – fast. Had Chaplin signed on with "Colonel" William Selig instead of heading out to Hollywood, he might have seen things differently. Selig, a vaudeville magician with entrepreneurial élan, made his first film in 1896. He hoped to make it big in the budding movie business, and researched the technology

Thanks to its opulent interiors, the landmark Chicago Theater is a popular film location.

Above: **Like Julia Roberts and Cameron Diaz in *My Best Friend's Wedding*, Chicagoans love to lunch in the elegant Walnut Room on the seventh floor of the Marshall Field's department store.**

needed to project moving pictures on a scale that would attract a sizeable paying audience. Machinist Andrew Schuster helped him to reproduce the latest in French film technology, and voilà: The cutting-edge Lumière Cinématographe was reborn as the slightly altered Selig Standard Camera and the Selig Polyscope projector. The colonel had found his niche.

Selig hit the jackpot with *Hunting Big Game in Africa* (1909), a flick based on President Teddy Roosevelt's hunting expeditions to the Dark Continent. After making the first film version of *The Wizard of Oz* (1910), Selig embarked on a project to recreate *The Coming of Columbus* (1912) on the shores of Lake Michigan. With three ships left over from the World's Columbian Exposition, he staged the explorer's landing despite overwhelming logistical difficulties. Popular acclaim rolled in, including kudos from the Pope. Selig had been to the coast of Southern California to make *The Count of Monte Cristo* (1908) and built a studio in Edendale, an area that has since become part of Hollywood. Out West, big players such as Universal and MGM would optimize the production and distribution of films in the teens and twenties, establishing the L.A. area as the center of the film industry. Warner Brothers hit it big in 1927 with the world's first-ever feature-length "talking" film, *The Jazz Singer,* starring vaudevillian Al Jolson. It was not long before other U.S. centers of film production faded into the background. The transition to sound would occur neither uniformly nor overnight in the movie-making industry, but the technological advancement was nonetheless a breakthrough powerful enough to shift the California-based film business into high gear.

Chicago's breathtaking skyline on Lake Michigan (left) **has aimed ever higher since the birth of the skyscraper here around the turn of the 20th century. Film locations such as Union Station** (below) **offer historic atmosphere as an alternative to sheer height.**

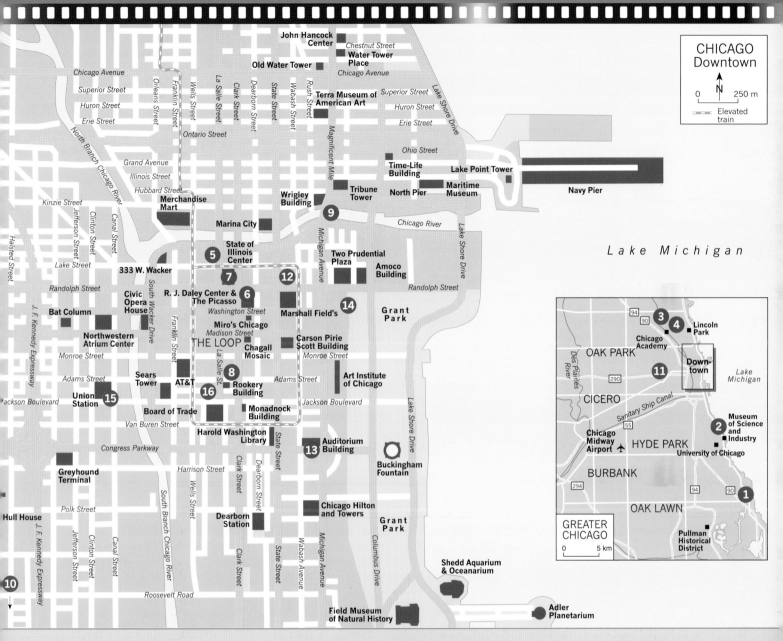

CHICAGO
Downtown

0   250 m

Elevated
train

Lake Michigan

GREATER
CHICAGO

0   5 km

OAK PARK

CICERO

Chicago
Academy

Lincoln
Park

Down-
town

Lake
Michigan

Des Plaines River

Sanitary Ship Canal

Chicago
Midway
Airport

HYDE PARK

University of Chicago

Museum
of Science
and Industry

BURBANK

OAK LAWN

Pullman
Historical
District

The Blues Brothers

1. Pilgrim Baptist Church, 3235 East 91st Street, South Side
2. Stone bridge in Jackson Park behind the Museum of Science and Industry, 5700 South Lake Shore Drive
3. Wrigley Field, 1060 West Addison Street
4. Curl Up & Dye, 2837 North Clark Street
5. Intersection of North La Salle and West Lake Streets
6. Richard J. Daley Center at 50 West Washington Street
7. City Hall-County Building, 121 North La Salle Street/118 North Clark Street

The Untouchables

8. Rookery Building, 209 South La Salle Street
9. Michigan Avenue Bridge
10. Malone's apartment, 1634 South Racine Street at Harrison Street
11. Our Lady of Sorrows Basilica, 3121 West Jackson Boulevard
12. Chicago Theater, 175 North State Street
13. Auditorium Building, 430 South Michigan Avenue
14. Chicago Cultural Center, 78 East Washington Street
15. Union Station, 210 South Canal Street
16. South La Salle Street before the Chicago Board of Trade Building, 141 West Jackson Boulevard

THE BLUES BROTHERS

Director   John Landis

Starring   John Belushi, Dan Aykroyd, James Brown, Cab Calloway, Ray Charles, Aretha Franklin, Carrie Fisher, John Candy

USA, 1980

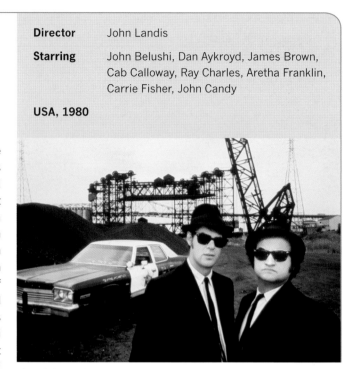

Elwood (Dan Aykroyd) and Jake (John Belushi) are on a mission from God.

The Blues Brothers is less a movie in the traditional sense than a $30-million musical rampage through the streets of Chicago. Blues enthusiast Dan Aykroyd, who created main characters Jake and Elwood, made the quixotic duo a hit in 1978 when he and John Belushi took their antics on stage in Los Angeles as the opening act for "wild and crazy" comedian Steve Martin. The album Briefcase Full of Blues produced from that performance went platinum, and the sketch, introduced in 1976 to warm audiences up for the show, became a staple of U.S. television's late-night review, Saturday Night Live. Aykroyd produced a mammoth film script based on the Blues Brothers act for Universal, and John Landis, who had directed Belushi as an irrepressible frat boy in Animal House (1978), whittled it down to the essentials. The result is a cult classic: two musical mobsters in black suits, madcap car chases, and a soundtrack featuring blues greats Aretha Franklin, Ray Charles, James Brown, Lou Marini, and more, all of whom make numerous cameo appearances in the film.

The action begins when reticent, harmonica-playing Elwood Blues (Dan Aykroyd) picks up his boisterous brother Jake (John Belushi) at the gates of Joliet prison. Jake has just finished serving a three-year sentence, and the brothers' first stop back in Chicago is the orphanage where they grew up. In a scene almost too silly to behold, the nun in charge, a.k.a. "the Penguin" (Kathleen Freeman), tells them that their childhood home will be closed unless they can come up with $5,000 in property

A slapstick showdown between the Blues Brothers and a gaggle of neo-Nazi nincompoops takes place on this stone bridge in Jackson Park.

taxes. Caretaker Curtis (Cab Calloway) advises them to seek help from above at the **Triple Rock Church,** in reality the **Pilgrim Baptist Church** at **3235 East 91st Street** on the South Side. Jake sees the light during an acrobatic gospel revival service led by Reverend Cleophus James (James Brown) and a choir angel played by pop princess Chaka Khan. The way to make money for the orphanage comes like a revelation: They must resurrect the Blues Brothers Band and tour the Chicago area on a paid musical review. After all, as the brothers insist throughout the film, they are on a mission from God.

What would seem like a matter of a few phone calls turns into a chase starting at the famous birthplace of the blues, the defunct **Maxwell Street Market,** where the legendary John Lee Hooker performs curbside. Aretha Franklin delivers her admonition to Matt "Guitar" Murphy to "Think" at the **Soul Food Restaurant,** filmed at the late great **Nate's Deli,** demolished by the ever-expanding University of Illinois in 1995. Ray Charles gets everybody dancing in the streets and ultimately provides the instruments the boys need for their shows. It is nothing short of a miracle that the Blues Brothers make it to their first gig at a honky-tonk roadhouse, survive a car chase in the Bluesmobile through the defunct Dixie Mall in Harvey, 20 miles (32 kilometers) south of downtown Chicago, and make it back to the city alive. Meanwhile, the Illinois State Nazi party is aching to take revenge for the disruption of its march on the stone bridge in **Jackson Park** behind the bombastic **Museum of Science and Industry, 5700 South Lake Shore Drive.** They fall for the false

Symbols of Chicago such as the baseball stadium at Wrigley Field embellish this cult film, but more than anything else, *The Blues Brothers* is about the music.

address on Elwood's driver's license and show up to duke it out at **1060 W. Addison Street,** baseball's **Wrigley Field.** Even Jake's disgruntled fiancée (Carrie Fisher) wants to get even, firing machine guns and flamethrowers when not doing perms at **Curl Up & Dye,** based on a real beauty salon of the same name at **2837 North Clark Street.** The law, led by Burton Mercer (John Candy), makes several befuddled attempts to collar the brothers, culminating in the famous monster pile-up of Chicago police cars under the elevated train at the intersection of **North La Salle and West Lake Streets.** With tanks, helicopters, and the National Guard in pursuit, Jake and Elmore crash their car through the windows of the **Richard J. Daley Center** at **50 West Washington Street,** and speed through the lobby en route to a final meeting with – who would have guessed? – a young Steven Spielberg. The now famous director makes a cameo appearance at the **City Hall-County Building,** accessible from both **121 North La Salle Street** and **118 North Clark Street.**

Iconic now, *The Blues Brothers* enjoyed great popularity with *SNL* fans but was panned by critics when it was released in June 1980. Despite the Blues Brothers Show Band's successful twenty-two-week musical tour in support of the film, Belushi was heartbroken by the reviews. His disappointment may have fueled an already raging drug habit, and an overdose of a lethal heroin and cocaine speedball at the Château Marmont Hotel on Sunset Boulevard in Los Angeles led to his death on March 5, 1982. Aykroyd continued his career in the movies, scoring multiple big-screen successes in such films as *Ghostbusters* (1984) and *Driving Miss Daisy* (1989), the latter winning him an Oscar nomination for the role of Boolie Werthan. Together with Belushi's widow, Judy, his brother James, and a co-founder of The Hard Rock Café, Aykroyd started an international restaurant chain called House of Blues in 1994, a far more successful enterprise than the film's sequel, *Blues Brothers 2000* (1998).

Even the little Pilgrim Baptist Church makes a lasting impression as the scene of the unforgettably raucous gospel service led by "the Godfather of Soul," James Brown, and featuring choir angel Chaka Khan.

THE UNTOUCHABLES

Director	Brian De Palma
Starring	Kevin Costner, Sean Connery, Robert De Niro, Andy Garcia, Charles Martin Smith
USA, 1987	

The historic Rookery Building (left) **and the soaring Chicago Board of Trade** (right, at center) **make for an impressive backdrop to the movie.**

Despite a humbling thumbs down from hometown critic Roger Ebert, *The Untouchables* captures Prohibition-era Chicago at its grimy best, with a stylized, high-action morality tale of mobster Al "Scarface" Capone and his good-guy nemesis, Eliot Ness. In real life, Ness literally wrote the book on bringing down the Mafia. His 1957 autobiography was the inspiration for the American TV series in the early sixties that Pulitzer Prize-winning playwright and Chicago native David Mamet would adapt to the big screen. In tune with the terse, hardboiled dialogue, director Brian De Palma pushed Paramount for the funds to film the story on location in Chicago.

The Windy City emerges as a maze of seedy back alleys contrasted with mighty towers, grandiose halls, and plush salons ruled by mobsters and their impeccably dressed underlings. Despite the rich visual drama, Academy Award nominations for art direction, costumes, and Ennio Morricone's score failed to produce awards, which went instead to the year's Best Picture, Bernardo Bertolucci's *The Last Emperor*. Sean Connery fared well anyway, taking home the flick's only Oscar for his supporting role as Jimmy Malone, an Irish cop with a hate-hate relationship with organized crime. Newcomer Kevin Costner didn't do too shabbily either: He was instantly propelled to stardom in his lead role as the handsome, principled Eliot Ness.

Al Capone (Robert De Niro) makes himself at home in a luxury hotel, the richly decorated interiors of which were shot at the Chicago Theater.

It's 1930, and Eliot Ness (Kevin Costner) is a Treasury Department agent assigned to solve the problem of organized crime in Chicago. Prohibition is still in full effect under the Volstead Act of 1919, and yet mob kingpin Al "Scarface" Capone (Robert De Niro) runs a booming brewery business that quenches the thirst of the corrupt Irish police force and a thriving crime syndicate. His speakeasies, bordellos, and gambling houses earn him a million bucks a week. Greenhorn Ness arrives ready for action at police headquarters, the historic **Rookery Building** at **209 South La Salle Street** in Chicago's Loop district, but finds himself surrounded by stooges on Capone's payroll.

While bemoaning a raid that turned up parasols instead of barrels of booze, Ness meets beat cop Jimmy Malone (Sean Connery) on the **Michigan Avenue Bridge.** Impressed by his words of wisdom, Ness tracks Malone down at his apartment at **1634 South Racine Street at Harrison Street,** close to Addams Park. With some arm-twisting, and a heart to heart under the barrel vault of **Our Lady of Sorrows Basilica, 3121 West Jackson Boulevard,** Ness hires Malone to help him recruit a few good, uncorrupted "untouchables" to clean up the city. Fresh-faced rookie George Stone (Andy Garcia) and mousy accountant Oscar Wallace (Charles Martin Smith) join the ranks for a fearless, if unlikely, foursome. Meanwhile, Capone is living it up amid oriental carpets, gilt furnishings, and butler service at the Lex-

University providing the grand staircase where Ness memorably threatens Capone in person.

Before Capone takes it out on the boys from Treasury, he brutally purges his own ranks at a banquet using a baseball bat. Later he celebrates at the opera, filmed at the Tiffany-domed **Chicago Cultural Center** on **78 East Washington Street.** Even as he sips bubbly at the opera with a tenor who sings "Vesti la giubba" from Leoncavallo's *I Pagliacci,* Ness is hot on his trail. A critical victory comes during a dramatic shootout at **Union Station** at **210 South Canal Street,** De Palma's cinematic tribute to the "Odessa Steps" scene in *The Battleship Potemkin* (1925) that involves a baby carriage, a clock, a set of marble steps, and bullets raining down. Tax evasion proves to be Capone's swan song, but not before Malone pays the ultimate price at his Racine Street apartment. Ness takes revenge on the roof of the **Chicago Cultural Center,** sending the dapper assassin Frank Nitti (Billy Drago), a character symbolic of the entire mob scene, to a vertiginous death.

Ironically for Ness, Prohibition's unpopular restrictions would be repealed anyway in 1933 with the passage of the 21st Amendment. Never mind, he jokes with a reporter on **South La Salle Street** before the magnificent **Chicago Board of Trade Building** at **141 West Jackson Boulevard.** If alcohol really does become legal, then he too can have a drink.

Left: Mafia boss Capone celebrates with pomp and circumstance at the Chicago Cultural Center.

Center and below: Eliot Ness (Kevin Costner) fights for justice at Union Station.

ington Hotel, the mobster's real-life headquarters at the corner of Michigan Avenue and 22nd Street. The Lexington was not demolished until 1995, but these scenes were filmed inside a 1920s movie house instead, the beaux-arts **Chicago Theater** at **175 North State Street,** just as its magnificent 1933 décor was being restored. An 1890 landmark by architects Adler & Sullivan that shares a building with Roosevelt University, the white terracotta clad **Auditorium Building** at **430 South Michigan Avenue** stood in for the Lexington's exterior, with the adjoining **Roosevelt**

FLORENCE

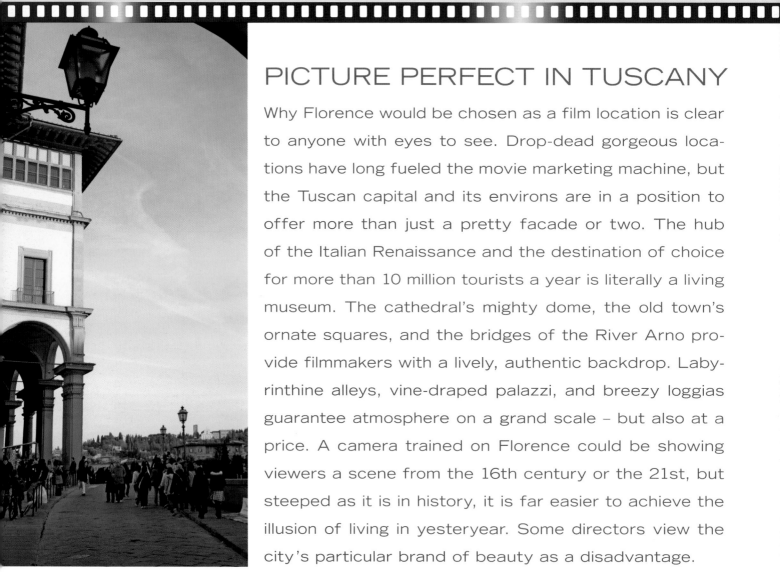

PICTURE PERFECT IN TUSCANY

Why Florence would be chosen as a film location is clear to anyone with eyes to see. Drop-dead gorgeous locations have long fueled the movie marketing machine, but the Tuscan capital and its environs are in a position to offer more than just a pretty facade or two. The hub of the Italian Renaissance and the destination of choice for more than 10 million tourists a year is literally a living museum. The cathedral's mighty dome, the old town's ornate squares, and the bridges of the River Arno provide filmmakers with a lively, authentic backdrop. Labyrinthine alleys, vine-draped palazzi, and breezy loggias guarantee atmosphere on a grand scale – but also at a price. A camera trained on Florence could be showing viewers a scene from the 16th century or the 21st, but steeped as it is in history, it is far easier to achieve the illusion of living in yesteryear. Some directors view the city's particular brand of beauty as a disadvantage.

Exactly because it is so beautiful and ancient, surprisingly few international films are made amidst the marble cladding and graceful towers of Florence. Directors shy away from palaces and monuments as too distracting from characters and plot. Not so with heritage films: James Ivory and Ismail Merchant adapted E.M. Forster's 1907 novel *A Room with a View* to the silver screen with enough sensory overload and strong performances for an Academy Award. The directing and producing duo's 1985 film captured the sense of adventure and naughtiness abroad under the guise of an educational English holiday, with Lucy Honeychurch's most important lessons set before pretty churches and ravishing landscapes.

Much the same can be said of Kenneth Branagh's romantic comedy *Much Ado About Nothing* (1993), set not, as Shakespeare would have liked, in Messina, Sicily, but at Villa Vignamaggio on a Tuscan hilltop a good stone's throw from Florence. The lush gardens and splashing fountains of the Chianti manor house are a delightful playground for the Bard's cavorting lovers and a perfect foil to Don John's dastardly plots.

In the end, looks aren't everything. On the international market, it is the English who have made the most out of filming in Florence, an extension of a love affair with Italy that became serious during the days of the Grand Tour. That 18th-century convention requiring young men of means to see the world but especially Italy fostered an extraordinary flowering of expatriate genius. The birthplace of Dante, Michelangelo, and Leonardo da Vinci became a second home to such stars of British literature as Byron, Shelley, the Brownings, and many more.

Where some have succeeded, others have failed. Franco Zeffirelli's *Tea with Mussolini* (1999) employs the Florentine town hall square, the Piazza della Signoria, and other hallowed sites to conjure World War II Italy, but casting and plot failed to live up to history or place. Based on the classic tale by Henry James, Jane Campion's *The Portrait of a Lady* (1996) tosses in scenes of the Tuscan capital the way an Impressionist might add a dash of unexpected color to a canvas. A carriage careens past the marble facade of the cathedral and over the historic stones of Piazza SS. Annunziata – and yet the effect is unsatisfying. In its long Florentine sequence, the film fails to achieve a clear sense of place, a curious miscalculation considering the strong presence the city exudes. No one has ever claimed that filming in a "living museum" was easy, however.

Director Ridley Scott plunged the city on the Arno into terror when he sent Anthony Hopkins abroad as *Hannibal* (2001). In the sequel to *The Silence of the Lambs* (1991), Hollywood's most fascinating serial killer, Dr. Hannibal Lecter, carries out a ritual murder from the balcony of the Palazzo della Signoria, Florence's storied town hall. The fatally attractive FBI agent Clarice Starling (Julianne Moore) must stay on his trail, but is permitted to track him only from her offices in Washington, D.C. The gorgeous palaces and traditional markets leave only a fleeting impression of the city, and Moore's performance pales in comparison with Jodie Foster's Oscar-winning job in the original

Above: **The Ponte Vecchio showcases Florence's tranquil side, especially when used in a movie like *Hannibal.***
Left: **The Galleria degli Uffizi on the banks of the Arno.**

film – perhaps because she's simply not allowed to pursue her diabolical subject at close range.

Our collective memory of older films made in Florence may be much faded, but Florence was by no means a new location for filmmakers in the late 20th century. The legendary sisters Lillian and Dorothy Gish had performed on location here in the twenties while filming the Renaissance drama *Romola* (1924). Two decades later Roberto Rossellini would film his six-episode film *Paisà* (1946), choosing Florence as the backdrop for some of the movie's most dramatic scenes. In one of the film's tragic tales, an English nurse fights for her life and the survival of others as bullets rain down amid the historic monuments of the city. Love blossomed here well before *A Room with a View*; Joan Fontaine and Joseph Cotten fled reality for Florence and Capri for a *September Affair* (1950).

In the seventies, directors decided that the mood in Florence was dark and gloomy, perhaps like Visconti's Venice, and their films show a decidedly macabre shift. In *Obsession* (1976), director Brian De Palma sends an obsessed Cliff Robertson to the Tuscan capital where he meets a young woman who he thinks is a reincarnation of his murdered wife. Al Pacino didn't have a much cheerier time in *Bobby Deerfield* (1977) as a race car driver who finds love in the shadow of the Florentine cathedral, but a little too late. Sydney Pollack's film didn't really sit right in Florence, though, making audiences wonder again whether Florence is simply too immersed in history to work well as a location for modern films.

More than any other film, *A Room with a View* (bottom right) captures the romantic flair of Florence. Soak up the historic atmosphere on an evening stroll through the old town (left) or by taking in the panoramic view from Piazzale Michelangelo at sunrise (below).

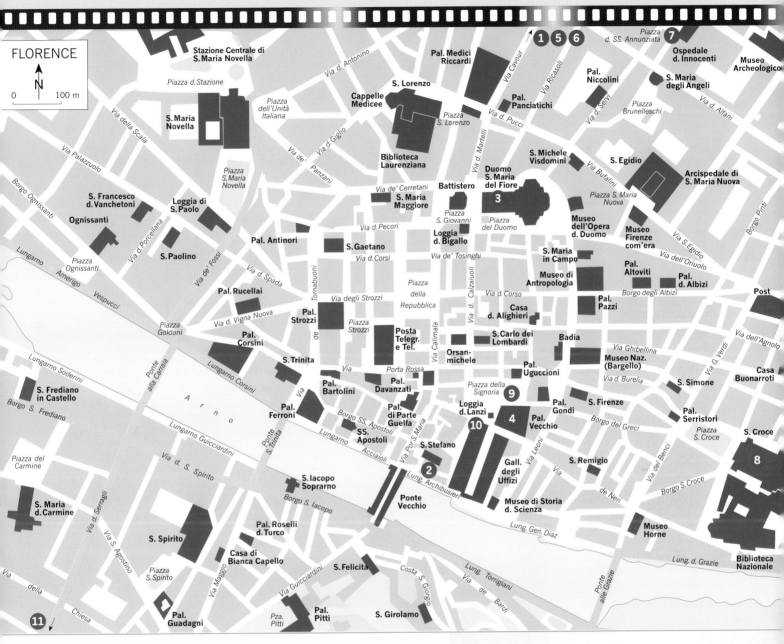

FLORENCE

N

0   100 m

Stazione Centrale di S. Maria Novella

Piazza d. Stazione

Via della Scala

Via Palazzuolo

Via d. Antonino

Pal. Medici Riccardi

Via Cavour

Via Ricasoli

① ⑤ ⑥

Piazza d. SS. Annunziata

⑦

Ospedale d. Innocenti

Museo Archeologico

S. Maria Novella

Piazza dell'Unità Italiana

Cappelle Medicee

S. Lorenzo

Piazza S. Lorenzo

Pal. Panciatichi

Pal. Niccolini

Via d. Servi

S. Maria degli Angeli

Piazza Brunelleschi

Via d. Alfani

Via d. Pucci

Piazza S. Maria Novella

Via d. Giglio

Via de' Panzani

Biblioteca Laurenziana

Via d. Martelli

Duomo S. Maria del Fiore

S. Michele Visdomini

Via Bufalini

S. Egidio

Arcispedale di S. Maria Nuova

Via de' Cerretani

Battistero

③

Museo dell'Opera d. Duomo

Piazza S. Maria Nuova

S. Maria Maggiore

Via d. Pecori

Piazza S. Giovanni

Piazza del Duomo

Museo Firenze com'era

Via S. Egidio

Borgo Pinti

S. Francesco d.Vanchetoni

Loggia di S.Paolo

Via d. Porcellana

Pal. Antinori

S. Gaetano

Via d. Corsi

Loggia d. Bigallo

Via de' Tosinghi

S. Maria in Campo

Via dell'Oriuolo

Ognissanti

Borgo Ognissanti

S.Paolino

Via de' Fossi

Via d. Spada

Tornabuoni

Pal. Altoviti

Pal. d. Albizi

Piazza Ognissanti

Lungarno Amerigo Vespucci

Piazza Goldoni

Via d. Vigna Nuova

Via degli Strozzi

Piazza della Repubblica

Via d. Calzaiuoli

Via d. Corso

Museo di Antropologia

Borgo degli Albizi

Post

Pal. Rucellai

Pal. Strozzi

Piazza Strozzi

Casa d. Alighieri

Pal. Pazzi

Via dell'Agnolo

Lungarno Soderini

Borgo S. Frediano

Pal. Corsini

S. Trinita

de

Via

Posta Telegr. e Tel.

S. Carlo dei Lombardi

Via d. Burella

Via Ghibellina

Museo Naz. (Bargello)

Via G. Verdi

Casa Buonarroti

Arno

S. Frediano in Castello

Pal. Bartolini

Pal. Ferroni

Via

Porta Rossa

Orsan-michele

Via Calimala

Pal. Davanzati

Pal. Uguccioni

Piazza della Signoria

⑨

Loggia d. Lanzi

Pal. Gondi

S. Simone

S. Firenze

Pal. Serristori

S. Croce

Ponte alla Carraia

Lungarno Corsini

Lungarno Guicciardini

Ponte S. Trinita

Borgo SS. Apostoli

Pal. di Parte Guelfa

SS. Apostoli

⑩

④

Pal. Vecchio

Piazza S. Croce

Borgo del Greci

⑧

Piazza del Carmine

S. Iacopo Soprarno

Borgo S. Iacopo

Via Por S. Maria

Lungarno Acciaioli

S. Stefano

②

Lung. Archibusieri

Gall. degli Uffizi

Via Leoni

S. Remigio

de Neri

Via del Benci

Borgo S. Croce

S. Maria d.Carmine

Via d. Serragli

Via d. S. Spirito

Pal. Roselli d.Turco

Ponte Vecchio

Museo di Storia d. Scienza

Museo Horne

Via d. Agostino

S. Spirito

Casa di Bianca Capello

S. Felicita

Costa S. Giorgio

Lung. Gen. Diaz

Lung. Torrigiani

Ponte alle Grazie

Lung. d. Grazie

Biblioteca Nazionale

Piazza S. Spirito

Via Maggio

Via Guicciardini

Via d. Bardi

Pal. Guadagni

Pza. Pitti

Pal. Pitti

S. Girolamo

⑪

A Room with a View

1. Villa Maiano, Via Benedetto da Maiano 11, 6 miles (10 km) northeast of Florence near Fiesole
2. Hotel degli Orafi, Lungarno Archibusieri 4
3. The duomo, or cathedral, of S. Maria del Fiore
4. Palazzo Vecchio, town hall
5. Villa I Tatti, Harvard University, near Fiesole
6. Barley field near Fiesole
7. Ospedale degli Innocenti, Piazza della SS. Annunziata
8. Church of Santa Croce
9. Neptune Fountain, Piazza della Signoria, town hall square
10. Loggia dei Lanzi, Piazza della Signoria

Much Ado About Nothing

11. Villa Vignamaggio, Via Petriolo 5, near Greve in Chianti, 20 miles (32 km) south of Florence

A ROOM WITH A VIEW

Director	James Ivory
Starring	Helena Bonham Carter, Julian Sands, Daniel Day-Lewis, Simon Callow, Maggie Smith, Rosemary Leach, Judi Dench
UK, 1985	

The unforgettable kiss in a field near Fiesole.

What's a girl in a corset to do? Why, fall in love with the wrong man, of course, as English rose Lucy Honeychurch promptly did amid the fountains and squares of Florence in *A Room with a View*. Rosy cheeked and demure, newcomer Helena Bonham Carter plays the heroine on a tour of Italy with her spinster cousin, Charlotte Bartlett (Maggie Smith), in what is known as the quintessential Merchant-Ivory film. The producer-director duo adapted E.M. Forster's 1907 classic novel and made highbrow "art cinema" palatable to a broad audience with the help of stunning period detail, sweeping musical scores, and gorgeous locations, a formula they would use to thrill audiences again in two more movies about the clash of England's social classes, *Howards End* (1992) and *The Remains of the Day* (1993).

The comedy of manners pokes fun at stuffy Edwardian society on holiday but not at all enjoying it despite the charms of the Tuscan capital. Lucy and her chaperone check in at the fictitious Pensione Bertolini to discover that their rooms, contrary to the assurances of their Cockney hostess, do not have a view. Help arrives when the decidedly lower class Mr. Emerson (Denholm Elliott) and his brooding son George (Julian Sands) offer to exchange accommodations. The plush hotel interiors were shot at the 15th-century **Villa Maiano** at **Via Benedetto da Maiano 11** some six miles (ten kilometers) to the northeast near the pretty

Miss Lavish and Cousin Charlotte pay a visit to Piazza della SS. Annunziata. Unaccompanied by her chaperone, Lucy ventures forth to the Church of Santa Croce (right) **to visit some of Florence's most precious works of art.**

After fainting away at the Neptune Fountain, Lucy regains consciousness on the steps of the Loggia dei Lanzi, a famous 14th-century monument.

town of Fiesole. But the view that became legendary from the final scenes of the film was shot at a Florentine hotel, formerly the **Quisisana e Ponte Vecchio** and now called the **Hotel degli Orafi,** located close to the Uffizi on **Lungarno Archibusieri 4** at the corner of **Arco delle Carrozze.** The view from **Room 412** still gazes across to the **cathedral** and the **Palazzo Vecchio,** or town hall, as does the picture window in the cozy bar on the fifth floor. To Mr. Emerson, trading rooms is perfectly logical: "Women like looking at a view. Men don't." Charlotte, a stickler for protocol, thinks there's some Victorian reason to resist. Perhaps it's that George can't keep his eyes off of Lucy, and any involvement, no matter how innocent seeming, could compromise her honor.

Common sense and convention clash again when, after a long drive that passes by the Harvard University-owned **Villa I Tatti,** George sweeps Lucy into his arms and kisses her in a barley field near **Fiesole.** Romance was inevitable, after all, but not before the camera has had a good flirt with Florence. Charlotte and eccentric novelist Miss Lavish (Judi Dench) salute a statue of Grand Duke Ferdinand by the **Ospedale degli Innocenti,** the orphanage that the Renaissance architect Brunelleschi built after he designed the tricky cathedral dome. As the two older women leave the **Piazza della SS. Annunziata,** Lucy ventures forth unescorted to **Santa Croce,** the church where French writer Stendhal famously fainted from too much sightseeing, and where Giotto's frescoes and a monument to Dante make it a must-see monument for conscientious tourists. Later, Lucy witnesses a knife-fight in the **Piazza della Signoria** that ends

tragically at the **Neptune Fountain.** George comes to the rescue just as she swoons by the town hall, and sets her gently down beneath the cool arches of the **Loggia dei Lanzi.** Their Italian adventures return to haunt them back home in Surrey when Lucy's priggish fiancé Cecil Vyse – brilliantly played by Daniel Day-Lewis – recites passages from Lavish's new book, *Under a Loggia.* True love ought to prevail over class differences, but Lucy's not so sure. The final scenes with their gorgeous view from the Hotel degli Orafi offer a pretty answer to a silly problem.

Made for a mere $3 million, *A Room with a View* was nominated for eight Academy Awards and won three: for long-time collaborator Ruth Prawer Jhabvala's outstanding screenplay, for art direction, and for costumes. The Oscars recognized Merchant-Ivory's contribution to the silver screen, but foreign places, grand manors and period dress already had a dedicated following in the 1980s. The genre that has since produced hits like Ang Lee's *Sense and Sensibility* (1995), Robert Altman's *Gosford Park* (2001), and *Pride & Prejudice* (2005) owes a debt of style to the BBC's *Brideshead Revisited,* a literary television mini-series first aired in 1981. Americans who had thrilled to PBS's *Masterpiece Theatre* since the 1970s were enchanted by the accents and manners of the English cast when *Brideshead* made its debut in the U.S. in 1982. Never mind that the late Merchant was Bombay-born, and that Ivory hails from California: Their trademark "heritage films" were marketed as exotically European and quintessentially British, a recipe for success that has stood the test of time.

A stone's throw from the Ponte Vecchio, the famous view from the Hotel degli Orafi shows the cathedral dome and the tower of the Palazzo della Signoria. It is here that Lucy and George find their happy ending.

MUCH ADO ABOUT NOTHING

Director   Kenneth Branagh

Starring   Kenneth Branagh, Emma Thompson,
Denzel Washington, Keanu Reeves,
Richard Briers, Kate Beckinsale,
Robert Sean Leonard, Michael Keaton

UK/USA, 1993

How better to popularize Shakespeare than to film his best-loved comedy in a beautiful Tuscan villa? Kenneth Branagh chose **Villa Vignamaggio** at **Via Petriolo 5** just south of **Greve in Chianti** and 20 miles (30 kilometers) south of Florence en route to Siena, a hilly, wine country setting that captured the "hot-tempered Italianate qualities" of the 400-year-old play. Today the noble house is a bed and breakfast offering wine tastings and country tours, as much a popular stop for film aficionados as it is for fans of the good life. Teaming up with then-wife Emma Thompson, Branagh drew upon his roots as a player in the Royal Shakespeare Company and in his own troupe, the Renaissance Theatre Company, to adapt the Bard's tone and wit to the silver screen.

Shakespeare's comedy comes to life under the Tuscan sun.

The play had been filmed before, a full four times between 1926 and 1973, but under limited circumstances – mostly East German and Russian productions – and never to great acclaim. Branagh's clear sense of purpose was crucial to the film's success when it was released in 1993. His aim, to convince a mass audience that Shakespeare is fun and vividly alive, had already won him Academy Award nominations for Best Director and Best Actor in *Henry V* (1989). Critics dubbed him "the next Olivier," alluding to Laurence Olivier's legendary role as director and king in the 1944 film production of the same Shakespeare play.

When Branagh said that he wanted his fifth movie to be "sexy, fleshy, and sensuous" with none of the usual "incomprehensible booming and fruity-voiced declamation" usually ascribed to Shakespearean acting, he meant it. *Much Ado* is nothing if not a joyful romp under the Tuscan sun. This is Chianti before Frances Mayes and the floods of summer visitors, predating even the literary Grand Tourists like Byron, Shelley, and the Brownings. Splendidly isolated on a hilltop, the 14th-century Villa Vignamaggio overlooks olive groves and a gently undulating landscape. A daughter of the Gherardini clan exiled from Florence, the pretty Madonna Lisa, was born here in 1479, and went by the nickname Mona when she sat for the famous portrait by Leonardo da Vinci. To Branagh, these facts were academic. He never meant to connect the golden era of a wealthy

Director Kenneth Branagh found the perfect stand-in for Sicilian Messina at pretty Villa Vignamaggio, just south of Florence.

Tuscan family with Shakespeare's original setting, Sicilian Messina. Instead, the villa, the costumes, and the props had to provide a uniform appearance, creating what he described as "an imaginary world that could have existed almost anytime between 1700 and 1900."

The villa looks every bit a bucolic heaven in the opening scenes. Leonato (Richard Briers), the governor of Messina who owns the villa and runs the farm together with his brother Antonio (Brian Blessed), is picnicking with family and friends as good news arrives: The Prince of Aragon has won the war and is coming home. Moreover, the prince has reconciled with his odious half-brother, Don John (Keanu Reeves), and his victorious band plans to stay for a month of rest and relaxation. Leonato's family – in particular his daughter Hero (Kate Beckinsale), who has just come of age, and his sharp-tongued niece, Beatrice (Emma Thompson) – mean to oblige. Each anticipates the arrival of a beau: the chivalrous Claudio (Robert Sean Leonard) for Hero, and his comrade, Benedick of Padua (Kenneth Branagh), for Bea.

Much of the film's fun derives from the "merry war" of words between Benedick (Kenneth Branagh) and Beatrice (Emma Thompson). Will the witty rivals part as enemies, or succumb to Cupid's arrows?

Sparks fly between Branagh and Thompson (now long since divorced), who wage a "merry war" of words as the prince tricks them into their worst fear: falling in love. The **manicured gardens** at Vignamaggio provide a perfect setting with high hedges for eavesdropping, broad vistas for dreaming, and grand fountains for splashing and dancing in. Central to the story is the betrothal of Claudio to Hero. Their tale unfolds more formally in the **court** and **chapel yard,** using the rose-colored villa as the stage for banquets, balls and the fateful wedding day. Evil Don John wanders the cold **stone cellars** of the house with his henchmen at night, hatching the perfect plan: to convince Claudio that Hero is no maiden but a wanton woman instead. The farcical constable Dogberry (Michael Keaton) comes to the rescue, or at least makes a few comical attempts. Honor plays a central role in the story, and pride; and while both fail to spoil the romance, they succeed in proving, as Shakespeare notes in the guise of Benedick, "that man is a giddy thing."

Left: **Keanu Reeves is the odious Don John.**
Above: **The classically designed gardens of Villa Vignamaggio serve as a cheerful green setting for the dramatic twists and turns of the Bard's plot.**

HAVANA

FLAIR OF THE CARIBBEAN

Havana films beautifully, its colonial facades, colorful Malecón waterfront, and zest for life providing a vibrant foil to a nation fallen on hard times. Exotic cityscapes and decadent nightlife drew international attention to the Paris of the Caribbean before the revolution in 1959, but the attraction seems only to have grown since Cuba's capital began to fall into decay. As with Venice, the glory days of old have been replaced with a morbid charm that local filmmakers cultivate to fire social criticism. Foreign directors, on the other hand, tend to play it safe, sticking to the commercial certainty of well-crafted beauty shots.

A filmmaker's find: the decrepit charm of the once opulent colonial buildings along the waterfront promenade of the Malecón.

And yet contrast has always been a byword for Cuban history. Today, Cuba's *máximo lider* insists on a politics of strict separation from America, the despised "imperialist class enemy." But not even Castro can deny that American culture held *La Habana* in its sway before the revolution, and nowhere was U.S. influence more dominant than in the movies. Cuba didn't have much of a home-grown film industry until the 1960s, but cinema did get an early start on the island. For a city of just half a million inhabitants, Havana was well on its way to movie madness in 1920 with fifty movie theaters and an overall seating capacity of 23,000.

Most cinemas showed only Hollywood productions, some of them filmed on location especially for the Latin American market. American movie stars were spoiled habitués of the city's premier luxury hotel, the Nacional, and as late as 1959, the Cuban capital provided the backdrop for Graham Greene's spy parody, *Our Man in Havana*. Director Carol Reed even received permission to film on location from Castro himself. But that was practically the end of the road. Cuban-American relations declined rapidly shortly thereafter – the ill-fated Bay of Pigs invasion was but two years away – and the American embargo on trade with Cuba would cap such projects indefinitely.

The foundation in 1959 of the Cuban Institute of Cinematographic Arts and Industry (ICAIC) marked the official birth of a national film industry. The agenda was clear: Foreign films would be bumped from the program by locally made movies that celebrated Cuban culture and strengthened national identity. Nonetheless, censors banned the homespun film *P.M.* (1961) from the cinemas with the claim that a movie about nightlife in Havana's working-class neighborhoods was incompatible with

"Papa" Hemingway visits the Cuban capital for the shooting of *Our Man in Havana* (1959) and chats with actors Alec Guinness and Noel Coward.

The Malecón seaside promenade, beloved of filmmakers.

the revolutionary spirit. Still, the government insisted that artistic freedom and creativity would be promoted at all costs, and many early movies were indeed bitterly critical of contemporary politics, something almost unheard of today.

In *Memorias del Subdesarollo* (*Inconsolable Memories*, 1968), Tomás Gutiérrez Alea tells the story of an intellectual disillusioned by the revolution. Protagonist Sergio Corrieri observes the city through a telescope from his luxurious apartment, takes leisurely drives along the seaside Malecón, complains of empty shop windows, parties in the La Rampa red-light district, and visits Hemingway's villa in San Francisco de Paula beyond the city limits. He grows estranged from the bland "new Havana" that Gutiérrez Alea presents as a multiethnic city of workers, a perspective refreshingly honest for what would later become a suffocatingly restrictive regime.

By the 1970s and '80s, critical perspective had worn out its welcome. Films like Juan Carlos Tabío's *Se Permuta* (*House for Swap*, 1984) on the shortage of apartments in Havana were the exception. By the early 1990s, filmmakers had managed to regain some measure of artistic freedom. Popular movies such as *Fresa y chocolate* (*Strawberry and Chocolate*, 1994), *Guantanamera* (1995), *La vida es silbar* (*Life is to Whistle*, 1998)

and *Lista de espera* (*The Waiting List*, 2000) addressed taboo topics like homosexuality and exile head on while reflecting on life in modern Cuba. The absurdities of everyday life thanks to bureaucracy gone wild, a dearth of even the most basic goods, and the breakdown of public transportation were among the recurring themes. In *La vida es silbar*, director Fernando Pérez traces the paths of four subjects on their search for happiness through Havana, a quest that culminates in all of them meeting, ironically, on the Plaza de la Revolución. At the Havana International Festival of New Latin American Cinema, where the film won numerous awards, the director told the press that the only thing of significance regarding the film was that he was allowed to march to the beat of his own drum.

Creativity, a talent for improvisation, and the charm of light-hearted satire sometimes encourage the observer to forget how much the Cuban movie industry has suffered from the severely depressed economy of recent years. Funding during this "periodo especial" often allows no more than one movie to be produced each year. No wonder Cuban filmmakers have to rely increasingly on international co-productions. Still, it's an uneasy relationship. U.S. trade restrictions kept Sydney Pollack out of the Cuban capital in the late '80s, forcing the director to reconstruct *Havana* (1990) in the Dominican Republic, a popular Central American holiday destination. Wim Wenders fared better: His blockbuster documentary filmed on location with the aging musicians of the *Buena Vista Social Club* (1999) rekindled pop culture's passion for Cuba, perhaps inspiring Steven Spielberg's comment at the Havana film festival in 2002 that he, too, expected to be making films in Cuba very soon.

Cuba loves going to the movies: Theaters sell out of tickets and stay that way once films by big-name international directors finally make it into town.

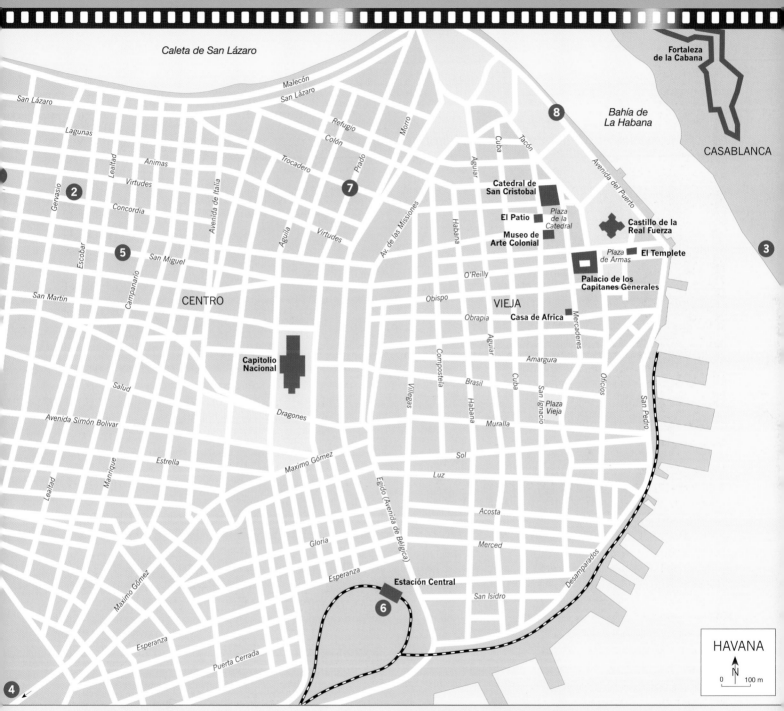

Caleta de San Lázaro

Fortaleza
de la Cabana

Bahía de
La Habana

CASABLANCA

Malecón
San Lázaro

San Lázaro

Lagunas

Refugio

Colón

Prado

Cuba

Tacón

Avenida del Puerto

Morro

Gervasio

Lealtad

Animas

Virtudes

Concordia

Trocadero

Aguila

Virtudes

Aguiar

Habana

 Av. de las Missiones

Catedral de
San Cristobal

El Patio

Plaza
de la
Catedral

Castillo de la
Real Fuerza

Escobar

Campanario

San Miguel

San Martin

Avenida de Italia

CENTRO

Museo de
Arte Colonial

O'Reilly

Obispo

VIEJA

Plaza
de Armas

El Templete

Palacio de los
Capitanes Generales

Salud

Capitolio
Nacional

Dragones

Villegas

Compostela

Obrapia

Aguiar

Brasil

Cuba

San Ignacio

Casa de Africa

Amargura

Plaza
Vieja

Mercaderes

Oficios

San Pedro

Avenida Simón Bolivar

Estrella

Maximo Gómez

Habana

Muralla

Sol

Luz

Lealtad

Manrique

Maximo Gómez

Egido (Avenida de Bélgica)

Acosta

Merced

Desamparados

Gloria

Esperanza

Esperanza

Estación Central

San Isidro

Puerta Cerrada

HAVANA

N

0   100 m

Strawberry and Chocolate

1. Coppelia ice cream parlor, Parque Coppelia,
   Calle 23 on the corner of Calle L

2. La Guarida, Calle Concordia 418,
   between Gervasio and Escobar streets

3. Estatua de Cristo, Casablanca

Buena Vista Social Club

4. Buena Vista neighborhood in west Havana

5. Egrem Studios, Calle San Miguel 410,
   between Lealtad and Campanario streets

6. Estación Central (main train station) on Avenida de Bélgica

7. Escuela Nacional de Gimnástica on the Prado at the corner of Trocadero

8. Malecón seaside promenade

STRAWBERRY AND CHOCOLATE

Fresa y chocolate

Directors	Tomás Gutiérrez Alea and Juan Carlos Tabío
Starring	Jorge Perugorría, Vladimir Cruz, Mirta Ibarra, Francisco Gattorno

Cuba / Mexico / Spain, 1993

Two very different worlds collide when the buttoned-down student David (Vladimir Cruz) meets a gay artist, Diego (Jorge Perugorría), at the Coppelia ice cream parlor.

Fidel Castro's secretary is said to have come up with the idea in the wake of the revolution's success: Why not establish the Coppelia ice cream parlor as a meeting place of the people, so that Habañeros both black and white, students and workers, could congregate in sweet harmony? Two completely different worlds meet at this popular locale in *Strawberry and Chocolate,* the most successful Cuban film of all time. Diego (Jorge Perugorría), a gay artist, takes a seat next to buttoned-down student David (Vladimir Cruz) and coaxes him into conversation. That Diego does not exactly fit in with David's friends in the Young Communists is something he recognizes at first glance: "There was chocolate and he ordered strawberry."

Even today there are seldom more than two flavors of ice cream to choose from at the **Coppelia** ice cream parlor located at **Calle 23** on the corner of **Calle L.** Nonetheless, on hot days, long lines form in front of the popular café set in the pretty **Parque Coppelia** near La Rampa in the villa quarter of **Vedado.** This emblem of Communist ideals – hailed by the Cuban leadership as "the revolution's gift to the people" – made the proud claim in the sixties that it offered more flavors than Baskin-Robbins, the famous purveyors of ice cream in the archenemy

America. Not much of the futuristic Coppelia is shown in the film, its odd concrete structure redolent of a spaceship sitting on stilts under the breezy palms. Like many Habañeros, Diego and David prefer the tables on the leafy terrace to the barstools at the long counter indoors.

When Diego describes to his straight-laced friend some of his treasured possessions, such as photographs from a play and an unusual book, David cannot resist. He agrees to go to Diego's, following him up the broad, curving stair to the third floor of a grand but decrepit 19th-century apartment house at **Calle Concordia 418,** between Gervasio and Escobar streets. "Welcome to my cave," says Diego, opening the door to an apartment full of forbidden books, records, and sculpture, the walls cluttered with Christian icons cheek by jowl with abstract art and photographs of Cuban literati and American film stars. This private Bohemian world fascinates David, a student of political science who expects dutifully to serve his land upon graduation but whose secret dream is to become a novelist. David's visits to Diego's apartment become a fixture of his routine. Initially he plans to spy on the politically seditious artist; Diego, for his part, still harbors hopes of seducing David. In time, and despite the odds, a deep friendship develops between the two antithetical-seeming men.

Enrique Nuñez, who permitted the filmmakers to use his apartment as a location in 1992, never dreamed that the film's runaway success would change his life. As the stream of fans

The Coppelia ice cream parlor, located in a park in the leafy Vedado quarter, is one of the city's best-loved hangouts on hot days.

Fresa y chocolate is the most successful Cuban film of all time. All Havana flocked to the city's cinemas to see it.

knocking at his door to take a peek at Diego's "cave" swelled, Nuñez made a decision laced with typical Cuban pragmatism: to open a restaurant on the premises. His apartment has since been known as **La Guarida,** "the cave," and has been regarded for years as one of Havana's very best *paladares,* as the tiny, private-home eateries with speakeasy character are known. It's as though the cameras are still rolling: Inside, the stucco in the vast marble staircase is still crumbling, and the restaurant itself is hung with film stills from *Strawberry and Chocolate* and snapshots of famous visitors, such as Jack Nicholson. Guests dine by candlelight in darkened rooms, a setting reminiscent of the scene in which Diego invites David and his neighbor Nancy (Mirta Ibarra) to a dinner party.

Strawberry and Chocolate ends on a bittersweet note with Diego's reluctant decision to leave Cuba. At one of their last meetings, the two friends sit side by side across the bay from downtown Havana. Diego casts a wistful glance at the city he calls home, a place he may never see again. This lookout point in the **Casablanca** neighborhood is well known, especially for the white marble **Estatua de Cristo** which, like the towering figure of Christ in Rio de Janeiro, keeps watch over the city.

In the film's final scenes, David observes that each Cuban should have the right to live as he or she sees fit – a statement met with frenetic applause at the Havana film festival. Diego responds that the revolution needs more militants like David. It is surprising that a comedy that does not mince words in its critique of the government was allowed to be shown at all; permission was granted only after long discussions at the highest levels of the Communist Party. The Cuban public showed its thanks by storming the cinemas in full force. Nor did the international community withhold its approval: In 1995, *Strawberry and Chocolate* was the first Cuban film ever nominated for an Oscar, and remains the country's most successful movie.

The story of an unusual friendship ends on a bittersweet note in the Casablanca neighborhood on a hill with a view across the bay to downtown Havana.

BUENA VISTA SOCIAL CLUB

Director   Wim Wenders

Starring   Ibrahim Ferrer, Rubén González,
Compay Segundo, Eliades Ochoa,
Ry Cooder, Omara Portuondo,
Juan de Marcos González, Pio Leyva

Germany/USA/UK/France/Cuba, 1999

In the 1930s and '40s, Havana's hilly **Buena Vista neighborhood** was home to the city's most famous *sociedad* dance club. In the opening scenes of this film, aged guitarist Compay Segundo cruises the streets of this quarter in a vintage American car on the lookout for the legendary locale. "We should ask the old people," he suggests, but memories of the big parties are all they can offer. The club itself, one of the places where Afro-Caribbean *son* music was born, no longer exists.

Thanks to musician-producer Ry Cooder, the Buena Vista Social Club has emerged from the memories of Habañeros to become synonymous with Cuban music the world over. In 1996 Cooder traveled to Cuba to track down the forgotten musical legends of a pre-revolutionary golden era. When the native Californian who has worked with the Rolling Stones and Eric Clapton got the elderly musicians together for a jam session, many hadn't played an instrument in years. In fact, crooner Ibrahim Ferrer relates that he drove to the studio straight from a day's work at his shoeshine stand. Cooder passed on his passionate regard for the music of these *super abuelos*, or mighty grandfathers, to friend and filmmaker Wim Wenders, who decided to discover the fading musical tradition for himself as the subject of a documentary. Two years later, Cooder and Wenders returned to the island nation to make a film.

Rubén González plays the piano for the little ballerinas at the Escuela Nacional de Gimnástica on the Prado.

Ry Cooder and his son Joachim explore the Old City.

Wenders wanted to craft a documentary that would allow the music to speak for itself. Lacking a clear concept and any serious movie-making equipment, he and cameraman Jörg Widmer roamed the city with nothing but a couple of digital cameras and a hand-held Steadicam. Wenders followed the musicians to recording sessions at the **Egrem Studios** at **Calle San Miguel 410** in **Centro Habana** between Lealtad and Campanario streets, later contrasting these scenes with those from a concert in Amsterdam, the first live performance of the newly formed Buena Vista Social Club outside of Cuba, and another concert at New York City's Carnegie Hall.

Each of the five main musicians waxes poetic on life and his ongoing love affair with music. Eliades Ochoa strolls the derelict railroad tracks behind Havana's **Estación Central**, the main train station on **Avenida de Bélgica** in **Habana Vieja**.

The camera loves Havana's historic promenade, the Prado.

The Buena Vista Social Club on world tour: Omara Portuondo and Compay Segundo crooning at New York City's Carnegie Hall.

Meanwhile, singer Omara Portuondo breaks into an impromptu duet with a charming passerby in Havana's Old Town. Rubén González, who hadn't played the piano for years because of crippling arthritis, tinkles the ivories in the grand hall of the **Escuela Nacional de Gimnástica** on the **Prado** at the corner of Trocadero amidst little girls at ballet lessons and boys fencing in the vast columned hall. Interspersed with the ongoing stories of the musicians are Wenders's impressions of the city: children roller-skating across the Prado's leafy promenade, a woman smoking a fat cigar while sweeping the sidewalk, men engrossed in a game of dominoes. As the camera takes in the **Malecón,** waves break on the quay and spray a misty patina over the crumbling facades of colonial-era townhouses.

The movie would be the surprise hit of 1999, but Wenders noted with regret that during the three weeks of filming, he had had only a vague, postcard-like view of Havana as a metropolis. For him, the sojourn in Cuba was primarily about people making music. For the audience, it is exactly this look at a group of nearly forgotten musicians – their passion, their suffering, and their wisdom – that is the key to the city and the lively rhythms that are its pulse. Without trying to paint a too-pretty picture of the Havana of today, Wenders conjures the decadent times before the revolution, when the music and nightlife of the city boasted an unrivaled élan.

Havana's lively streets and genteel facades offered Wim Wenders a colorful backdrop for his musical documentary. Audiences were treated to an eyeful of the city's charm.

HONG KONG

Jeremy Irons plays a cynical journalist covering an event central to the plot of *Chinese Box:* the 1997 handover of Hong Kong to the People's Republic of China.

Below: **Hong Kong is a city of contrasts in which monumental colonial buildings such as the proud neoclassical parliament stand cheek by jowl with modern skyscrapers such as Norman Foster's HSBC Headquarters Building.**

MOVIE CAPITAL OF THE FAR EAST

The very first movie filmed in Hong Kong dealt with a topic typical of the city: *Stealing the Roasted Duck* (1909) related the tale of thieves hungry for the chance to make off with the cooked fowl so commonly seen hanging in the windows of local restaurants. The comedy was inspired by Chinese opera, but produced by an American. Shortly after the film's debut, World War I broke out and brought the city's fledgling film industry to an abrupt halt. Cosmopolitan Shanghai took its place, and was dubbed the "Hollywood of the Orient" for the next two decades, until the fighting between China and Japan forced many filmmakers to flee to the crown colony.

Vibrant masks and costumes that take their cue from traditional Chinese opera exert a powerful influence on films made in Hong Kong.

The influx of moviemakers was a major impetus for the film business in Hong Kong, but as luck would have it, this new heyday didn't last. From 1941 to 1945 Japan occupied Hong Kong and imposed a moratorium on all film production. The movie-making industry did not begin to recover until the close of World War II. Only after another exodus of directors and screen talent from mainland China – a land under Communist rule as of 1949 – did the film business become firmly established in Hong Kong. Next to Hollywood and India's Bollywood, Hong Kong now numbers among the top three filmmaking metropolises of the world.

To call Hong Kong a fast-paced city is a gross understatement. Trends of today are forgotten tomorrow, and the film industry ups the tempo with a new spate of films premiering every few weeks. Rapid camera work and innovative editing techniques are de rigueur, producing a style that finds resonance in Hollywood films like *The Matrix* (1999). How better to reflect a city that floods the senses with visual stimulation, where streaming masses of people seldom focus on anything for longer than a fraction of a second? Given Hong Kong's ultramodern atmosphere, it is surprising that stories of China's history are so overwhelmingly popular here. Although the narratives have little in common with day-to-day life in contemporary Hong Kong, the cinema offers a brief means of escape, trading crowded living conditions and hectic schedules for a cinematic journey to quieter, if not necessarily more peaceful, times.

Chinese history and culture inform modern movies more often than not. The heroes of the sort of martial arts films that made Bruce Lee, Jackie Chan, and Jet Li stars in the West are often based on centuries-old legends and storylines borrowed from Chinese opera. Even choreographed fight scenes trace their heritage to the genre's acrobatic performances. One such hero is Wong Fei Hung, a doctor and kung-fu master who made his screen debut in 1949 in *The True Story of Wong Fei Hung*. There have been more than a hundred Wong Fei Hung films since the initial blockbuster, all showcasing well-known kung-fu greats in the role of the eponymous master. Jackie Chan made a name for himself in *Drunken Master* (1978) as the young and less-than-heroic Wong Fei Hung while developing his own inimitable kung-fu comedy style. Jet Li would step up to take the part of Wong in the six-part historical drama and action series *Once Upon a Time in China* (1991-93).

Popular comedies provide yet another way to escape reality for an hour or two. This Hong Kong genre is barely known in the West but fiercely loved at home, with films such as *Private Eye* (1976) with Michael Hui and *King of Comedy* (1999) with superstar Stephen Chow employing slapstick of the one-gag-after-another variety as the main draw. Storylines are relegated to "prop" status. In contrast to these lighthearted flicks, home-grown corruption and organized crime find their way to the silver screen in action films such as *A Better Tomorrow* (1986) and *The Killer* (1989), both starring Chow Yun Fat. Social issues are examined on celluloid, too, with films such as Ann Hui's *Boat People* (1982) telling the story of Vietnamese refugees.

Hong Kong's film stars, actresses in particular, jump effortlessly from genre to genre. From a Western perspective, it may seem improbable that Maggie Cheung could successfully play a character role in *In the Mood for Love* (2000) after her performance as an innkeeper selling dumplings filled with human flesh in *Dragon Inn* (1992) and as a superhero in *The Heroic Trio* (1993) shortly thereafter. But in Hong Kong this kind of adaptability is standard fare. In contrast with how filmmaking works in the West, actors in Hong Kong tend to do their own stunts, even if it means putting their lives at risk. Not only male stars go in for derring-do. Michelle Yeoh of *Crouching Tiger, Hidden Dragon* (2000) fame jumps her motorcycle onto a speeding train in *Police Story III* (1992) and takes a death-defying leap from a highway overpass in *The Stuntwoman* (1996).

Despite the increasing popularity of films made in Hong Kong with audiences beyond Asia, the nineties was an era of crisis for the island's movie-making industry. Numerous factors snowballed to create great financial losses. A general air of uncertainty after the handover of Hong Kong to the People's Republic of China, the economic crisis in Asia, and a growing preference for videos and DVDs over trips to the cinema made an impact. Luckily, a city as dynamic as Hong Kong is always good for a surprise, if not a comeback. Audiences look to recent successes such as the kung-fu comedies *Shaolin Soccer* (2001) and *Kung Fu Hustle* (2004) as evidence of an optimistic trend.

Kar-Wai Wong's film *2046* starring Faye Wong (right) shows the many faces of Hong Kong, spanning its at times seedy nightlife and its modern – even futuristic – world of private clubs and stunning architecture. The movie was nominated for the Golden Palm in Cannes in 2004.

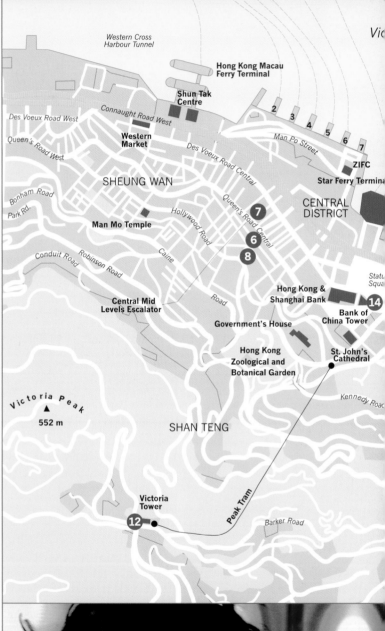

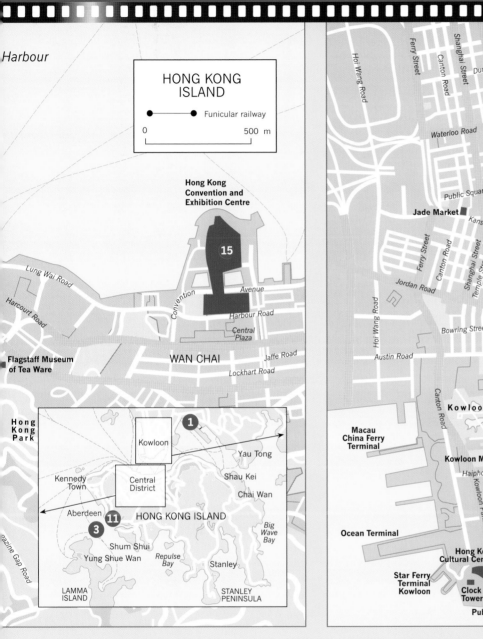

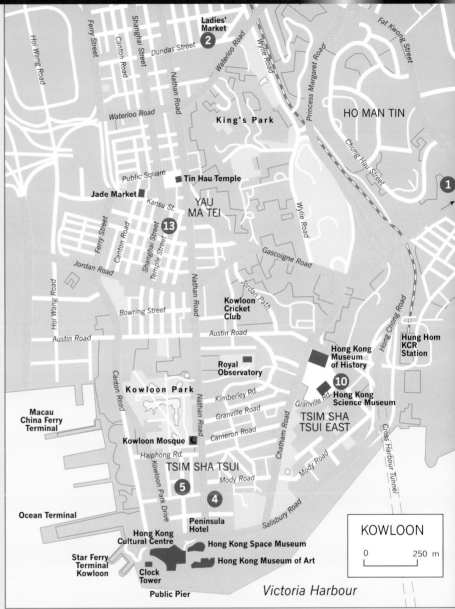

HONG KONG ISLAND

●━━━━● Funicular railway

0 ————— 500 m

Harbour

Hong Kong Convention and Exhibition Centre

15

Lung Wai Road

Harcourt Road

Flagstaff Museum of Tea Ware

Convention Avenue

Harbour Road

Central Plaza

WAN CHAI

Jaffe Road

Lockhart Road

Hong Kong Park

1

Kowloon

Yau Tong

Kennedy Town

Central District

Shau Kei

Chai Wan

Aberdeen **11**

HONG KONG ISLAND

Big Wave Bay

3

Shum Shui

Yung Shue Wan

Repulse Bay

Stanley

azine Gap Road

LAMMA ISLAND

STANLEY PENINSULA

Ferry Street

Shanghai Street

Canton Road

Dundas Street

Ladies' Market 2

Waterloo Road

Wylie Road

Fat Kwong Street

Hoi Wang Road

Nathan Road

Waterloo Road

King's Park

Princess Margaret Road

HO MAN TIN

Chung Hau Street

Public Square

Tin Hau Temple

Jade Market

Kansu St.

YAU MA TEI

Wylie Road

1

Ferry Street

Canton Road

Shanghai Street

Temple Street

13

Jordan Road

Gascoigne Road

Jordan Path

Hoi Wang Road

Bowring Street

Nathan Road

Kowloon Cricket Club

Hong Chong Road

Austin Road

Austin Road

Hung Hom KCR Station

Canton Road

Kowloon Park

Kimberley Rd.

Royal Observatory

Hong Kong Museum of History

Chatham Road

Macau China Ferry Terminal

Kowloon Mosque

Granville Road

Cameron Road

Granville Rd.

Hong Kong Science Museum

10

TSIM SHA TSUI EAST

Haiphong Rd.

TSIM SHA TSUI

Mody Road

Cross Harbour Tunnel

Ocean Terminal

Kowloon Park Drive

5

4

Mody Road

Salisbury Road

Mody Road

KOWLOON

0 ————— 250 m

Peninsula Hotel

Hong Kong Cultural Centre

Star Ferry Terminal Kowloon

Clock Tower

Public Pier

Hong Kong Space Museum

Hong Kong Museum of Art

Victoria Harbour

Enter the Dragon

1. Former Kai Tak Airport
2. Shop-lined streets in Kowloon
3. Junk port in Aberdeen Harbour

Chungking Express

4. Chungking Mansions, 40 Nathan Road, Tsim Sha Tsui
5. Bottoms Up Bar, Mohan's Building, 14-16 Hankow Road, Tsim Sha Tsui
6. Midnight Express fast-food restaurant, 3 Lan Kwai Fong, Central
7. Central Mid-Levels Escalator
8. California Bar, 24-26 Lan Kwai Fong, Central

Chinese Box

9. Central Mid-Levels Escalator (see point 7)
10. BBoss club, New Mandarin Plaza, 14 Science Museum Road, Tsim Sha Tsui
11. Jumbo Restaurant, Aberdeen Harbour
12. Victoria Peak, overlooking the Central district
13. Temple Street Market, Yau Ma Tei, Kowloon
14. China Club, Old Bank of China Building, 1 Bank Street, Central
15. Hong Kong Convention and Exhibition Centre, Harbour Road, Wan Chai

ENTER THE DRAGON

Director   Robert Clouse

Starring   Bruce Lee, John Saxon, Jim Kelly, Kien Shih, Ahna Capri, Angela Mao, Robert Wall

Hong Kong/USA, 1973

Kung-fu films are the cinematic symbol of Hong Kong, and no actor is more identified with the genre than Bruce Lee. Born in San Francisco, but raised in Hong Kong, Lee made a name for himself in the U.S. playing small parts in films and in a minor role as Kato in television's *The Green Hornet* (1966-67). When he was passed over in favor of David Carradine to be the star of the TV series *Kung Fu* – supposedly because he was "too Chinese" – he packed his bags and returned to Hong Kong, the city of his childhood. The decision could not have been better: He rapidly made the jump to movie star and then to international legend. *Enter the Dragon* is the last of four films Lee made before his untimely death at thirty-two years of age, one month before the release of the movie. The first co-production between studios in Hollywood and Hong Kong would take in some $90 million worldwide.

Bruce Lee plays the Shaolin fighter known, conveniently, as Lee. In accordance with his contract with the British authorities, he enters a kung-fu competition held by Han (Kien Shih), a shady character who hides out on a private island. Lee has his own agenda, as well: Han is a renegade student of the Shaolin philosophy, and his evil ways must be opposed. Moreover, Han's bodyguard (Robert Wall) drove Lee's sister to suicide years ago. Two fighters from the United States enter the tournament, too: the opportunistic and financially troubled Roper (John Saxon) and an African-American fighter named Williams (Jim Kelly).

The director cleverly used the Americans' arrival in Hong Kong to show the city with sweeping, atmospheric shots of the island metropolis. Williams's airplane slowly approaches **Kai Tak Airport,** long a symbol of Hong Kong before the new airport opened in 1998; it also makes an appearance in *Chinese Box* (1997). As anyone who has flown into Kai Tak will recall, the approach was legendary. Pilots had to undergo special training to land at the airport, and when the planes descended, they were forced to fly so close to the apartment towers of Kowloon that their wings seemed to graze the colorful washing lines hung from the balconies.

Top: **Bruce Lee fights his diabolical enemy Han using every kung-fu trick in the book.**

Left: **Houseboats bob in Aberdeen Harbour, south of Hong Kong Island. Shaolin fighter Lee and the other contestants pass by the floating villages in water taxis en route to the tournament.**

Even decades after his premature death at 32 years of age in 1973, Bruce Lee is still revered worldwide, as the German poster below indicates, as a martial arts icon and the unassailable master of kung fu.

Shortly afterwards Williams visits a street market and walks along a busy shop-lined avenue in **Kowloon** teeming with over-the-top neon ads – scenes typical for the quarter even today. In the meantime, Roper relaxes in a rickshaw, arriving at the harbour in style. In the seventies, rickshaws still served as taxis in Hong Kong; today they are hardly in use at all. The fighters row past the water-borne throngs in the **junk port in Aberdeen Harbour** on their way to the competition, watching as the resident Tanka boat people go about their lives amidst houseboats and floating restaurants, such as the Jumbo Restaurant also seen in the film *Chinese Box*.

In James Bond style, Han's island compound is crawling with treacherous beauties and scowling fighters. The fight scenes that Bruce Lee choreographed outpace all earlier kung-fu films for their realistic quality. Not everything was just acting: After Robert Wall inadvertently injured Lee with a bottle during one scene, Lee pulled out the stops for the duration of the fight. When both Lee and Roper finally decide to battle Han head on, the drug baron sets his kung-fu army on them. Bruce Lee is often shown in slow-motion during the fight scenes – possibly as a courtesy to the audience, whose chance of following the action is much improved as a result. Lee's preternatural speed was one reason he became such a legend on the kung-fu scene. The film's final showdown takes place in Han's hall of mirrors, a fight to the death between Lee and Han. More than 8,000 mirrors were used to construct the hall, an effect that made the fight scenes seem even more dynamic.

Bruce Lee's death and the immense success of his films prompted a flood of imitators. Films starring Bruce Li, Bruce Lai, Bruce Le, and Dragon Lee attempted to meet the demand for kung-fu films. Even years after Lee's death, leftover footage showing Lee in numerous fight scenes was used to create one last, albeit poor movie, *Game of Death* (1978), created with the help of a look-alike actor. As late as 1981, a few minutes of footage was enough to compile yet another unremarkable film, *Game of Death II*. In comparison, though, the copies were but pale reflections of the originals, at best serving to embellish the legend of Bruce Lee and the cult status of his films. Fans still yearned for a talented successor for Lee, but fate worked against them. Tragically, Brandon Lee, who might have followed in his father's footsteps as an actor and kung-fu artist, was killed at the age of twenty-eight on the set of *The Crow* (1994) in an accident involving a faulty prop gun.

CHUNGKING EXPRESS

Director   Kar-Wai Wong

Starring   Brigitte Lin, Takeshi Kaneshiro,
Tony Leung Chiu Wai, Faye Wong

Hong Kong, 1994

Chungking Express is the tale of two love stories as well as a portrait of Hong Kong. Filmed mostly with a hand-held camera, cleverly arranged sequences capture the energy of this densely populated metropolis, a city that is home to some seven million denizens in a space roughly six times the size of the District of Columbia. The Hong Kong of director Kar-Wai Wong is not the heroically modern commercial powerhouse of business magazines, a place soaring ever-skyward with its glittering skyscrapers. Instead, it is the Hong Kong of regular people and their hopes and dreams.

The film was an international breakthrough for Kar-Wai Wong, who grew up in Hong

Chinese pop star Faye Wong as the character Faye riding the Central Mid-Levels Escalator.

Kong and whose reputation as a filmmaker was already well-established in Asia. His subsequent movies also met with great success in the West: *Fallen Angels* (1995), a film that employs a plot line originally meant for *Chungking Express*, *In the Mood for Love* (2000), a love story set in Hong Kong of the 1960s, starring big-name actors Maggie Cheung and Tony Leung, and *2046* (2004), a dream-like set of narratives that alternates between Hong Kong of the future and of the past.

The film location that dominates the first half of *Chungking Express* is **Chungking Mansions** at **40 Nathan Road,** an apartment complex in the tumultuous **Tsim Sha Tsui** quarter, where a blonde in dark glasses (Brigitte Lin) outfits a group of Indians as drug mules. Backpackers know Chungking Mansions for its numerous mini-hotels, but the area is also popular for its restaurants and shops selling everything from tailor-made suits to video cameras. Even small factories are wedged into this labyrinthine housing complex. The film starts with a chase scene:

**Alone in a teeming metropolis:
Everyone in *Chungking Express*
seems to be looking for love.**

Officer 223, He Qiwu (Takeshi Kaneshiro), is chasing a criminal through Chungking Mansions and almost runs headlong into the mysterious blonde. The action comes to an abrupt halt when He Qiwu rather enigmatically declares that he will fall in love with the woman in exactly fifty-seven hours.

Hong Kong's nightlife served as the backdrop to Wong's love story.

pathetic act of exorcism. He Qiwu and the blond woman meet that same night in the **Bottoms Up** bar in the **Mohan's Building, 14-16 Hankow Road** in **Tsim Sha Tsui,** a striptease joint that also makes an appearance in the James Bond flick *The Man with the Golden Gun* (1974). The couple decide to go to a hotel, but in the end, there's no spark. People living in Hong Kong are forced into constant contact with one another on the city streets, but the exhausted sleeping woman and He Qiwu don't even touch. When he leaves the hotel at the break of dawn, He Qiwu realizes that he still doesn't even know the woman's name.

If Chungking Mansions and its milieu of crime, broken dreams, and hopes for a better future is the hub of the film's first half, then the fast-food restaurant **Midnight Express, 3 Lan Kwai Fong** in the Central district is the focal point of the second half. Faye (played by Faye Wong, one of Asia's most famous pop stars in one of her first film roles) works in her cousin's eatery and spends most of her time daydreaming about moving to California. Officer 633 (Tony Leung), another broken-hearted policeman, stops in daily at Midnight Express for a cup of coffee. Alone in his apartment, he tries to get over the irrefutable fact that his girlfriend has left him – by talking to inanimate objects. While he confers with his soap and his bath towel, people float by on the **Central Mid-Levels Escalator** right outside his window. The contrast is striking: He's isolated in a city where it's never really possible to be alone.

When Officer 633's ex-girlfriend drops off a letter and his apartment key at Midnight Express, Faye makes an unusual attempt to gain his attention and his affections. She repeatedly sneaks into his apartment and makes small changes to how things are arranged. Too blinded by self-pity, Officer 633 fails to notice the changes and Faye's love. When he finally realizes that he has fallen in love with Faye, he asks her to meet him at the **California Bar, 24-26 Lan Kwai Fong.** But she doesn't show. She's already on her way to the real California, the land of her dreams.

Before that can happen, He Qiwu continues to pine for his ex-girlfriend May, who he is certain will come back to him in time for his birthday on May 1. Once a day he buys a can of pineapple with a sell-by date that matches his birthday, and when the time is up, he eats the contents of all the cans in a rather

Viewers would never guess that Kar-Wai Wong filmed *Chungking Express* in a mere twenty-three days while on break from his martial arts epic *Ashes of Time* (1994). The film's energy and creative camera work make *Chungking Express* a memorable experience, conjuring the feeling of having been immersed in the exciting rhythms of the fast-paced metropolis, if only briefly. At the Hong Kong Film Awards, Kar-Wai Wong's masterpiece won the award for Best Picture, with Wong receiving Best Director kudos and Tony Leung taking the Best Actor title.

Faye meets the man of her dreams in Midnight Express. But will Officer 633 (Tony Leung) seize his chance at happiness in time?

CHINESE BOX

Director	Wayne Wang
Starring	Jeremy Irons, Li Gong, Maggie Cheung, Michael Hui, Rubén Blades

France / USA / Japan, 1997

Pretty Vivian (Li Gong) hopes to marry a successful Hong Kong businessman, but must face her feelings for John (Jeremy Irons).

It was high time for a homecoming. After several successful films in the U.S., including *The Joy Luck Club* (1993) and *Smoke* (1995), Wayne Wang returned to the city of his childhood to make *Chinese Box*. Filmed shortly before and during the handover of Hong Kong to China on July 1, 1997, the movie adroitly mixes documentary scenes with screenplay dialogue in an homage to the old Hong Kong that simultaneously looks to the future of this dynamic and ever-changing city.

Jeremy Irons is John, a cynical old hand among the foreign journalists living in Hong Kong. The title of his book, *How to Make Money in Asia*, is hardly a subtle indication of his self-assured stance towards a city he considers ripe for Western exploitation. He lives in an old-fashioned apartment with a view of the **Central Mid-Levels Escalator** connecting the Central and Mid-Levels districts, a location also important in the film *Chungking Express* (1994). He has a wife and children back in England,

but it is clear that John loves his life as an "outsider" in the teeming metropolis of Hong Kong. Shortly before the handover of Hong Kong to China, John is diagnosed with leukemia, and his world as well as his tough-guy demeanor begin to fall apart. He attempts to win back Vivian (Li Gong), the love of his life and the mistress of a successful businessman. At the same time he starts to record what he considers to be "the real Hong Kong" with a handheld video camera. He becomes obsessed with Jean (Maggie Cheung), a young street vendor with a scarred face whom he meets during one of his rambling tours through the city streets. He insists that she allow him to film her story, even though the memories are obviously a great source of pain.

It isn't easy to sympathize with the main protagonist; John's motives leave a lot to be desired, or at least explained. Vivian may be the love of his life, but he humiliates her in front of her clients and her boyfriend with a photo from her days as a pros-

A brooding ex-pat journalist, John wanders the streets of Hong Kong and discovers a completely new side to a city in transition.

titute. When he tries to apologize the next day, he is so arrogant that the only option left to Vivian is to reject him completely. But Vivian's feelings are hard to read, too: Her attempt to seduce John by putting on the clichéd act of an Asian siren in the **BBoss** hostess club **(New Mandarin Plaza, 14 Science Museum Road** in **Tsim Sha Tsui)** is either calculated to get her a ticket out of Hong Kong or a confused expression of her devotion to him.

A number of typical tourist attractions make appearances in the film, such as the floating **Jumbo Restaurant** in **Aberdeen Harbour, Victoria Peak, Temple Street Market** (Yau Ma Tei, Kowloon), and the seemingly endless shop-lined alleys and boulevards. Many scenes capture sides of the city that tourists seldom see, like Jean's small garden off a narrow city street, tiny apartments where inhabitants play hours upon hours of mah-jongg, and deals being sealed in elite watering holes such as the **China Club (Old Bank of China Building, 1 Bank Street, Central).** Many of the sequences have a documentary quality

that blurs the line between fiction and reality. In one of the film's finest scenes, Jeremy Irons appears amidst a throng of real journalists on July 1, 1997, as the Chinese army is rolling its tanks into the city. Filming took place in the **press center** that was specially opened for the handover in the **Hong Kong Convention and Exhibition Centre** on Harbour Road in Wan Chai. And yet, despite the advent of communist rule on the morning of July 1, in Hong Kong life continued as usual. The only difference seemed to be that from that day forward, some 150 years of British governance belonged irretrievably to the past.

Above: **Symbols of the city and tourist highlights such as the Jumbo Restaurant in Aberdeen Harbour lend the film a uniquely Hong Kong flair.**

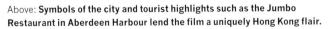

The handover of Hong Kong from the United Kingdom to the People's Republic of China provided an exhilarating contemporary context for Wayne Wang's melodrama.

LAS VEGAS

Glamorous showgirls and Little Venice: Las Vegas celebrated its 100th birthday in 2005.

SIN CITY IN THE DESERT

Of the world's most cinematic cities, Las Vegas is probably the least forgiving. This is the place where dreams die – on the silver screen, at any rate – and even the most upstanding characters deviate from the path of righteousness. And how many of them make it through the movie with their money, their sanity, and their life intact? Behind the glittering facade of this desert city, a dark world of roulette wheels, strip bars, slot machines, and greedy gangsters awaits. In numerous screenplays, Vegas becomes a kind of moral proofing ground. Good men give in to the siren's song of big bucks or are forced

to wager the love of their life. Nicolas Cage loses his fiancée in a poker game in *Honeymoon in Vegas* (1992), and Woody Harrelson takes a wealthy bachelor (Robert Redford) up on his *Indecent Proposal* (1993) to lend him his wife (Demi Moore) for one night – and a million dollars. Even the hardboiled gangsters of Scorsese's *Casino* (1995), for whom Vegas is a singular paradise, fall victim to their own insatiable greed, forfeiting fortune and influence in the process.

A couple gets married in one of the city's many chapels every five minutes. Elvis impersonators are the most popular witnesses.

Only Johnny Depp, who plays gonzo journalist Hunter S. Thompson's alter ego in *Fear and Loathing in Las Vegas* (1998), stumbles unscathed through the seamy casino underworld, possibly because his character is high as a kite for most of the film. He of all people feels bad for the suckers who crowd the gambling tables at four in the morning, still clinging to the impossible dream of hitting the jackpot in the last minutes before sunrise. For all its attractions, though, the shimmering, illusory image that Las Vegas projects fails to impress the world-weary. In the award-winning drama *Leaving Las Vegas* (1995), Nicolas Cage plays an alcoholic whose steadfast goal is to drink himself to death beneath the city's neon lights. Even his love affair with a call girl (Elisabeth Shue) fails to divert him from his grim intentions.

The city whose dark side would fascinate filmmakers in the nineties was all fun and games three decades earlier. In the

Tommy (Nicolas Cage) and his fiancée (Sarah Jessica Parker) finally step up to the altar in the comedy *Honeymoon in Vegas*. Most of the movie was filmed at Bally's Casino.

sixties, Vegas was a glamorous entertainment hub where stars like Frank Sinatra and Sammy Davis Jr. rode the carrousel of nightly performances at numerous clubs and casinos. The films made here were staged as sideshows: All the stars were in town anyway, and Las Vegas made for an exotic backdrop to singing race car drivers such as Elvis Presley in *Viva Las Vegas* (1964) or tuneful casino thieves like the nonchalant Rat Pack in the original *Ocean's Eleven* (1960). Filmmakers began to examine the squalid aspects of the desert city in the late seventies, when the place first tried to clean up its act and cut its ties to the mob. Only decades later would the dark side of Vegas become a fixture in major feature films. *Bugsy* (1991) is one such flick, a gangster saga starring Warren Beatty that depicts the early days of the Mafia-controlled gambling capital in the postwar years, when Ben "Bugsy" Siegel built the Flamingo Casino. In *Casino* (1995) Las Vegas is a quagmire of violence and corruption during its heyday of organized crime.

Robert Redford helped to paint a picture of the city as a place of disillusionment in his performance as a washed-up rodeo rider in *The Electric Horseman* (1979). To the Hollywood veteran, the city was a symbol of American consumerism and excess. While on location for *Indecent Proposal* (1993), he told

the *Las Vegas Review-Journal* that the city is "often like a rich dessert dumped in your lap. But, when you think of it, that is very American." Even for Monty Python's Terry Gilliam, Las Vegas is a depressing place where the American dream becomes a nightmare. After directing *Fear and Loathing in Las Vegas*, the comedian commented that the casino-rich city was remarkable for having no connection to reality.

Despite the cultural critique often leveled against it, the tawdry, artificial world of Las Vegas delivers the perfect backdrop for movies such as *Mars Attacks!* (1996) and *Austin Powers* (1997). The desert, too, which surrounds the city on all sides, has always attracted Hollywood filmmakers – Los Angeles is, after all, only 270 miles (435 kilometers) away. In the 1920s, Westerns were filmed just beyond the city limits. But even the broad sandy plains and jagged canyons of the Mojave Desert are complicit in Vegas's dark dealings: "Meeting in the middle of the desert always made me nervous. It's a scary place," said Ace (Robert De Niro) in *Casino*. "I knew about the holes in the desert, of course, and everywhere I looked it could have been a hole." His friend Nicky (Joe Pesci) was wise to what lay beneath, noting that there were "a lot of holes in the desert, and a lot of problems are buried in those holes."

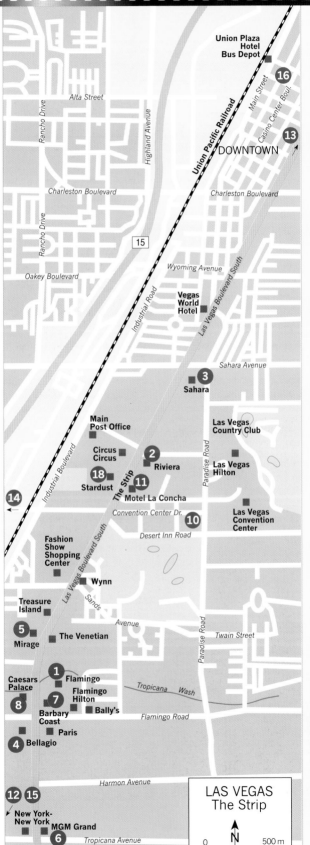

Vegas theme hotels like Circus Circus (left), which Terry Gilliam had hoped to use as a film location in *Fear and Loathing in Las Vegas*, are considered old hat today. The new casinos are opulent palaces like the Bellagio (center), where Julia Roberts works as a curator in the remake of *Ocean's Eleven*.

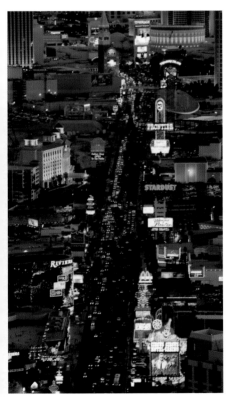

Ocean´s Eleven

1. Flamingo Hotel
2. Riviera Hotel & Casino
3. Sahara Hotel & Casino
4. Bellagio Hotel & Casino
5. Mirage Hotel & Casino
6. MGM Grand Hotel & Casino
7. Barbary Coast Hotel & Casino
8. Caesars Palace Hotel & Casino

Casino

9. Riviera Hotel & Casino (see point 2)
10. Piero's, 355 Convention Center Drive
11. Former Motel La Concha,
   2955 Las Vegas Boulevard South

Fear and Loathing in Las Vegas

12. Blue Diamond, 24 miles (39 km) southwest of Las Vegas
13. Moapa, 52 miles (84 km) northeast of Las Vegas
14. Red Rock Canyon, 23 miles (37 km) west of Las Vegas
15. Goodsprings and Lake Jean, 32 miles (51 km) and 38 miles (61 km) southwest of Las Vegas, respectively
16. Binion's Horseshoe Casino, 128 East Fremont Street
17. Riviera Hotel & Casino (see point 2)
18. Stardust Resort & Casino
19. Flamingo Hotel (see point 1)

OCEAN'S ELEVEN

Director	Lewis Milestone
Starring	Frank Sinatra, Dean Martin, Sammy Davis Jr., Peter Lawford, Joey Bishop, Angie Dickinson
USA, 1960	

Danny Ocean (Frank Sinatra) woos the ladies at the Sands.

If you like the 2001 remake of this film starring George Clooney and Brad Pitt, you'll love the original, for nothing was cooler in the early 1960s than the Rat Pack. The hard-partying singing troupe that included Frank Sinatra, Dean Martin, Sammy Davis Jr., Peter Lawford, and Joey Bishop was renowned for all-night crawls through nightclubs in sharp suits and broad-brimmed fedoras. At the height of their fame, the swinging bachelors so epitomized cool that not even a leather-jacketed newcomer to Las Vegas called Elvis Presley could hold a candle to them. The entertainment capital of America was their playground, and it seemed a natural step to immortalize the nonstop party by committing it to celluloid. The idea for *Ocean's Eleven* was born.

With a cast like the Rat Pack, no storyline could ever be more than a sideshow. With this film, the casting made all the difference. In fact, when studio boss Jack Warner read the original screenplay for *Ocean's Eleven*, he was skeptical, to say the least. He joked that it might be better to carry out the reckless five-casino robbery described in the story than to make a film about it. But when he found out that Frankie and company would be headlining the act, he changed his tune. Jerry Weintraub, who worked with Sinatra back then and would produce the remake forty years on, confirmed that the role of the Rat Pack was the film's ace in the hole. "They could have been reading the telephone book and it would have been exactly as successful," he claimed in a 2001 statement to the press. No wonder the boys would go on to film three more movies together.

Performances by the five legendary entertainers at the Sands Hotel and Casino in Las Vegas were reverently called "Rat Pack summits."

FRANK SINATRA
DEAN MARTIN
SAMMY DAVIS JR.
PETER LAWFORD
JOEY BISHOP

Sands Hotel, Las Vegas

The film's narrative shortcomings go largely undetected. The plan for the heist is revealed a good fifty minutes into the film, and the robbery itself is not all that exciting. For audiences this was no big deal since what the flick offered was the Rat Pack in top form, doing what they did best: delivering smooth as silk lines, knocking back mixed drinks, and hitting on blondes. Guest appearances by Red Skelton, George Raft, and Shirley MacLaine upped the ante, as did memorable musical performances by Sammy Davis Jr. ("E-O Eleven") and Dean Martin ("Ain't That a Kick in the Head"). Odd that Frank "The Voice" Sinatra failed to showcase his singing talents in the film.

But of course Sinatra had his hands full. He was on the set during the day, and at night he and his sidekicks starred in two shows in the packed **Copa Room** at the **Sands Hotel and Casino,** a legendary venue that was demolished in 1996. Afterwards it was bottoms up into the wee hours at private parties at the Sands. Even handsome young Senator John F. Kennedy took a break from his presidential campaign for a flying visit. Crew and fellow actors often waited for hours until the hung-over Rat Packers finally showed up for work at midday, transforming the set into the current stop on their party circuit.

Not only did Frank Sinatra and Dean Martin have financial interests in the **Sands,** but along with the **Flamingo,** the now defunct **Desert Inn,** the **Riviera,** and the **Sahara,** it features at the center of the film's plot: Eleven former Army buddies make big plans to rob all five casinos simultaneously on New Year's Eve. *Ocean's Eleven* is a monument to the five members of the Rat Pack and the five casinos considered "big" in those days. How close the film came to mirroring reality is evident in the final scene. With inimitable nonchalance, Sinatra and his buddies saunter by the Sands, not even batting an eye at the billboard plastered with their real names. Director Quentin Tarantino paid homage to this monumental display of cool in a slow-motion scene in *Reservoir Dogs* (1992) in which his gangsters strut down the street wearing slick suits and dark shades.

The Bellagio is the key location for the remake of *Ocean's Eleven* starring George Clooney as Danny Ocean.

The Rat Pack's music and lifestyle enjoyed a renaissance at the start of the 21st century. After Tarantino's subtle tribute, Steven Soderbergh decided to film a remake. The director of *Erin Brockovich* (2000) and *Traffic* (2000) was well aware of the cult status of the 1960 movie, and made no attempt to emulate the original Rat Pack cast. Instead, he insisted on big-name stars such as George Clooney, Brad Pitt, Matt Damon, Andy Garcia, and Julia Roberts for the new *Ocean's Eleven* (2001). Nor are the locations the same, since the remake is set in the Vegas of today: Danny Ocean (George Clooney) and his compadres plan to rob the three best-known, new casinos on the Strip – the **Bellagio,** the **Mirage,** and the **MGM Grand.** Most of the filming took place in the plush Bellagio, although some twenty complex sets had to be integrated into the premises. Soderbergh and his production designer decided to use the **Barbary Coast,** the **Flamingo,** and the entry to **Caesars Palace** for filming flashbacks to the sixties, seventies, and eighties. Seen together, the Sinatra original and Soderbergh's film sample four exhilarating decades of Las Vegas casino history. A sequel, *Ocean's Twelve* (2004), took the gang on a series of heists in Europe.

In 1996 the Sands, a casino classic, closed its doors for good.

CASINO

Director Martin Scorsese

Starring Robert De Niro, Sharon Stone, Joe Pesci, James Woods, Don Rickles

USA, 1995

Las Vegas in 1973: A twinkling oasis in the desert that is irresistible to gamblers and rip-off artists, soldiers of fortune, and card sharks. A city of corrupt politicians and trade unionists where the Mafia, above all other crooks, has the last word. Heaven on earth for the very kind of small-time gangster that director Martin Scorsese had transformed into heroes in *Mean Streets* (1973) and *Goodfellas* (1990). In *Casino*, the last episode of his celebrated "crime trilogy," he gives his hoodlums a taste of paradise in a nearly three-hour-long epic of greed, crime, and betrayal.

Casino is also a meticulously rendered portrait of Las Vegas in its most felonious heyday, before faceless corporations bought up the casinos and the city was transformed bit by bit into a family-friendly Disneyland. Scorsese worked together with Nicholas Pileggi on the screenplay, a follow-up to their joint effort in *Goodfellas*. Pileggi had already spent years researching the story of the rise and fall of a real casino boss and his connections with organized crime. Scorsese dipped into the cast of *Goodfellas* for talent, hiring on old gangster hands Robert De Niro and Joe Pesci to play key roles in the new movie.

Sam "Ace" Rothstein (Robert De Niro) is tapped by Midwest mob bosses to take over the Tangiers Casino in Las Vegas. Ace has the right attitude for the job: "Back home, they put me in jail for what I'm doing. Here, they give me awards." Ace's brief is to run the casino as smoothly and inconspicuously as possible, and to divert some of the monthly take to his bosses in the Midwest. His best friend, the hot-tempered shyster Nicky Santoro (Joe Pesci), is supposed to watch Ace's back and make sure all goes smoothly.

Everything runs like clockwork – at first. With great expectations of living a life of luxury, Ace wins the affections of Ginger (Sharon Stone), a beautiful call girl. But Las Vegas trots out a parade of temptations and corrupts them all in the end. The more power and money the casino brings in, the more the gangsters' ambition, greed, and distrust of one another grows. Just when Nicky decides that he too wants to be a major player in the casino business, and win Ginger away from Ace, the house of cards collapses on their heads.

The Las Vegas of *Casino* is the city of a bygone era. Nevertheless, Scorsese managed to place it in the Vegas of the nineties. The fictitious Tangiers Casino is really the **Riviera Hotel & Casino** at **2901 Las Vegas Boulevard South** at the north end of the Strip, where Frank Sinatra and the Rat Pack filmed scenes for the original *Ocean's Eleven* in 1960. Its "historic look" has been painstakingly maintained ever since, receiving another layer of polish with a major renovation in the early nineties. The film team transformed the gaming hall of the Riviera into a set between midnight and ten a.m. for more than six weeks, with the casino's business running as usual in the background all the while. Capturing the atmosphere and energy of an authentic casino was more important to Scorsese than having the degree of "quiet on set" usually considered the norm in the industry. Even the documentary-style scenes, such as when the camera

Ace (Robert De Niro) runs the fictitious Tangiers Casino, for which director Martin Scorsese found the perfect stand-in at the Riviera. Ginger (Sharon Stone) risks it all, both in gambling and in love.

follows a Mafia money courier through the back passages of the casino, were shot at the Riviera. Standing in for the exterior shots of the Tangiers was the then defunct **Landmark Hotel,** a futuristic multistory building from the sixties whose spectacular demolition features in the sci-fi spoof *Mars Attacks!* (1996).

Scorsese and his team took no shortcuts with *Casino,* filming at more than 120 locations in and around Las Vegas. Even the comparatively low-key locations such as the hideouts of the Midwest Mafia bosses were filmed here. Classic Vegas locales make appearances as well: Joe Pesci's Leaning Tower Mafia hangout is in fact the Italian restaurant **Piero's** at **355 Convention Center Drive,** located on a side street off the Strip. The shell-shaped **Motel La Concha, 2955 Las Vegas Boulevard South** next to the Riviera, a well-loved sixties kitsch dream in white and pink, is another such location, serving as the love nest for Nicky and Ginger's short but dangerous affair. The landmark motel was torn down at the end of 2004 to make way for the new forty-five-story Hotel Majestic.

Filmmakers love the Riviera for its retro look, which can credibly convey a casino from the seventies.

In the end, the Las Vegas of *Casino* is far more than a sum of its parts. Scorsese immerses the viewer in the city's underground and revives the heyday of organized crime, memories lost between the pyramids of Egypt, the canals of Venice, and pirate ships à la Treasure Island of today's theme-park casinos.

FEAR AND LOATHING IN LAS VEGAS

Director	Terry Gilliam
Starring	Johnny Depp, Benicio Del Toro, Tobey Maguire, Ellen Barkin, Christina Ricci

USA, 1998

If you go looking for the American dream in Las Vegas under the influence of various illicit substances, you have to be prepared to settle for the American nightmare instead. Bringing gonzo journalist Hunter S. Thompson's drug-addled view of Vegas to the silver screen turned out to be a hard nut to crack – Martin Scorsese and Jack Nicholson had already taken a shot at it, as had Dan Aykroyd and John Belushi; but none of them followed through to produce a film. With Monty Python's Terry Gilliam, the story finally seemed to have landed in the right hands. The actor-director had already proven his range and a penchant for the bizarre as a member of the legendary British comedy troupe and in films like the Orwellian *Brazil* (1985) and the apocalyptic thriller *Twelve Monkeys* (1995).

In the cinematic version of Thompson's 1971 cult novel *Fear and Loathing in Las Vegas*, oddball journalist Raoul Duke (Johnny Depp) and his shady attorney Dr. Gonzo (Benicio Del Toro) set out for Las Vegas with a trunk full of drugs. Their mission: to report on the Mint Hotel's "Mint 400" desert motorcycle race. As a sideline, as Duke earnestly explains to an increasingly frightened hitchhiker played by Tobey Maguire, he also plans to write the decisive account of his generation. The southern tip of Nevada provided plenty of locations for scenes of Duke and Dr. Gonzo speeding through the desert in a cherry-red convertible en route to Las Vegas. Filming took place outside the city at **Blue Diamond,** at **Moapa,** at **Red Rock Canyon,** and in the ghost town of **Goodsprings,** with the dry lake bed of **Lake Jean** providing the ideal setting for the dusty Mint 400 desert speedway.

Filming was less simple in Las Vegas itself. Since the famous Mint Hotel & Casino no longer existed, Gilliam and his team had to find a credible stand-in. They settled on the neighboring **Binion's Horseshoe Casino** at **128 East Fremont Street,** a venue that had long since purchased the Mint and incorporated it into its premises. During filming it was business as usual at the casino, with actors and extras placing real bets. The director later

Duke (Johnny Depp) takes the "high" way to Vegas.

joked that this provided the unique opportunity either to double the film's budget or see it all go down the drain.

Because Binion's Horseshoe didn't fit the bill for all of the interior shots, Gilliam looked for an alternate location that was equally as effective as Binion's in evoking authentic early seventies flair. Like Scorsese with *Casino* (1995), Gilliam decided on the **Riviera Hotel & Casino** at **2901 Las Vegas Boulevard South.** The classic gambling palace had the look of the era down pat, and even plugged the filming as an attraction for its guests. The open casting call at the Riviera Comedy Club was further evidence that *Fear and Loathing in Las Vegas* was a totally different breed of film, with contortionists, fire eaters, midgets, and showgirls auditioning for parts alongside gaming table attendants and Hell's Angels types.

As the film does not exactly show Vegas from its best side, other casinos were far less enthusiastic than the Riviera about participating in its creation. Circus Circus, site of a very bizarre drug trip in Thompson's novel, barred the crew from using its famous entrance as backdrop to these scenes. Gilliam used the **Stardust** at **3000 Las Vegas Boulevard South** instead, changing the name of the casino to the Bazooka Circus to sidestep legal issues. He ordered a mammoth clown's head to be erected so that its mouth could serve as the portal into a wacky circus world. Set designers even built a copy of the carrousel bar at Circus Circus for the memorable scenes in which Dr. Gonzo refuses to jump off the revolving watering hole.

In a stingingly satirical episode, the two anarchical coke-heads attend a drug conference for district attorneys in the

Hunter S. Thompson's novel is set at Circus Circus, but the casino wouldn't allow the oddball satire to be filmed on its premises.

conference hall of the **Flamingo Hotel** at **3555 Las Vegas Boulevard South.** The sequence swings manically between paranoia and sheer hysteria, with the two protagonists nearly losing their grip on reality in a flurry of wild hallucinations: Boozy barflies seem to be transforming into lounge lizards, with scales, claws, and all, and even the psychedelic pattern on the casino carpet springs to life, winding its tendrils around Duke's leg. Gilliam's efforts to stay as close to the "unfilmable" original novel as possible make the most of a city that can justifiably be described as artificial on many levels. The zoned-out reporter's final insights provide a ringing confirmation: "This is not a good town for psychedelic drugs. Reality itself is too twisted."

Exteriors were filmed in front of the Stardust Casino. The Riviera, which opened in 1955, was the perfect choice for the interior shots.

LONDON

SEX, SPIES AND HIGH SOCIETY

With comic talents such as Alec Guinness, Peter Sellers, and Peter Ustinov; troupes like Monty Python, and actors such as Merle Oberon and Laurence Olivier, no one can claim that the United Kingdom hasn't contributed mightily to the silver screen. The list of greats goes on: Peter O'Toole, Maggie Smith, John Gielgud, Michael Caine, Daniel Day-Lewis, Helen Mirren, Ben Kingsley, Jeremy Irons, Bob Hoskins, Kenneth Branagh, Hugh Grant, and Emma Thompson are just a few of the top names who have earned the island nation its sterling cinematic reputation. Moviemaking in the U.K. includes productions from studios like Ealing and Shepperton, masterpieces from big names of the postwar era like Carol Reed and Alfred Hitchcock, and entertaining blockbusters from today's directorial darlings such as Roger Michell of *Notting Hill* (1999) fame and Sharon Maguire, whose film debut was the smash hit *Bridget Jones's Diary* (2001). As a film location, London's star is only just rising, a phenomenon that parallels the capital city's new-found popularity as a center of art, cuisine, fashion, and design.

Back when film left its silent phase and entered the "talkie" era, London was a far cry from being an important film location. Britain was, however, the largest overseas market abroad for U.S. films, and Hollywood led the global trade. By the time *The Jazz Singer* wowed audiences with synchronized sound in 1927, the U.K. would account for one third of American films' foreign income. And yet the nation known for its trade savvy had its own movie-making industry, one rooted in the ingeniousness of Robert W. Paul. The English film pioneer copied Thomas Edison's Kinetoscope movie-viewing technology and introduced it to astonished viewers at London's Earls Court in the 1890s.

For Paul it was no easy job to stay a step ahead of the French. The Lumière brothers, who were busily masterminding the new art of film distribution in France, sent an agent to premiere their Cinématographe machine at London's Regent Street Polytechnic in 1896. They even initiated a movie program at the Empire Theatre on Leicester Square that same year. Most films were made by the same companies that produced the projection equipment, so Paul followed suit and went into film production. He established the city's first studio in 1899 with competitor Cecil Hepworth on his heels – Hepworth would found his innovative and commercially successful studios in London just one year later. Brighton would also become a center of British filmmaking, an industry whose ties to the U.S. were always much closer than to continental Europe. As a result, American

John, Paul, George, and Ringo brought the Beatles phenomenon to the silver screen in movies such as *A Hard Day's Night* and *Help!* No one could resist the charm of the Fab Four.

films flooded the British market, providing great variety for U.K. audiences but stiff competition for domestic productions.

This "special relationship" nearly eclipsed Britain as a film-making society, forcing it into the shadow of the United States for decades. London Films and its Hollywood-hating boss, the Hungarian producer Alexander Korda, would win international renown for U.K.-made films with *The Private Life of Henry VIII* (1933) and other costume pageants that promoted the careers of British actors such as Laurence Olivier and Vivien Leigh. London-born Alfred Hitchcock made films in England from 1925 to 1939, but his biggest hits, such as *Rear Window* (1954) and *Psycho* (1960), were done in Hollywood.

The "new wave" that revived French and Italian film in the sixties barely got under way in the U.K. before more "swinging" trends catapulted *Dr. No* (1962), starring a dashing young Sean Connery as James Bond, and the Beatles' *A Hard Day's Night* (1964) into the limelight. The Fab Four would abandon the recording studio for the silver screen again in *Help!* (1965), but it was Connery who would light up the cinemas in the long term. With five more Bond films under his belt, he helped to create a commercial streak for British filmmaking that maintains a distinctly English character even in today's Hollywood-generated sequels. Difficult to believe that the creator of James Bond, author Ian Fleming, feared that Connery would be utterly wrong for the job, a concern the press has adopted to haunt the new Bond man, the talented and handsome Brit Daniel Craig.

Top: **A panorama of the city on the Thames from Tower Bridge.**
Center: **The best views of London are from the glassed-in cabins of the London Eye, a gigantic Ferris wheel.**
Right: **007 inspects his latest automotive plaything in the Tube.**

James Bond's brief Thames-side encounters and the Beatles' romps notwithstanding, it would be Stanley Kubrick who would make us sit up and pay attention to London's presence in film, even if the impressions are not all pleasant. The American director unleashed his ill-mannered droogs in the unforgettable *A Clockwork Orange* (1971), a film that hardly showed London from its prettiest side but used the city as a location in a multifaceted way that the cult punk flick *Quadrophenia* (1979) would fail to do. London locations would not play an important role in the small-time Brit production *Chariots of Fire* (1981), but the film did take the Oscars by storm, followed the next year by Richard Attenborough's epic blockbuster *Gandhi* (1982). Suddenly U.K. productions were in the limelight again.

Despite a resurgence in international acclaim, few British filmmakers were choosing London as a cosmopolitan backdrop to their films. Instead, England made it big as a location in literary and historical films such as *Howards End* (1992), *The Remains of the Day* (1993), and *Gosford Park* (2001), movies that used landscapes and manor houses as backdrops. Another successful genre was social criticism: Films such as *Brassed Off* (1996), *The Full Monty* (1997), and *Billy Elliot* (2000) told the stories of lovable, resilient underdogs fighting for survival in industrial settings ravaged by unemployment.

Filmmakers would occasionally turn to London for multicultural topics, such as narratives surrounding the millions of Pakistani and Indian immigrants trying to make ends meet in the big city. Poor neighborhoods and run-down suburbs play a central role in films such as *My Beautiful Laundrette*

(1985) and *Bend It Like Beckham* (2002). What London lacks in certain qualities – such as the immediate charm of Paris or the vertiginous grandeur of New York City – it makes up for in character. And yet perhaps the city's lack of obvious, picture-postcard prettiness is the very reason it has waited so long for extended big-screen exposure in a series of box-office hits.

Since the nineties, London has had to wait no longer: *Shakespeare in Love* (1998) showcases many of the city's grand historical sights, peering inside its hallowed halls and stately houses to conjure a nostalgic atmosphere. *Notting Hill* (1999) starring Julia Roberts and Hugh Grant treats the viewer to a tour of the eponymous neighborhood, unlocking the secrets of its quaint antiques arcades and bookshops before zipping downtown to hit the luxury hotels and hip eateries. Almost no film is more synonymous with workaday London than the original *Bridget Jones's Diary* (2001), which, *Notting Hill*-like, offers a lighthearted introduction to the bustle and fun of lively Borough Market, as well as a sampling of trendy restaurants. *Harry Potter and the Sorcerer's Stone* (2001) takes a more traditional route through London's railway stations, embassies, and zoos, delivering a fresh, magical new view of a venerable old city. Even diehard New Yorker Woody Allen succumbed to the charms of life along the Thames, tossing Scarlett Johansson and Jonathan Rhys-Meyers into a tangled web of love and lies in the remarkable thriller *Match Point* (2005).

Above: **Ingrid Bergman and Cary Grant during the filming of *Indiscreet* (1958).**
Below: **Tower Bridge, one of the enduring symbols of London, made a memorable appearance in *Bridget Jones's Diary.***

A Clockwork Orange

1. Wandsworth Bridge Roundabout, Trinity Road
2. Taggs Island, 16 miles (26 km) from London
3. Skybreak House, The Warren, Radlett, 24 miles (38 km) from London
4. Former Chelsea Drugstore, King's Road and Royal Avenue
5. Thamesmead South housing towers
6. Shenley Lodge, Rectory Lane, Shenley, near Radlett, 21 miles (33 km) from London
7. Brunel University, Uxbridge
8. Cheyne Walk
9. Albert Bridge
10. Edgwarebury Hotel, Barnet Lane, Elstree, 14 miles (23 km) from London

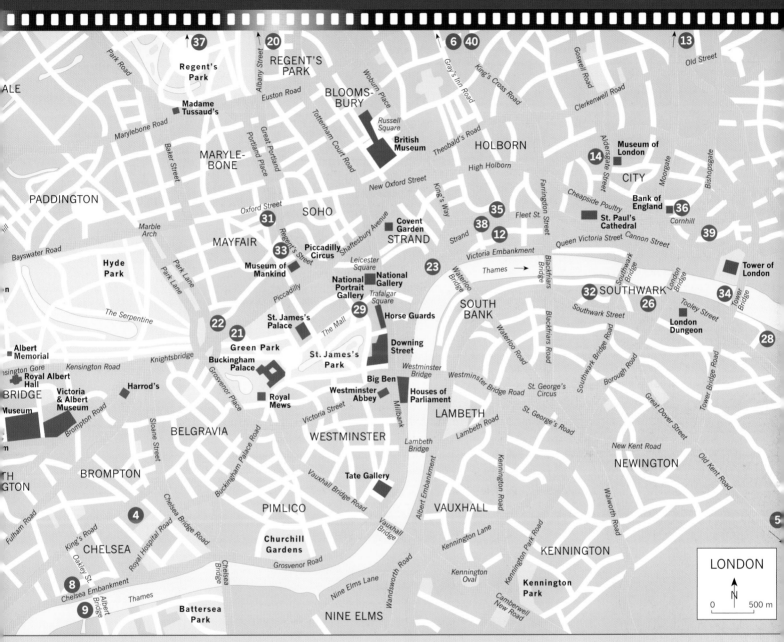

37 Regent's Park

20

REGENT'S PARK

6 40

13 Old Street

Park Road

Madame Tussaud's

BLOOMS-BURY

Russell Square

British Museum

Goswell Road

Gray's Inn Road

King's Cross Road

Clerkenwell Road

Marylebone Road

MARYLE-BONE

Euston Road

Great Portland Street

Portland Place

Woburn Place

Tottenham Court Road

Theobald's Road

HOLBORN

High Holborn

Museum of London

CITY

14

Aldersgate Street

Moorgate

Bishopsgate

PADDINGTON

Baker Street

New Oxford Street

King's Way

Farringdon Street

Cheapside Poultry

Bank of England

36

Cornhill

Oxford Street

SOHO

31

Shaftesbury Avenue

Covent Garden

35

Fleet St.

St. Paul's Cathedral

Queen Victoria Street Cannon Street

39

Marble Arch

33

Regent's Street

Piccadilly Circus

Leicester Square

STRAND

38

12

Strand

Victoria Embankment

Bayswater Road

MAYFAIR

Museum of Mankind

National Portrait Gallery

National Gallery

Trafalgar Square

23

Waterloo Bridge

Thames

Blackfriars Bridge

32 SOUTHWARK

26

Southwark Bridge

London Bridge

Tower of London

34

Tower Bridge

Hyde Park

Park Lane

Piccadilly

22

21

St. James's Palace

29

The Mall

Horse Guards

SOUTH BANK

Southwark Street

London Dungeon

Tooley Street

Tower Bridge Road

28

The Serpentine

Green Park

Buckingham Palace

St. James's Park

Downing Street

Westminster Bridge

Westminster Bridge Road

Blackfriars Road

Southwark Bridge Road

Borough Road

Knightsbridge

Kensington Road

Grosvenor Place

Royal Mews

Big Ben

Westminster Abbey

Houses of Parliament

St. George's Circus

Albert Memorial

Kensington Gore

Royal Albert Hall

Harrod's

Buckingham Palace Road

Victoria Street

LAMBETH

Lambeth Road

Kennington Road

Great Dover Street

NEWINGTON

Old Kent Road

Victoria & Albert Museum

BRIDGE

BELGRAVIA

WESTMINSTER

Millbank

Lambeth Bridge

Albert Embankment

New Kent Road

BROMPTON

Sloane Street

Vauxhall Bridge Road

Tate Gallery

VAUXHALL

Kennington Park Road

Walworth Road

4

CHELSEA

King's Road

Royal Hospital Road

Chelsea Bridge Road

Chelsea Bridge

PIMLICO

Churchill Gardens

Grosvenor Road

Vauxhall Bridge

Kennington Lane

Kennington Oval

KENNINGTON

Kennington Park

Camberwell New Road

8

Fulham Road

Oakley St.

Chelsea Embankment

Albert Bridge

Thames

9

Battersea Park

Nine Elms Lane

Wandsworth Road

NINE ELMS

Kennington Park Road

LONDON

N

0   500 m

Shakespeare in Love

11. Broughton Castle, near Banbury in the Cotswolds, 90 miles (150 km) from London
12. Great Hall, Middle Temple, Inns of Court
13. Hatfield House, Hertford-shire, 21 miles (34 km) from London
14. St.-Bartholomew-the-Great, West Smithfield

Notting Hill

15. Portobello Road
16. William's apartment, 280 Westbourne Park Road
17. Gong, 142 Portobello Road
18. Travel Bookshop, 13 Blenheim Crescent
19. Coronet Cinema, 103 Notting Hill Gate
20. Kenwood House, Hampstead
21. The Ritz, 150 Piccadilly
22. Nobu, Metropolitan Hotel, 19 Old Park Lane
23. The Savoy, on the riverside Strand
24. Hempel Hotel, 31-35 Craven Hill Gardens
25. Private gardens off of Rosmead Road in Notting Hill

Bridget Jones's Diary

26. Bridget Jones's apartment above The Globe pub, 8 Bedale Street
27. Snowshill, Cotswolds, 90 miles (150 km) from London
28. Cantina del Ponte, 36c Shad Thames
29. Institute of Contemporary Arts, The Mall
30. Stoke Park Club, 25 miles (40 km) from London
31. Dickens & Jones department store, 224 Regent Street
32. Restaurant at the Tate Modern museum, Bankside
33. Momo's, 25-27 Heddon Street
34. Tower Bridge
35. Royal Courts of Justice, The Strand and Fleet Street
36. Mont Blanc shop, 11 Royal Exchange

Harry Potter and the Sorcerer's Stone

37. Reptile House at the London Zoo, Regent's Park
38. Australia House, corner of Aldwych and the Strand
39. Optician's shop, Bull's Head Passage 42, Leadenhall Market
40. King's Cross Station, Platform 4
41. Divinity School of the Bodleian Library and the Great Hall of Christ Church College, Oxford University, 60 miles (100 km) from London

A CLOCKWORK ORANGE

Director	Stanley Kubrick
Starring	Malcolm McDowell, Warren Clarke, James Marcus, Michael Tarn, Patrick Magee
UK, 1971	

Alex and his pals toast "Ludwig Van" in the Korova Milk Bar.

Black humor, disturbing imagery, a penchant for Beethoven, and the old "in-out, in-out" secured the late Stanley Kubrick and his breakthrough film enduring cult status. The flick has lost none of its shock value over the decades. Scenes of gang rape and violence seem, at first, gratuitous. But what distinguishes *A Clockwork Orange* is its message: Free will, even if used for evil ends, must be preserved at all costs.

The story pitting a lawless young man named Alex against a repressive society confuses as it enlightens, a paradox British author Anthony Burgess wove into his 1962 novel of the same name. The story is based on the rape of his wife in 1944, and was written in haste as doctors had mistakenly diagnosed him as having a fatal brain tumor. The odd and at times disturbing dialect spoken throughout the film – a Cockney-Russian patois – conjures a pervasive strangeness that Bronx-born director Kubrick underscored with his innovative use of lenses and lighting. He also insisted on filming at locations in and around London, sites with a futuristic look that were also convenient to his Abbots Mead house just north of the city. Rumor has it he was afraid to fly and preferred to stick close to home.

Still enjoying the success his sci-fi cult classic *2001: A Space Odyssey* (1968), Kubrick launched into filming *A Clockwork Orange* with the intensity and perfectionism that had made his two previous projects, *Lolita* (1962) and *Dr. Strangelove or: How I Learned to Stop Worrying and Love the Bomb* (1964), so popular with audiences. The Orwellian tale opens with Alex (Malcolm

Alex on his first day in the bizarre Ludovico Institute.

McDowell) gearing up for a night of "ultra-violence" with his obsequious droogs, Dim, Georgie, and Pete (Warren Clarke, James Marcus, Michael Tarn). The pals meet at the fictitious Korova milk bar, one of only a few sets constructed for the film. After roundly beating up a drunk in an undepass at **Wandsworth Bridge Roundabout,** Trinity Road, Wandsworth, the boys interrupt a gang of hoodlums preparing to rape a distraught woman. The brutes forget the girl and indulge in an expertly choreographed rumble instead at the since demolished **Casino Hotel** on **Taggs Island** in the Thames, opposite the historic royal residence of Hampton Court Palace. The nocturnal tour of terror continues with a wild car ride to a modernist mansion called "Home" whose sleek interiors were filmed at **Skybreak House,** an early building by star architect Norman Foster at The Warren, Radlett, Hertfordshire, just north of London. The masked "Singin' in the Rain" rape scene that so outraged Gene Kelly, star of the original 1952 movie, takes place here, leaving its two unfortunate victims, a subversive author, Mr. Alexander (Patrick Magee), and his wife (Adrienne Corri), physically and emotionally destroyed.

Back at the Korova, Alex is rendered speechless with wonder as a woman at the next table sings part of Beethoven's Ninth, his favorite, a piece best remembered in later scenes in composer Walter (later "Wendy") Carlos's synthesized renditions. Music plays a vital role when Alex picks up two girls at a music shop, filmed at the trendy **Chelsea Drugstore, King's Road** and **Royal Avenue,** now sadly transformed into a McDonald's. Rossini's

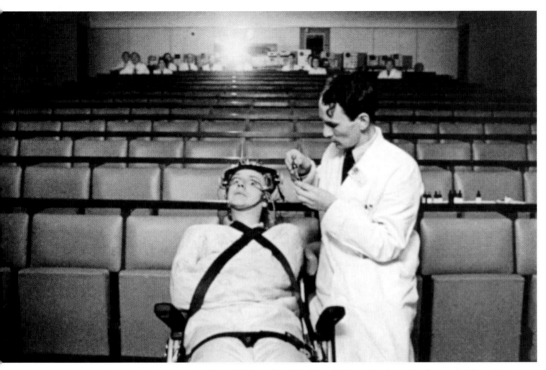

Darth Vader in the original *Star Wars* trilogy). His wife has since died from injuries incurred during the attack, and Alexander himself is confined to a wheelchair. The vengeful writer plots to have young Alex done away with once and for all, and prods him to take a suicidal leap from a window of the Tudor-style **Edgwarebury Hotel** on **Barnet Lane** in **Elstree,** Hertfordshire, simply by playing Beethoven's Ninth. Miraculously, Alex survives, and his bizarre treatment is painstakingly reversed. He returns to his old, violent self, leaving audiences to ponder the moral consequences of his time spent in the hands of the well-meaning but misguided authorities.

In reality, the Ludovico Institute is Brunel University, Uxbridge, in West London. Alex is reconditioned to become a good citizen in Lecture Theatre E.

William Tell Overture accompanies their high-speed orgy that originally earned the film a dreaded "X" rating, followed by a slow-motion fight in which Alex pitches his disobedient droogs into a marina at the grim Corbusian **Thamesmead South** housing towers in southeast London. Subdued, the droogs propose a heist that night at a health farm. Alex gains entry to the house, in reality **Shenley Lodge** on **Rectory Lane** in Shenley, just inside the M25 near Radlett. He wallops the feisty Cat Lady (Miriam Karlin) with an enormous phallus after she threatens him with a bust of – you guessed it – Ludwig Van. When his pals betray him, Alex ends up in the hands of the authorities and is sentenced to spend fourteen years behind bars.

Alex is a model prisoner, and during a visit by the Minister of the Interior (Anthony Sharp) he volunteers to be the guinea pig for a newfangled form of corrective "treatment." Guards haul him off to the ugly Ludovico Institute, actually the brutalist Central Lecture Block building at **Brunel University,** Uxbridge, in West London. In **Lecture Theatre E** he is reconditioned by means of filmed scenes of violence set to the music of Beethoven. The treatments work, at least initially. Whenever Alex is tempted to commit a crime, he becomes physically ill. His family rejects him, and after a stroll along **Cheyne Walk** on the Thames, strange coincidences force him to confront his victims.

The tramp he traumatized at the beginning of the film accosts him at the neoclassically adorned **Albert Bridge,** and Alex eventually finds himself at the mercy of former victim Mr. Alexander and his muscle-bound bodyguard, Julian (David Prowse, later

NOTTING HILL

Director	Roger Michell
Starring	Julia Roberts, Hugh Grant, Richard McCabe, Rhys Ifans, James Dreyfus, Tim McInnerny, Gina McKee, Emma Chambers, Hugh Bonneville

UK/USA, 1999

William (Hugh Grant) still has no idea that the Hollywood star (Julia Roberts) who just walked into his bookshop will end up being the love of his life.

Romantic comedy made a rollicking comeback when the filmmakers of *Four Weddings and a Funeral* reunited for this 1999 box office hit. *Notting Hill* is film title and location in one, giving audiences a whirlwind tour of a hip, multi-ethnic global village in West London. The leafy neighborhood is famous for Europe's biggest street party, the Notting Hill Carnival, an annual summer celebration of Caribbean culture and music started by Trinidadian immigrants in 1964 that draws attention from the international press but curiously enough goes unmentioned in the flick. Candy-colored townhouses, market stalls selling beads, flowers, and antiques, especially on Saturdays, hip eateries like 192 and treasure-trove bookshops specializing in cooking and, of course, travel, make main artery **Portobello Road** a nonstop carrousel of new-age fun. Not exactly down-at-heel during filming, the quarter has boomed since the movie's six-week shooting in 1998 and subsequent success, attracting stars like Robbie Williams to call Notting Hill home.

Maybe real estate was on author Richard Curtis's mind when he wrote his flat at **280 Westbourne Park Road** – practically at the corner of Portobello Road – into the script. The world hunger charity he co-founded, British Comic Relief, could have profited from the sale of the famous blue door and the property itself, which went on the market during initial screenings of the film for $2 million. The improbable storyline turned the apartment into a monument to love: Anna Scott (Julia Roberts), the world's

A romantic break-in at the private gardens on Rosmead Road.

most glamorous movie star, falls head over heels for the man in the street, William Thacker (Hugh Grant), a struggling bookstore owner with floppy hair and a sweet, sheepish grin. After inadvertently dousing her with orange juice on the sidewalk, William invites Anna to clean up at his house, a.k.a. the director's house, just across the street. His store is in reality the Gong interior décor shop (previously the Nicholls Antique Arcade) at **142 Portobello Road,** and is based on the real **Travel Bookshop** around the corner at **13 Blenheim Crescent.** Before she leaves, Anna surprises William with a steamy Hollywood kiss, and that's when the real trouble begins.

The story is based on a tale Grant allegedly once told the screenwriter, an anecdote of movie star and mere mortal having an affair in a London flat. Curtis imagined himself in the same situation, dating Madonna, for example, and still negotiating the day-to-day hurdles of any new relationship. Anna's a celebrity, and her star status gets in the way at every turn. Determination to find love keeps her coming back to William, and to Notting Hill, delivering heartbreaking lines that the soppy Englishman finds impossible to resist: "The fame thing isn't real, you know," Anna intones. "Don't forget – I'm also just a girl standing in front of a boy, asking him to love her." Cynics may cringe, but audiences loved it. Dinner with William's friends, movies at the plush velvet **Coronet Cinema** at **103 Notting Hill Gate** at the corner of Hill

Above: **The corner shop at 142 Portobello Road stood in as William's travel bookshop in the film. The real Travel Bookshop around the corner was the original inspiration.** Right: **William poses exactly the right question at the press conference in the Lancaster Ballroom of the Savoy hotel.**

Gate Street, and jokes at the breakfast table lead them to believe that they have found true love, at least until Anna's obnoxious boyfriend arrives on the scene. Break-ups punctuate the love affair, and it seems Thacker is always chasing her down, as when she's filming a costume drama set before stately **Kenwood House** in Hampstead, North London.

Grand hotels play a key role in telling the story of Anna's life: pursued by paparazzi, interviewed from dusk until dawn by anxious reporters, and never really at peace anywhere in the world. The arcaded **Ritz**, at **150 Piccadilly**, is Anna's "Trafalgar Suite" home away from home – not a bad choice of pied-à-terre given that luminaries from King Alfonso of Spain to the Aga Khan and Paul Getty also liked to reside here when in London. The **Metropolitan**, at **Number 19** in Mayfair's **Old Park Lane**, is the site of the trendy Japanese restaurant **Nobu** where Anna gives impolite diners a piece of her mind. Her last-chance press conference takes place in the Lancaster Ballroom of **The Savoy**, on the riverside **Strand**, a hotel where Elizabeth Taylor famously spent her honeymoon in 1950 with first husband and hotel heir Nicky Hilton. Wedding bells ring in the Zen-like green beside the **Hempel Hotel** at **31-35 Craven Hill Gardens** in **Bayswater,** and true bliss is found on a park bench amid the private gardens off **Rosmead Road** back in good old Notting Hill.

Londoners flock to the Notting Hill neighborhood for its colorful market stands, antiques shops, and quaint bars.

SHAKESPEARE IN LOVE

Director	John Madden
Starring	Gwyneth Paltrow, Joseph Fiennes, Colin Firth, Geoffrey Rush, Judi Dench, Ben Affleck

USA/UK, 1998

The 16th-century equivalent of bread and circuses, claims the proprietor of the revered Rose Theatre, is "love and a bit with a dog." Whatever keeps the ticket sales rolling and stage-loving benefactress Queen Elizabeth (Judi Dench) in good humor is what the rival Rose and Curtain playhouses crave in 1593. When up-and-coming playwright William Shakespeare (Joseph Fiennes) purports to have a smash hit in the works – albeit entitled *Romeo and Ethel, the Pirate's Daughter* – everyone's got to have it. And the sooner the better.

Dubbed Best Picture at the Academy Awards – it won seven Oscars in all – *Shakespeare in Love* is the endearing, fictional tale of how the Bard beats writer's block to produce a timeless romantic tragedy. He cannot hope to write a convincing love story unaided by his muse, the winsome Viola De Lesseps (Gwyneth Paltrow). London locations that survived the Great Fire of 1666 rounded out painstakingly designed sets in the production of this film, as did great estates outside the city limits. The delightful tale of the birth of show business comes wrapped in the attractive package of a period piece resplendent in opulent costumes and prettily delivered lines.

The poet and his muse: Will (Joseph Fiennes) and his Viola (Gwyneth Paltrow).

Even the critics who tapped *Saving Private Ryan* (1998) for Best Picture applauded *Shakespeare*'s Oscar for art direction. Some 115 workers labored eight weeks to recreate an Elizabethan street on a back lot at Shepperton Studios near London, a feat

Above and right: **Queen Elizabeth (Judi Dench) waits impatiently in the Great Hall of the Middle Temple in the Inns of Court for the performance of Shakespeare's latest play to begin.**

Left: **Shakespeare is thought to have premiered his play *Twelfth Night* in 1602 in the Great Hall of the Middle Temple, just through these doors on Fountain Court.**

that included full-scale replicas of the Rose and Curtain theaters. The only "real" theater in the city that achieves the same level of atmosphere is The Globe on the South Bank at 21 New Globe Walk, a masterful re-creation that visitors sought out in droves after the release of the film. For authentic period atmosphere, director John Madden looked elsewhere: Shakespeare first spies Viola dancing in the Great Hall of her parents' estate, in reality **Broughton Castle,** a manor house near Banbury in Oxfordshire's Cotswolds (90 miles or 150 kilometers northwest of London) that has been in actor Joseph Fiennes's family for centuries.

Viola, secretly an aspiring actress, had already spotted the playwright before, scowling at a limp production of *Two Gentlemen of Verona* at the **Great Hall** of **Middle Temple** at Fountain Court, **Middle Temple Lane.** The magnificent clubhouse of the intellectual elite was completed in 1573 as part of the lawyerly **Inns of Court,** and records claim it was the venue of the "sweet Swan of Avon's" *Twelfth Night* premiere in 1602, probably starring Shakespeare himself. The Queen cackles in delight at the play's comic relief – a dog in a stiff white ruff – and dozes off during a soliloquy as Viola considers how she might make a career on the stage. Women are forbidden to work as players, but hearing of an audition at the Rose, she disguises herself as a man and wins the part of Romeo. Shakespeare and Viola fall madly in love, but the bliss doesn't last. In the wood-paneled **Oak Room** back at Broughton Castle, Viola learns she is to marry the Earl of Wessex (Colin Firth). The dastardly colonial landowner needs her cash to jump-start his American investments; for him, the ravishing Viola's charms are merely incidental.

Convention requires that Viola appear before the Queen as Wessex's bride-to-be at Greenwich Palace. The opening scene of the sequence shows a grand party with fireworks set up on the garden side of **Hatfield House,** the great Jacobean pile in Hertfordshire where Elizabeth spent her childhood years. With her fate as good as sealed, Viola dumps the poet – despite a charming scene on a wooden balcony over the formal gardens at the southwest corner of the great house at Broughton. The slings and arrows of outrageous fortune rain down on Shakespeare all at once when he discovers that a rival playwright, Christopher Marlowe (Ben Affleck), has been mistakenly killed in his stead by the jealous Wessex. Wessex thinks he's seen a ghost when the writer appears at a prayer service in the venerable medieval church in the City, **St.-Bartholomew-the-Great, West Smithfield,** also a key location in *Four Weddings and a Funeral* (1994). But Viola is ecstatic, and declaring her undying love for Shakespeare, delivers a stunning performance to a packed house at the Rose – not as Romeo, of course, but as Juliet. All's well that ends well, except it doesn't. Social obligation delivers one final blow before the film is through, a hard lesson in the vagaries of life at the royal court.

Top right: **Viola (Gwyneth Paltrow) dances with her husband-to-be (Colin Firth) at Broughton Castle.**

Right: **A glittering party kicks off with fireworks in the gardens of Hatfield House.**

BRIDGET JONES'S DIARY

Director	Sharon Maguire
Starring	Renée Zellweger, Colin Firth, Hugh Grant, Gemma Jones, Jim Broadbent, Embeth Davidtz

UK / France, 2001

Bridget Jones is a one-woman disaster area, a walking, talking chronicle of crisis. Her weight, her drinking, her work, and her love life are the stuff of this year-in-the-life diary that rings all too true with the over-thirty crowd. Renée Zellweger of *Jerry McGuire* (1996) and *Nurse Betty* (2000) fame achieves full stardom in a film that casts her as a goofy, desperate singleton alongside the ubiquitous British heart-throbs Colin Firth and Hugh Grant. Were it not for the novel that preceded the film, you might suspect that the movie was screenwritten simply to showcase Zellweger's superb comic timing. And yet there's more to it.

Journalist Helen Fielding published the best-selling novel *Bridget Jones's Diary* in 1996 based on her successful newspaper column in *The Independent*. True to her goal, to craft a modern-day take on Jane Austen's early 19th-century classic *Pride and Prejudice*, Fielding wrote the character of Mark Darcy especially for Colin Firth – a splendid choice, as Firth had acted the part of Austen's original Mr. Fitzwilliam Darcy in the 1995 TV series *Pride and Prejudice*. Little was left to chance in the collaborative creative endeavor that would become a box-office hit: First-time movie director Sharon Maguire is Fielding's best friend; screenwriting support came from pal Richard Curtis, who penned London cult flicks *Notting Hill* (1999) and *Four Weddings and a Funeral* (1994); and the locations are places where this gang of media insiders lived and hung out. Could it be that art was imitating life to produce the film's many charms, or was it the other way round?

Bridget Jones, hero of all single women over thirty.

Because Bridget's workaday struggles are anything but heroic, Maguire deliberately avoided using London's grand monuments and squares as locations, preferring instead the cafés, shopping streets, and neighborhoods she knew the real Bridget would frequent. Zellweger, who put on a posh British accent and twenty pounds for the part, fits right in to the Borough Market milieu and lives in a flat above **The Globe** pub at **8 Bedale Street.** It is here she bemoans what she thinks is a certain fate: to die a spinster and be discovered half eaten by dogs.

Love almost finally comes her way in the form of Mark Darcy (Colin Firth), a childhood pal turned boring barrister who attends her parents' Christmas party in **Snowshill,** a picturesque hamlet in the **Cotswolds** some 90 miles (150 kilometers) northwest of London. After a disastrous introduction to Darcy, she returns to London and her job as a publicist at a publishing house, a dull grind but for the opportunity to flirt with handsome boss Daniel Cleaver (Hugh Grant). Bridget narrates the entries in her diary, recording a romantic riverside dinner with Daniel at **Cantina del Ponte, 36c Shad Thames,** an encounter that somewhat makes up for a mortifying public speaking gaffe earlier that evening. The disastrous book launch for *Kafka's Motorbike* was filmed in the glitzy **Institute of Contemporary Arts** on The Mall across

Bridget sees her former childhood playmate Mark Darcy (Colin Firth) in a whole new light at her parents' Christmas party in Snowshill, a picturesque hamlet in the Cotswolds.

from St. James's Park, a set of unforgettable scenes in which literary bigwigs Salman Rushdie and Lord Archer cameo themselves, complete with condescending smirks.

All is forgotten by the time Bridget and her boss-turned-lover take a weekend mini-break at the august **Stoke Park Club,** 25 miles (40 kilometers) west of London, the very same golf club where *Goldfinger* (1964) challenged Bond (Sean Connery)

girl in this complex tale of false expectations and constant misunderstandings gives Bridget an unforgettable kiss in the snow after buying her a new diary at a real London location: the **Mont Blanc shop** at **No. 11 Royal Exchange.** The happy ending holds until the sequel throws Bridget back into the dating game once again. In *Bridget Jones: The Edge of Reason* (2004), the same cast returns for another ride on the relationship carrousel.

Torn between two lovers: Bridget with "boring" barrister Mark in front of the Mont Blanc shop, and at the snazzy Italian eatery Cantina del Ponte with playboy publisher Daniel.

to a tough turn on the fairways. Infuriatingly, Mark Darcy shows up at the same hotel with legal gal pal Natasha Glenville (Embeth Davidtz), and Bridget begins to fear that nothing is going according to plan. But what is? Bridget's mum humiliates her with a suggestive egg-peeling gadget in the venerable **Dickens & Jones** department store at **224 Regent Street** before dumping dear old Dad for a home-shopping buffoon. And when a stick-insect American shows up at the office and is introduced as Daniel's fiancée, Bridget makes a stand and quits her job.

After emergency chat sessions with friends at the panoramic restaurant of the **Tate Modern** museum, **Bankside,** and under faux tents at the trendy Moroccan eatery **Momo's** at **25-27 Heddon Street,** near Regent Street, things finally begin to look up. Bridget records it all faithfully in her diary: new job, still no progress on losing weight, a bit less alcohol .... As she walks across **Tower Bridge** grinning at her new job prospects, it seems as though her diary entries appear on the oversize billboards of Piccadilly – during filming, they actually did. Shots of the neo-gothic **Royal Courts of Justice** at **The Strand** and **Fleet Street** feature in Bridget's television breakthrough interview, an event that brings her closer to stodgy old Mark. Mark and Daniel finally duke it out in a fake Greek restaurant in hopes of determining who will win Bridget's fair hand. The man who gets the

Bridget's cosy apartment is located in the heart of the bustling Borough Market above The Globe pub.

HARRY POTTER AND THE SORCERER'S STONE

Director	Chris Columbus
Starring	Daniel Radcliffe, Rupert Grint, Emma Watson, Richard Harris, Robbie Coltrane, Maggie Smith, Ian Hart

USA, 2001

Adapting an international bestseller to the silver screen is no simple task, especially when the novel in question has already successfully captured the imaginations of millions of devoted readers. Anyone familiar with the *Harry Potter* series knows that these tales of a boy sorcerer simply beg to be filmed. Special effects were crucial in bridging the gap between the book and the film, transforming the very first of J.K. Rowling's popular series into a visually rich, magical world. Among the most memorable are the quirky ghosts who haunt the halls of the magical boarding school, Hogwarts, and fast-paced quidditch matches, a form of polo that the students play while flying on broomsticks.

The filmmakers were hesitant to try to create complex, atmospheric locales such as the Hogwarts School of Wizards and Witchcraft solely on the computer – with the exception of architectural oddities such as the mysteriously moving staircases. They searched high and low all over the British Isles for a location that would fit the bill. No match for the castle described by the author as the centuries-old home of the magical boarding school could be found. The good news was that the United Kingdom was full of excellent locations for the key sequences of the film. Getting to them would involve some travel, but like the disparate pieces of a puzzle, buildings and landscapes ranging from Oxford and London in the south all the way up to England's far north were viable and available for the project.

London is the very best starting point for following the footsteps of Harry Potter. The megalopolis on the Thames is the center of the Muggles' world – the world of non-wizards, that is. The film relates the tale of young Harry (Daniel Radcliffe), a

Harry at King's Cross Station on his way to Hogwarts boarding school.

boy who leads a rather joyless existence living under the stairs in the home of his Aunt Petunia (Fiona Shaw) and her distinctly unpleasant family. Exterior shots of the house were filmed at **12 Picket Post Close** in **Martins Heron** near **Bracknell, Berkshire**, some 40 miles (60 kilometers) west of London. On his eleventh birthday, Harry learns that his parents were wizards killed by the evil Lord Voldemort, and that he has been invited to attend the famous Hogwarts school of magic. The **Reptile House** at the **Zoo** at **Regent's Park** in the north of London, where Harry discovers that he can converse with snakes, is one of the few locations in the entire film that plays itself. Who would ever suspect that the

Left: **The sport of quidditch is taught before the imposing bastions of Alnwick Castle, one of the locations used to evoke the magical boarding school.**
Right: **The Divinity School of the Bodleian Library at Oxford University housed Madam Pomfrey's infirmary in the film's sequel.**

Australian Embassy in stately **Australia House** on the corner of **Aldwych and the Strand** is, in fact, just pretty frontage for the marble halls of **Gringott's Goblin Bank** hidden behind it?

Harry withdraws money from the spooky vaults and sets out with the friendly giant Hagrid (Robbie Coltrane) to shop for magical school supplies along Diagon Alley, filmed amid the picturesque arched passages of old **Leadenhall Market.** To

The ominous Platform 9¾ at King's Cross Station.

get to the winding little street, Harry must pass through The Leaky Cauldron pub, whose door belongs to an optician's shop at **Number 42** at the end of the Victorian market's **Bull's Head Passage.** Kitted out for his first day, the would-be wizard and new friends Ron (Rupert Grint) and Hermione (Emma Watson) make for **King's Cross Station,** where other students are already boarding the Hogwarts Express for the journey to the boarding school. A gorgeously maintained vintage steam locomotive and its passenger cars were brought down to London from North Yorkshire for the shoot. The train pulled in at **Platform 4,** right next to the familiar arcaded wall that Harry and his friends must somehow pass through to get to the ominous Platform 9 ¾. Muggles be warned – don't try this yourselves!

Hogwarts borrowed its distinguished atmosphere from the gothic architecture of **Oxford,** home to the oldest university in the English-speaking world roughly 60 miles (100 kilometers) to the west of London. The university's **Bodleian Library,** which houses more than eight million books, provided the Hogwarts library with its hallowed halls. Even Madam Pomfrey's infirmary, where students turned to stone lie silently in the sequel *Harry Potter and the Chamber of Secrets* (2002), was filmed at the **Divinity School** of the Bodleian. The film crews did their utmost not to disturb the classes at Oxford, working exclusively on weekends so that by Monday morning all the cameras were gone

The picturesque arched passages of old Leadenhall Market served as the location of Diagon Alley, where Harry shops for school supplies with the friendly giant Hagrid (Robbie Coltrane).

and every book was back in its proper place. The famous **Great Hall of Christ Church College,** the largest of the university's forty colleges, was the inspiration for the fantastic, vast dining hall at Hogwarts. The hall, with its long wooden tables, ornately vaulted roof, and cathedral-like windows was recreated at a much larger scale at Leavesden Studios near London.

Getting to the other Harry Potter locations involves going on the road to see some of England's most famous architectural landmarks. The gothic cloisters of the 900-year-old **Gloucester Cathedral** with its spectacular fan-vaulted ceiling 110 miles (180 kilometers) west of London provided the seemingly end-less corridors at Hogwarts. The cloisters of **Durham Cathedral** in England's far north make an appearance in the film, too, as does the chapter house, which stands in as Professor McGonagall's class-room. Further classrooms are supplied by the chapter house and sacristy of **Lacock Abbey** in Wiltshire, 105 miles (170 kilometers) west of London. The exterior shots of Hog-warts were provided by the imposing bastions of **Alnwick Castle,** easily identified in the famous high-speed quidditch scenes.

The famous Great Hall of Christ Church College was the inspiration for the vast dining hall at Hogwarts.

LOS ANGELES

MOVIE CAPITAL OF THE WORLD

"I love Los Angeles. I love Hollywood. They're beautiful. Everybody's plastic, but I love plastic. I want to be plastic." Ultimately, even pop-art prince Andy Warhol would have preferred gold, because it's the metallic allure of an Oscar and a shining star on the Walk of Fame that gives Tinseltown its glitzy cachet. The sprawling entertainment capital of the world is still home to the symbolic center of the movie industry, Hollywood, a holdout of old-school glamor ever since the earliest studios arrived in the first decade of the 20th century.

Tall palms and flashy skyscrapers define downtown Los Angeles.

Mammoths like Universal and MGM optimized film production and distribution in the teens and twenties, and were set to ride the wave when Warner Brothers hit it big in 1927 with the world's first feature-length "talking" film, *The Jazz Singer,* starring vaudevillian Al Jolson. The same year saw the formation of the Motion Picture Academy of Arts and Sciences and the inauguration of its annual awards ceremony. The star system was born, with fans and press alike packing Mann's Chinese Theater at 6925 Hollywood Boulevard for a glimpse of famous faces at the vaunted premieres.

Studios aside, directors love to shoot on location in L.A., where sun, surf, tall, skinny palms, and pretty people dazzle even seasoned auteurs. And why not? The smog of contradictions that envelops the tangled freeways, shining skyscrapers, and bright beaches of Santa Monica and Malibu offers a special brand of inspiration not found in New York, London, or Paris. Plus, there's nowhere better to make movies about The Industry, from classics like *Sunset Blvd.* (1950) to satires like *Get Shorty* (1995) and Steve Martin's *Bowfinger* (1999) as well as Martin Scorsese's masterpiece *Aviator* (2004), with Leonardo DiCaprio playing the eccentric movie mogul and aviation pioneer Howard Hughes.

When jaded tabloid reporter Sid Hudgens (Danny DeVito) welcomes the audience to "La-la Land" in *L.A. Confidential* (1997), it's the small-town hopes presented in a newly pressed suit that give the nickname its ironic charm. Nobodies still board buses in the middle of nowhere, headed for the Big Orange and a shot at stardom, like the character played by Naomi Watts

The star-studded Walk of Fame along Hollywood Boulevard.

Dustin Hoffman's breakthrough movie, picking up themes of family dysfunction from *Rebel* and transposing them into the upper-middle-class milieu that frequented luxury hotels like the Ambassador, the recently demolished legendary location where the doomed affair was filmed.

Film noir, too, found an unlikely home in sunny Southern California. *The Big Sleep* (1946) was filmed in the studios, but the dark places that detective Philip Marlowe (Humphrey Bogart) haunts were based on real locations. Private dick Jake Gittes (Jack Nicholson) makes a splash in L.A.'s notorious water feuds when he follows a key city official to Echo Park Lake and loses a shot at love on Ord Street down in *Chinatown* (1974). Russell Crowe and sexy Veronica Lake look-alike Kim Basinger try to keep their love affair hush-hush in *L.A. Confidential* (1997) as a murder mystery unravels between the Frolic Room, the Formosa Café, and élite residences like the Lovell Health House.

While *L.A. Confidential* looks back at the city in the fifties, *Blade Runner* (1982) fast-forwards to the grim, urban jungle that is Los Angeles in the year 2019. Amidst award-winning sets and special effects, Ridley Scott allows the real City of Angels to peek through with key scenes filmed at the historic Bradbury Building and Frank Lloyd Wright's stunning Ennis-Brown House in the Hollywood hills, a landmark of American architecture. The dramatic landscape just beyond the city proper fascinated one of the most original directors of our time: A car crash up on curvy *Mulholland Drive* (2001) kicks off David Lynch's enigmatic parody of Tinseltown, a fascinating film for which recognizable locations lend an irrefutable air of authenticity.

The elaborate Pantages Theatre, a piece of Hollywood history.

in *Mulholland Drive* (2001). Not many of the hopefuls manage to make a career of it, and fairytale happy endings à la *Pretty Woman* (1990), filmed between the penthouse suite of the Beverly Wilshire Hotel at 9500 Wilshire Boulevard and the tony boutiques around the corner on Rodeo Drive, are few and far between. Big dreams die hard, and L.A. native Marilyn Monroe was no stranger to the trade-offs: "Hollywood's a place where they'll pay you a thousand dollars for a kiss, and fifty cents for your soul. I know, because I turned down the first offer often enough and held out for the fifty cents."

James Dean held out for more, too, and got it. After *East of Eden* (1955), Dean scored his first big-screen success in *Rebel Without a Cause* (1955), a film about troubled youth made immortal by a knife fight and a fatal showdown at Griffith Observatory in the Hollywood hills. *The Graduate* (1967) was newcomer

Los Angeles laughs at itself in Steve Martin's bittersweet *L.A. Story* (1991), chock full of self-important media types who like to see and be seen. Woody Allen, who's in his element when he's in New York City, seems hilariously out of place in a trendy restaurant on Sunset Boulevard with Diane Keaton as *Annie Hall* (1977). Robert Altman takes a look behind the scenes in L.A. in *The Player* (1992) and in a celluloid series of short stories in *Short Cuts* (1993), both Oscar-nominated films.

Numerous "cop comedies" boast an L.A. connection, as well, from the *Beverly Hills Cop* films (1984-1994) with Eddie Murphy, to *Die Hard* (1988) starring Bruce Willis, and *Lethal Weapon 1-4* (1987-1998) with detective duo Mel Gibson and Danny Glover. Drugs and gang wars take center stage in *Boyz n The Hood* (1991), a drama set in the simmering ghettos of South Central L.A., while in *Training Day* (2001) Denzel Washington offers an Oscar-winning performance as a corrupt policeman who shows a rookie how to rule the neighborhoods. *Crash* (2004) cast Matt Dillon, Don Cheadle, and Ryan Phillippe as officers of the law who recognize how navigating good and evil in Los Angeles is much more difficult than any of them could have imagined.

Action films like *The Terminator* (1984), starring California's current governor, Arnold Schwarzenegger, and Quentin Tarantino's *Reservoir Dogs* (1992) and *Pulp Fiction* (1994), move far too fast to make location hunts much fun – and too many of the locations have been demolished in the meantime. Even the iconic Ambassador Hotel, a location in countless films, recently succumbed to the wrecking ball. Alfred Hitchcock's thriller *Psycho* (1960) offers some consolation: The home of creepy Norman Bates and his mom is a major highlight on the popular Universal Studios tour.

Above: **Richard Gere and Julia Roberts hit the shops on Rodeo Drive** in *Pretty Woman*.
Below: **The lovely lights of Santa Monica pier at sunset.**

LOS ANGELES

0   500 m

Rebel Without a Cause

1. Santa Monica High School, 601 Pico Boulevard
2. Griffith Park Observatory, 2800 East Observatory Road, Mount Hollywood

The Graduate

3. Ambassador Hotel (demolished), 3400 Wilshire Blvd.
4. University of Southern California
5. United Methodist Church at 3205 D Street in La Verne, 30 miles (48 kilometers) east of L.A.

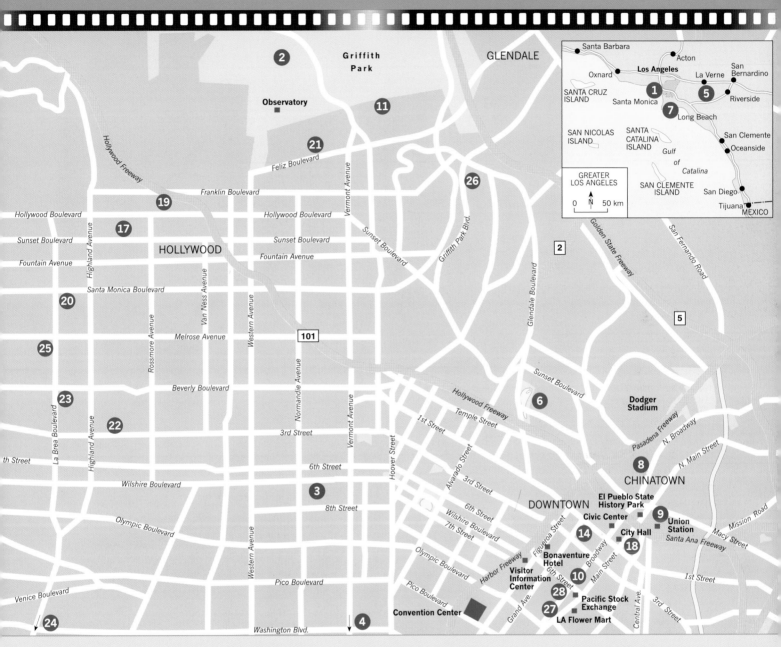

Chinatown

6. Echo Park Lake
7. Fermin Point, San Pedro Park, south of L.A.
8. Ord Street, Chinatown

Blade Runner

9. Union Station, 800 North Alameda Street
10. Bradbury Building, 304 South Broadway
11. Ennis-Brown House, 2655 Glendower Avenue

L.A. Story

12. Ambassador Hotel (demolished), (see point 3)
13. L.A. County Museum of Art, 5905 Wilshire Boulevard
14. Museum of Contemporary Art, 350 South Grand Street
15. Tail O' the Pup hot dog stand, 329 North San Vicente Boulevard (closed)
16. Hard Rock Café at the Beverly Center, 8600 Beverly Boulevard

L.A. Confidential

17. Crossroads of the World, 6671 West Sunset Boulevard
18. City Hall, 200 North Spring Street
19. Frolic Room, 6245 Hollywood Boulevard
20. Formosa Café, 7156 Santa Monica Boulevard
21. Lovell Health House, 4616 Dundee Drive in Los Feliz

Mulholland Drive

22. Mulholland Drive in the Hollywood Hills
23. Aunt Ruth's apartment, 450 North Sycamore Avenue
24. Caesar's Restaurant, 1016 West El Segundo Boulevard in Gardena
25. Pink's Hot Dogs, 709 North La Brea Boulevard
26. Sierra Bonita Apartments, 2900 Griffith Park Boulevard, Silver Lake
27. Tower Theater, 802 South Broadway
28. Palace Newsreel Theatre, 630 South Broadway

REBEL WITHOUT A CAUSE

Director	Nicholas Ray
Starring	James Dean, Natalie Wood, Sal Mineo, Jim Backus, Corey Allen, Dennis Hopper
USA, 1955	

Rebel Without a Cause will be forever synonymous with the brief life and fast times of James Byron Dean, whose premature death raised the aspiring young actor to the status of an American idol. The boy from Fairmount, Indiana, caused quite a stir in his first starring role as Cal Trask in *East of Eden* (1955). A handsome devil in his early twenties, he captured the spirit of angry postwar youth as *Rebel*'s red-jacketed Jim Stark.

Often mislabeled as the quintessential tough guy, Dean gave a performance alongside blushing brunette Natalie Wood that broke hearts across the nation and proved that real men have family problems, too. Los Angeles provided a bevy of choice locations, none more enduring than the Griffith Park Observatory, where a bust of Dean still evokes scenes from the film. As loved as he was despised by co-stars, directors, and press, Dean was posthumously nominated for two Academy Awards, Best Actor for both *East of Eden* (1955) and *Giant* (1956). Filming for *Giant* had just wrapped up when Dean's silver Porsche Spyder met another vehicle in a fatal head-on collision on September 30, 1955, a tragedy that made headlines around the world.

In *Rebel*, teen punk Jim Stark is in trouble – again. Drunk and disorderly, he's hauled down to the police station to the consternation of his parents. They've only just relocated to L.A. to escape the memory of their son's last embarrassing debacle, or so they say: Mrs. Stark (Ann Doran) and husband Frank (Jim Backus, Thurston Howell in the TV series *Gilligan's Island*) are constantly at each other's throats, and Jim will do anything to get their attention. Otherwise, he's just a nice guy. Down at the station, Jim offers his jacket to Plato (Sal Mineo), a disturbed child who has just offed a litter of puppies, and falls for Judy (Natalie Wood), a pretty girl who is also at odds with her parents. Jim meets Judy the next morning on the way to Dawson High, really **Santa Monica High School** at **601 Pico Boulevard** in Santa Monica. She spurns his offer of a ride and goes with "the kids" instead, a gang led by her bossy boyfriend, Buzz Gunderson (Corey Allen).

Jim (James Dean) and Judy (Natalie Wood) as troubled teens in a film that embodied an era.

Buzz and his pals, including a young Dennis Hopper, object to Jim's shenanigans during a school trip to the planetarium and challenge him to a gripping knife fight behind the **Griffith Park Observatory** at **2800 East Observatory Road, Mount Hollywood**. Plato the puppy killer tries to break it up and ends up befriending Jim – but it's too late. Jim has already agreed to meet Buzz that night for the ultimate test of manhood. After pressing his befuddled father for advice, Jim screeches off "for honor" and a deadly car race on the nearby bluffs, returning home for help when the contest goes horribly wrong. As usual, his parents fail him, and Jim turns to Judy for solace. They run off in the middle of the night to a derelict mansion nearby, and together with

Santa Monica High School (left), where Jim attends classes with Judy and has to fight to get respect from "the kids."

Plato they seem to form a sad little teenage family. Buzz's goons and the cops arrive, and the melee relocates to the Griffith Park Observatory where a tragic end awaits.

James Dean, often compared to his idol-rival Marlon Brando in *The Wild One* (1953) for his brooding manner and mumbling delivery, breathed new life into the "angry youth" flick as a film genre. His few films focused on the trials of a young man looking to connect with his parents, especially the father, a theme compatible with his own life. However widespread the cliché may be, Dean was, in fact, not a troublemaker. His reputation for ignoring cues and rearranging lines in the script has unfairly outlasted his standing as a highly admired method actor. Dennis Hopper, who would go on to star in such late sixties classics as *Easy Rider* (1969) after roles alongside Dean in *Rebel* and *Giant*, said it best: "He seemed to capture that moment of youth, that moment where we're all desperately seeking to find ourselves." Hopper's words dovetail beautifully with Dean's famous credo: "Dream as if you'll live forever. Live as if you'll die today."

The famous knife fight in *Rebel* (above) takes place on the terrace of the Griffith Park Observatory on a hill overlooking the smog-cloaked city.

THE GRADUATE

Director	Mike Nichols
Starring	Dustin Hoffman, Anne Bancroft, Katharine Ross, William Daniels, Murray Hamilton, Elizabeth Wilson, Buck Henry
USA, 1967	

Plus ça change.... This coming of age classic about Benjamin Braddock (Dustin Hoffman) and bored L.A. housewife Mrs. Robinson (Anne Bancroft) recently enjoyed a revival when Kathleen Turner bared it all on Broadway in the stage adaptation of *The Graduate*, a film as loved for its music as for its scandalous plot. Paul Simon penned the refrain "Here's to You, Mrs. Robinson" especially for the film, and with partner Art Garfunkel contributed songs from their Grammy-winning album *Sounds of Silence* to capture the mood of a generation confused by materialistic parents but schooled to become just like them. The youth of the Vietnam War era saw *The Graduate* as holding a mirror to their problems and tendering a revolutionary solution. Nichols was regaled as Best Director at the Oscars, another hit to follow his first film, the psychologically harrowing *Who's Afraid of Virginia Woolf?* (1966) starring Elizabeth Taylor and Richard Burton.

Charles Webb's 1963 novel translated beautifully into a screenplay about youth in well-heeled America. Ben Braddock (Dustin Hoffman) is a recent graduate from an East Coast college who has come home to confront his "future." Mom and Dad are the perfect upper middle class couple, with a gorgeously decorated home, a pool, and an attractive set of socialite friends. One of these is Mrs. Robinson (Anne Bancroft), a sexy, chain-smoking cynic who demands that Ben hop in the sack with her after his commencement party. Ben wants no part of it – at first, but soon arranges to meet her at the Taft Hotel where he sheepishly approaches the desk clerk (screenwriter Buck Henry) presiding over what was in reality the famed **Ambassador Hotel** at **3400 Wilshire Boulevard,** a recently demolished Mediterranean-styled grand auberge. In its long heyday, from the 1920s to the 1960s, the Ambassador's Cocoanut Grove lounge reigned as the ultimate star hangout featuring live music from Bing Crosby, who was discovered there. Marilyn Monroe signed her first modeling contract at the Ambassador, which was also the site of Robert F. Kennedy's assassination in 1968 at the hands of Sirhan Sirhan, a tragedy yet to occur when Ben Braddock took a room for a night and then all summer long to conduct an illicit affair. Little did he know that this rite of passage into adulthood would nearly cost him the love of his life.

Here's to you, Mrs. Robinson: The recently demolished Ambassador Hotel, where Ben (Dustin Hoffman) has an affair with an older woman (Anne Bancroft).

Ben waits for Elaine in front of USC's Doheny Memorial Library.

When Mrs. Robinson's daughter Elaine (Katharine Ross) returns home from school, Ben succumbs to pressure from his parents and takes her out on a date. The evening ends in two confessions: He declares his love for Elaine and admits that he's been having an affair with a married woman. "And it's all over now?" Elaine asks. Ben nods, and the film shifts into high gear. Mrs. Robinson threatens to tell everyone the truth if Ben insists on dating her daughter, but, thinking that love will conquer all, Ben does the job himself. Elaine is disgusted at the revelation and throws Ben out of her life. More like a stalker than a lover, Ben trails Elaine all over town before following her to college at Berkeley, across the Bay from San Francisco. The **University of Southern California** in downtown L.A. stood in for key shots in this sequence: After waiting by the fountain, Ben glimpses Elaine coming down the steps of **Doheny Memorial Library** in **Alumni Park** off of **Childs Way**.

war until Elaine's father shows up and forbids him to see his daughter ever again: Elaine and Carl have set a date for the wedding. Ben races his little red sports car up and down the coast of California in search of the ceremony, filmed at the modernist **United Methodist Church** at **3205 D Street** in **La Verne,** some 30 miles (48 kilometers) east of L.A. When Ben finally arrives, he finds the main doors to the church locked. Undaunted, the desperate suitor makes his way up to a balcony overlooking the nave. He screams Elaine's name while pounding on the plate glass dividing him from the wedding just ended below.

Elaine (Katharine Ross) and Ben make a break for it at the United Methodist Church in La Verne, east of downtown L.A.

Against her better judgment, Elaine realizes that she's in love with Ben – but she refuses his offers of marriage. She's also dating "make-out king" Carl Smith (Brian Avery), who has asked for her hand, too. Ben thinks he's winning the romantic tug of

Elaine is beside herself. The resolution is blissfully ambivalent, challenging the viewer to decide whether Ben has learned his lesson or whether he is hopelessly imprudent and destined to repeat the mistakes of the past.

CHINATOWN

Director	Roman Polanski
Starring	Jack Nicholson, Faye Dunaway, John Huston, Perry Lopez, Darrell Zwerling, Diane Ladd

USA, 1974

"Forget it, Jake. It's Chinatown." Neo-noir hit a high note in the seventies with this famous last line, one of many stellar quips in Roman Polanski's tour de force detective thriller. Nominated for eleven Academy Awards, *Chinatown* walked away with only one. Blame it on *Godfather II* (1974) because Robert Towne's Best Original Screenplay set in 1930s Los Angeles adds to murder and graft a dark romance between Jack Nicholson and Faye Dunaway so retro-stylish and deeply shocking as to make original 1940s L.A. noir novelist Raymond

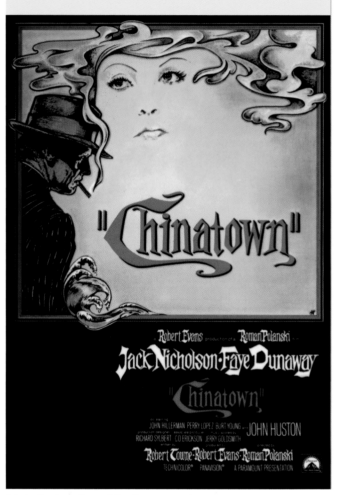

Jake (Jack Nicholson) and the mysterious Mrs. Mulwray (Faye Dunaway) in a twisted tale of murder and deceit.

Chandler green with envy. Out-of-doors locations add a raw, sun-bleached touch to the dark-toned sets where most of the flick's interior scenes were filmed.

Dapper private investigator Jake Gittes (Jack Nicholson) is duped into a dream job: A glamorous brunette posing as the wife of the water commissioner wants to know if her husband is, as she suspects, having an affair. Gittes and his operative trail the engineer, Hollis I. Mulwray (Darrell Zwerling), as he takes a "cute little twist" for a ride in a rowboat on **Echo Park Lake.** Snaps of the couple kissing hit the headlines, a boost to Jake's celebrity until the real Mrs. Evelyn Cross Mulwray (Faye Dunaway) turns up threatening to sue. So who was the looker

who hired him on? No natural laughingstock, Jake takes the case as a personal quest and follows Mulwray on inspections of reservoirs and river beds around the city. The city official seems agitated. Jake knows what Mulwray's worried about: Los Angeles is in the middle of a devastating drought, and farmers in the outlying San Fernando Valley are convinced that the city is getting more than its fair share of the water. The story is based on the real-life Owens River Valley scandal of 1908 involving the ambitious water commissioner William Mulholland.

Mulwray – the name a play on Mulholland – drowns in a man-made lake and Jake thinks the wife's behind it. More snooping gets Jake cornered by Water and Power Department toughs,

Jake stakes out the bad guys south of downtown Los Angeles at Fermin Point, near the port of L.A.

who had lost his mother and most of his family in the Nazi work camps of World War II – a topic he would revisit in his multiple-Oscar winning film *The Pianist* (2002). After studying film in Poland in the fifties, he made a splash in Europe with *Cul-de-Sac* (1966) and then in Hollywood with *Rosemary's Baby* (1968). Tragedy struck again in 1969 when members of Charles Manson's maniacal "family" brutally murdered Polanski's actress wife, Sharon Tate. The director's first self-imposed exile to Europe at the apex of his career ended when he returned to L.A. to produce *Chinatown,* considered his best-ever film.

What happened all those years ago in Chinatown? One of the film's many dark secrets.

and bit-part baddie and director Roman Polanski slices his nostril for nosing around at **Fermin Point, San Pedro Park,** near the port of L.A. south of the city. His comical bandage lands him in bed with the widowed femme fatale, but there are still too many questions to be answered: The coroner finds salt water in Mulwray's lungs, even though his body was found at a municipal reservoir; the mysterious mistress suddenly disappears, and Evelyn's father, rich and evil Noah Cross (veteran director John Huston), is offering to pay outrageous sums for her return. What the devil is going on, and why does Jake constantly refer to an incident years ago in Chinatown?

Hang on to the plot but don't despair if the incest and power mongering leave you grasping at clues. The only scene in the film that actually takes place in the eponymous and oft-mentioned Asian quarter is the final shootout on **Ord Street,** and nothing is really clear until Jake's old rival from the police department, Lieutenant Lou Escobar (Perry Lopez), drops charges against him and sends him home. The profoundly tragic outcome in Chinatown was Polanski's idea, written into the script just before filming despite protestations from writer Towne who had originally planned for a happy ending.

Perhaps catastrophe made the story more credible, or perhaps it came more naturally to Polanski, a Paris-born Pole

BLADE RUNNER

Director	Ridley Scott
Starring	Harrison Ford, Rutger Hauer, Sean Young, Daryl Hannah, Edward James Olmos, M. Emmet Walsh, William Sanderson, Joe Turkel
USA, 1982	

Former cop Deckard (Harrison Ford) takes on a bizarre manhunt in a spooky L.A. of the future.

Harrison Ford in a box-office flop? Perish the thought. *Star Wars* (1977) and *Raiders of the Lost Ark* (1981) were both megahits, but Ridley Scott's sci-fi thriller *Blade Runner* starring Ford as a hardboiled L.A. cop fell flat on its face when it debuted in 1982. Critics panned the tale of androids and lunar colonies as muddled and confusing, leaving it no chance at the Oscars against blockbuster *E.T.* despite spirited nominations for Best Art Direction and Visual Effects. As has been the case with many cult favorites, interest in the film adaptation of Philip K. Dick's 1969 novel *Do Androids Dream of Electric Sheep?* has skyrocketed since. The release of a modified director's cut in 1992 won cheers from fans who rate *Blade Runner* as the late 20th-century's greatest contribution to film noir, a genre perfected by Humphrey Bogart as private investigator Sam Spade in *The Maltese Falcon* (1941).

Vangelis's eerie sound track set the mood, and fantastical sets transformed a revamped back lot at Hollywood's Burbank Studios into L.A. in the year 2019. Masterfully crafted miniature buildings appear as densely packed skyscrapers hundreds of stories high, buzzing with police copters and flashing larger-than-life ads on oversize billboard screens. Special effects and modeling just about did the job, but Scott's scrupulous attention to detail demanded that the real City of Angels also feature in the sequencing right from the start.

The story opens with grumpy Rick Deckard (Harrison Ford) being hauled downtown to historic, Mission-style **Union Station** at **800 North Alameda Street** for the last thing he wanted as a former detective: a new assignment. Six escaped replicants – humanoid robots programmed for "off-world" labor in the planetary colonies and on the moon – must be hunted down and destroyed. Dapper cop Gaff (Edward James Olmos) folds an origami chicken to poke fun at his reluctance, and Deckard's

Deckard is dragged down to police headquarters at historic Union Station for an assignment he doesn't want: chasing down dangerous rogue replicants.

The awe-inspiring Bradbury Building, the scene of Deckard's showdown with muscle-bound replicant Roy (Rutger Hauer).

old boss Bryant (M. Emmet Walsh) won't take no for an answer. He recites a list of targets to include blond super-warrior Roy Batty (Rutger Hauer) and his pretty "pleasure model" girlfriend Pris (Daryl Hannah). A visit to the daunting Tyrell Corporation complex brings Deckard face to face with the androids' creator, Eldon Tyrell (Joe Turkel), and his female assistant. The lovely Rachael (Sean Young) is a forties-styled doll who has no idea that she, too, is an android. The detective suspects the truth: Rachael has a four-year lifespan, and implanted memories keep her convinced that she's human.

Meanwhile, robotic baddies Roy and Pris corner Tyrell Corporation programmer J.F. Sebastian (William Sanderson) in his spooky apartment complex, the landmark **Bradbury Building.** The 1893 brick pile at **304 South Broadway** is equipped with cage elevators, wrought-iron railings and piercing searchlights that add drama to the violence that unfolds within, a grisly counterpoint to the detective's romantic developments. Deckard falls head over heels for Rachael, and corners her into a kiss at his apartment located at the **Ennis-Brown House,** a textile-block-style villa built in 1924 by Frank Lloyd Wright at **2655 Glendower Avenue** in the sylvan Hollywood hills. After a mighty showdown with Roy at the Bradbury, the lovers decide to flee L.A., spurred on by the appearance of an origami unicorn as they depart, a sign they interpret to mean that time is running out.

To jazz up Los Angeles as a city of the future, production designer Lawrence Paull and "futurist visionary" Syd Mead borrowed heavily from the Orient. Except for certain specific locations, their L.A. of 2019 could have been Hong Kong, Shanghai, Tokyo, or any one of the densely populated, skyscraping capitals of the Far East obscured by smog and teeming with street life. In numerous scenes, noodle shops and market stalls hawking live animals can be seen thriving in the Technicolor glow of neon signs advertising sleazy hotels and casinos. Comparisons to Fritz Lang's film *Metropolis* (1927) abound, mostly because of the eerie futuristic effects. Los Angeles of 2019 is not the heroic city of modern aspirations, reflecting instead the director's view that humanity can easily lose its way in the forward rush of progress.

Closing scenes were filmed at the famous Ennis-Brown House, an architectural masterpiece by Frank Lloyd Wright that is considered an important landmark of American architecture.

L.A. STORY

Director	Mick Jackson
Starring	Steve Martin, Victoria Tennant, Richard E. Grant, Sarah Jessica Parker, Marilu Henner, Susan Forristal

USA, 1991

Detractors say Los Angeles is nothing more than urban sprawl with smog, but for Steve Martin it is the heady City of Angels. The screenplay he wrote over seven years is an ode to falling in love California-style with then-wife and co-star Victoria Tennant, the demure English rose he met on the set of *All of Me* (1984). *L.A. Story* is a classic Steve Martin star vehicle in the tradition of *The Jerk* (1979 – "I was born a poor black child") packed to the hilt with hilarious one-liners, but, in spite of all the wit, achingly soft in the middle. If you don't know that Martin is smitten with Tennant before you see the film, you'll know the minute she makes her appearance. And if you can't see that Martin is head over heels with Los Angeles for all the charming locations that give the city an otherworldly feel, then the joke's on you.

Martin lovingly pokes fun at the Angeleno lifestyle, and the cliché images couldn't be better: beautiful people meeting for social lunches in palm-fringed bistros, driving, never walking, even if only to a next-door neighbor's house, shooting at cars on the "open season" freeway, but most of all drifting in and out of romantic relationships with the unserious air of a prime-time sitcom. It's not SoCal superficiality, Martin intimates, it's just the palpable ennui of the incurably well-to-do. A hint as to what he's getting at appears during the opening credits: The giant hot dog being flown by helicopter over bathing beauties is an unsubtle reference to a similar sequence in Fellini's *La Dolce Vita* (1960), a classic film about the idle rich of Rome.

Harris (Steve Martin) is a slave to love – and shopping.

When celebrity weatherman Harris K. Tellemacher (Martin) meets visiting British journalist Sara McDowel (Tennant) at L'Idiot restaurant – filmed in the recently demolished **Ambassador Hotel** at **3400 Wilshire Boulevard** – he sees a chance to add meaning to his life. A highway sign spells it out for him in the form of a riddle, but for Harris the journey from halfhearted love affairs to a fulfilling relationship takes some doing. Meanwhile, he derives silly pleasure in roller-skating through the galleries of the **L.A. County Museum of Art** at **5905 Wilshire Boulevard** while a camera-wielding friend films it as "performance art." While whizzing through another temple to culture, the Arata Isozaki-

Harris flirts with irrepressibly bubbly California girl SanDeE* (Sarah Jessica Parker) at the Hard Rock Café in the Beverly Center.

Sara (Victoria Tennant) faces two types of temptation at the Tail O' the Pup hotdog stand.

designed **Museum of Contemporary Art** at **250 South Grand,** he runs into Sara, quite literally, knocking her flat.

It's clear that the two are falling in love, but there's a catch: Sara promises to spend a romantic weekend with her ex-husband, the annoying Roland Mackey (Richard E. Grant) over a wiener at the hot-dog shaped **Tail O' the Pup** stand, a fixture at **329 North San Vicente Boulevard** until it closed in 2006. They make plans to meet at a seaside resort. Harris becomes involved with Valley girl SanDeE* (Sarah Jessica Parker) at the **Hard Rock Café** at **8600 Beverly Boulevard** in the **Beverly Center** mall, and, peeved at Sara, arranges a tryst – also at a seaside

resort. Luck would have it that the couples choose the *same* seaside resort. Slapstick antics won't save Harris this time.

It's been called a counterpoint to Woody Allen's *Manhattan* (1979), but of course Martin's absurd comic timing makes for much lighter fare. A cameo appearance by Chevy Chase recalls Martin's wacky routines on television's *Saturday Night Live*, when 1970s audiences first got to know the irrepressible "wild and crazy guy." *L.A. Story* marks the actor's successful transition to serious characters who never get too serious while allowing the uninitiated to see Los Angeles as a place where dreams, and not just of stardom, really do come true.

Harris, Sara, and Roland (Richard E. Grant) form a love triangle that visits L.A.'s world-famous museums, such as the Museum of Contemporary Art (left).

L.A. CONFIDENTIAL

Director	Curtis Hanson
Starring	Russell Crowe, Kim Basinger, Guy Pearce, Kevin Spacey, James Cromwell, Danny DeVito

USA, 1997

An unlikely couple: Brute cop Bud White (Russell Crowe) and high-class hooker Lynn Bracken (Kim Basinger) find love against all odds.

Kim Basinger's Oscar-winning performance and director Curtis Hanson's clever use of famous Hollywood locations made *L.A. Confidential* a classier act than *Titanic*, even though the blockbuster boat flick starring Leonardo DiCaprio and Kate Winslet stole the show at the Academy Awards. Love may go on, if you believe Céline Dion's tear-jerking anthem, but murder is far more interesting, especially when committed in the 1950s movie star milieu that included gorgeous blondes like Lana Turner and gangsters à la Mickey Cohen. The mobster's jail term for tax evasion and the ensuing power vacuum described in James Ellroy's eponymous novel were director Hanson's ticket to a netherworld ruled by drugs, prostitution, and an intoxicating lust for fame. Hanson, who grew up in L.A., didn't set out to create high-style film noir. He wanted the City of Angels to appear "casual in its period look," with forty-five city locations creating a credible setting for the crises of human character that unfold in the film.

"Life is good in Los Angeles – at least that's what they tell you." Gossip columnist Sid Hudgens (Danny DeVito) sets a cynical tone in the opening scenes. His *Hush Hush* newsletter offices are situated under the spinning globe of the **Crossroads of the World** at **6671 West Sunset Boulevard,** a 1930s shopping center built to look like an ocean liner (it now houses offices). The L.A. police department is still reeling from corruption charges pinned on its vice squad in 1949, and four years on, the boys in blue based at the 1928 **City Hall** skyscraper at **200 North Spring Street** cannot shake the notoriety. Questionable methods employed by a trio of cops – Sergeant Jack Vincennes (Kevin Spacey), Officer Bud White (Russell Crowe), and Lieutenant Ed Exley (Guy Pearce) – end up righting the department's public image, but not before a few lives have been destroyed.

Vincennes moonlights as technical advisor to a television police drama – the fifties' classic *Dragnet* thinly disguised as *Badge of Honor* – and earns a few extra bucks making "celebrity busts" for reporter Hudgens. But Vincennes is not a morally indifferent man, and his conscience stares back at him in the mirror behind the bar at the **Frolic Room,** a neon-lit star haunt at **6245 Hollywood Boulevard** adjacent to **Pantages Theatre,** home of the Academy Awards in the 1950s. White, the muscle behind the unsavory antics of police chief Dudley Smith (James

Cromwell), fails to see the error of his ways until he, Vincennes, and Exley try solving a mass murder at the Nite Owl Café. Exley chases up clues at another classic Hollywood hangout, the **Formosa Café** at **7156 Santa Monica Boulevard,** on the corner of Formosa Avenue. After he and Vincennes encounter the wrath of Lana Turner at the Formosa, they are treated

Reporter Sid Hudgens (Danny DeVito) and Sergeant Jack Vincennes (Kevin Spacey) in front of the *Hush Hush* editorial offices at the Crossroads of the World, now a palm-fringed office complex (right).

to another icy reception at the villa of pimp Pierce Patchett (David Strathairn), the **Lovell Health House,** an icon of California architecture at **4616 Dundee Drive** in **Los Feliz** built by the designer Richard Neutra in 1929.

Standing amid all the sleaze and underhanded activity like a beacon of hope is high-class hooker Lynn Bracken (Kim Basinger), a dead ringer for screen star Veronica Lake. Tough-nut White, a hopeless case for damsels in distress, falls head over heels in love with Lynn and starts to dream of a better life somewhere else. Meanwhile, Exley, the golden boy gunning for a promotion, taps the wrong suspects for the Nite Owl crimes and accidentally stumbles over a clue to the real root of L.A. corruption. Director Hanson masterfully juxtaposes pretty Hollywood imagery with hard reality all the way up to the explosive final scenes, where onetime enemies and police department rivals become allies in defeating organized crime.

L.A. Confidential succeeded on the strength of ensemble acting with some eighty speaking parts, and also brought Russell Crowe big-screen fame that had eluded him in his first two American films. Hanson, who liked Crowe in the Australian skinhead flick *Romper Stomper* (1992) and took a well-calculated chance on Eminem in *8 Mile* (2002), is an old hand at launching new stars, including Tom Cruise in *Losin' It* (1983) and Tobey Maguire in *Wonder Boys* (2000).

The star-studded Formosa Café (left) **and art-deco City Hall** (right): **classic Los Angeles at its best.**

MULHOLLAND DRIVE

Director David Lynch

Starring Naomi Watts, Laura Elena Harring,
Justin Theroux, Ann Miller, Dan Hedaya

France / USA, 2001

Director David Lynch offers a few pointers to his stars.

Director David Lynch erases the line between dream and reality in a parody of Hollywood that begins with a car crash above the glittering lights of L.A. on Mulholland Drive, the famous street named for the city's legendary water commissioner. Comparisons with Billy Wilder's *Sunset Blvd.* (1950) extend only to an aura of glamour and the choice of a famous thoroughfare for the title, as the creator of *Blue Velvet* (1986) and *Lost Highway* (1997) paints a sinister portrait of Tinseltown set to the rumbling mood music of composer Angelo Badalamenti. Originally planned for television like Lynch's *Twin Peaks* series (1990), a film was born when skittish American networks backed out of the project and France's Studio Canal stepped in. Night views onto L.A. from the scenic causeway in the Hollywood Hills are set against mundane eateries and offices downtown, a gloomy contrast that underscores the desperation of the movie's star-struck protagonists.

Who doesn't want to be a star? Blond ingénue Betty Elms (Naomi Watts) arrives from Deep River, Ontario, to audition for film parts, and discovers Rita (Laura Harring) cowering in her Aunt Ruth's shower in an apartment at **450 North Sycamore Avenue.** The mysterious brunette admits that she adopted the name after a car accident – she couldn't remember who she was. Nor can she explain why there are stacks of cash and a weird blue key in her purse. Betty takes on the case of unknown identity like a sisterly Nancy Drew. She scans the papers for news of the car accident over coffee with her amnesiac pal at

Right: **Rita (Laura Harring) and Betty (Naomi Watts) pose questions of identity at Caesar's. Visitors beware: There's a monster in the parking lot.**

Below: **The once glittering Tower Theater on South Broadway, where Rebekah Del Rio croons Roy Orbison's "Crying" in Spanish.**

Winkies, a fifties-style diner filmed at **Caesar's Restaurant, 1016 West El Segundo Boulevard** in Gardena. The diner harbors a monster living in its parking lot, star of an earlier sequence and one of several odd characters who emerge like creatures from a nightmare throughout the film.

The best way to follow the film's developments may be not to try at all. The Cowboy (Monty Montgomery, who produced Lynch's 1990 *Wild at Heart*) emerges as another such inexplicable character, and advises young director Adam Kesher (Justin Theroux) to choose a new leading lady for his film, or else. Lynch adds another layer to a story already brimming with

what appear to be non sequiturs: A bumbling assassin (Mark Pellegrino) interviews a hooker on the whereabouts of a mysterious brunette at **Pink's Hot Dogs,** run by friendly Gloria Pink at **709 North La Brea Boulevard.** Now who could that be? None of it makes sense except to heighten the tension surrounding Betty and Rita, who have since developed alter egos – the washed-up

Few fans recall anything about the film with much accuracy: just that they loved it or hated it, and that Rita, former Miss America Laura Harring, arrived at the Oscars in a pair of diamond-studded pumps worth a cool million and a $27-million diamond necklace. For David Lynch, the 2002 Academy Awards at Los Angeles's Shrine Auditorium were a bit of a letdown. Although

Storied Mulholland Drive, where all the trouble begins. The famous view is not of downtown L.A., but of the San Fernando Valley.

Diane Selwyn and her elusive girlfriend, Camilla Rhodes. The pair embarked on a lesbian love affair at the half-timbered Sierra Bonita apartments at **2900 Griffith Park Boulevard,** Silver Lake, as well as having broken into apartments and the movie business in the course of their investigation. The dizzying events grow more bizarre still after a midnight trip to Club Silencio, where the two women watch as Rebekah Del Rio croons Roy Orbison's "Crying" in Spanish on the ornate stage of the **Tower Theater, 802 South Broadway,** with exterior shots done at the **Palace Newsreel Theatre, 630 South Broadway.** Betty discovers a blue box in her purse. Now, where was that key ...?

he had shared the prize for Best Director with Joel Coen at the prestigious Cannes Film Festival and had been nominated for Best Director by the Academy, the Oscars for Best Picture and Best Director went to Ron Howard, director of *A Beautiful Mind.* To Naomi Watts, *Mulholland Drive* was the break she had been hoping for. Subsequent roles in *Le Divorce* (2003) and *I ♥ Huckabees* (2004) culminated in her performance as Ann Darrow in Peter Jackson's major motion picture *King Kong* (2005), and a memorable photo on the cover of *Vanity Fair* magazine.

The Sierra Bonita Apartments in the Silver Lake neighborhood, scene of a steamy love affair between two mysterious women.

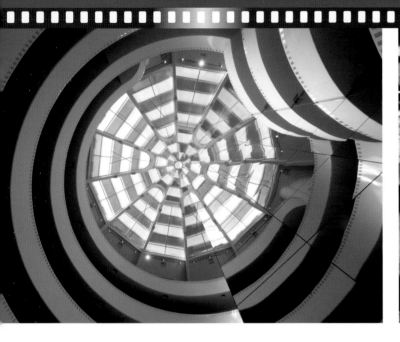

THE ULTIMATE URBAN BACKDROP

From Marilyn Monroe in a billowing, low-cut dress, to Robert De Niro as a *Taxi Driver* losing it amidst the neon lights of Times Square, and Audrey Hepburn gazing at the Tiffany's display in the early morning hours, the movies have profoundly affected the way we see New York. Film fans around the world know the Big Apple like no other city. Even those who have never visited the mighty island metropolis recognize the skyscraper canyons, the brownstones with their cast-iron fire escapes, the ubiquitous yellow cabs, and the steam rising ominously from manhole covers as typically Manhattan.

Top left: **Frank Lloyd Wright's Guggenheim Museum spirals upwards like a strip of celluloid.** Top right: **Marilyn Monroe in a famous scene from *The Seven Year Itch* at the corner of Lexington Avenue and East 52nd Street.** Below: **The southern tip of New York City with the Manhattan Bridge in the foreground.**

New York City has played an important role in filmmaking since cinema's earliest days. Currently more than 150 feature films are shot here each year, a figure especially impressive considering that it was just over a century ago – starting in 1888 – that inventor Thomas Edison began to experiment with film technology in his lab just outside the city. Six years later he opened a trailblazing theater on Broadway, the first-ever venue to be equipped with his pioneering Kinetoscope film-viewing machines. New York City immediately established itself as the center of the American film industry, eventually ceding its position to new studios in sunny California in the years just before World War I.

But even as filmmakers abandoned the East Coast, New Yorkers would play a vital part in establishing the burgeoning

For the most part, though, filmmakers were not satisfied unless their cameras could scan the breathtaking skyline of the real Manhattan. Brooklyn-born Woody Allen, the quintessential New York director, has been portraying the narrow isle for more than thirty years in films such as *Annie Hall* (1977), *Manhattan* (1979), and *Mighty Aphrodite* (1995). The Upper East Side in particular provides an elegant backdrop to his endearing and quirky tales whose characters represent the city's famously liberal – and endearingly neurotic – intelligentsia.

Martin Scorsese's view is poles apart. In *Mean Streets* (1973), the New York native tells the complex tale of two small-time crooks in Little Italy, masterfully played by Robert De Niro and Harvey Keitel. Three years later the legendary director exposed audiences to the paranoid fantasies of De Niro as a *Taxi*

Yellow cabs are a fixture on the streets of New York – not only since Martin Scorsese's cult film *Taxi Driver.*

film industry in Hollywood. Key players from Cecil B. De Mille to William Fox and Samuel Goldwyn would maintain a strong connection and deep sense of nostalgia for the teeming streets and landmark bridges of their hometown back east. No wonder that the Big Apple featured so prominently in early 20th-century films, and that its signature skyscrapers, distinctive brownstones, verdant parks, and busy waterfronts were rebuilt with an obsessive attention to detail on numerous L.A. studio lots.

Driver (1976) losing his mind. Taking a completely different tack, *The Age of Innocence* (1993) explores the world of fin-de-siècle elites, with Daniel Day-Lewis and Michelle Pfeiffer dallying in the privileged salons of 19th-century New York. Scorsese abandoned hopes of filming on location in favor of the studios at Cinecittà in Rome, where elaborate sets helped recreate the slums and flophouses of immigrant New York during the Civil War for his epic *The Gangs of New York* (2002).

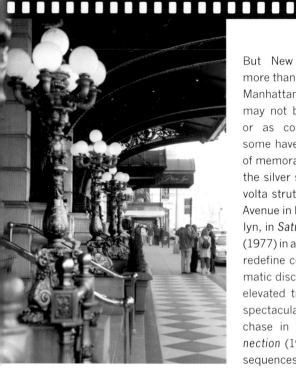

From *North by Northwest* to *Barefoot in the Park,* the Plaza Hotel has always been a popular movie location.

But New York is much more than just the island of Manhattan. Other boroughs may not be as glamorous or as cosmopolitan, but some have had their share of memorable moments on the silver screen. John Travolta strutted down Fourth Avenue in Bay Ridge, Brooklyn, in *Saturday Night Fever* (1977) in a scene that would redefine cool for the phlegmatic disco era. Brooklyn's elevated trains hosted the spectacular high-speed car chase in *The French Connection* (1971), hair-raising sequences that have since become the stuff of legend. Spike Lee put Brooklyn in the spotlight again in *Do the Right Thing* (1989), a moving account of racial tension in a multiethnic neighborhood. African-American stories like *Harlem* (1939), *Cotton Comes to Harlem* (1970), *Shaft* (1971), and *Black Caesar* (1973) have paid tribute to Harlem's distinctive history and character as a quarter that, while not a separate borough, in many ways has been treated as one.

New York has many faces. Whether making a lighthearted comedy or a disaster flick, this is where filmmakers come to find a big-town backdrop to fit their purposes. In the charming musical *On the Town* (1949), Frank Sinatra and Gene Kelly explore the Big Apple as sailors on shore leave. Meg Ryan, who starred alongside Billy Crystal in the popular New York romance *When Harry Met Sally* (1989), finds true love with Tom Hanks on the viewing platform of the Empire State Building in *Sleepless in Seattle* (1993). The panorama deck had already served as a rendezvous for Cary Grant and Deborah Kerr in the heart-rending melodrama *An Affair to Remember* (1957). The modern Romeo-and-Juliet tale portrayed in *West Side Story* (1961) was shot among the derelict tenements that were torn down to make way for the Lincoln Center right after filming had ended.

Despite its polished image these days, New York was considered a dangerous place for many years. The first gangster films were shot here in the thirties, but it was mostly through movies like *Serpico* (1973) and Sergio Leone's violent saga *Once Upon a Time in America* (1984) that film noir found its home in the dark, rainy streets of New York. Heroes like Superman and Spider-Man feel right at home here, as does Batman, whose futuristic Gotham City is a comic-strip version of NYC. Horror flicks such as Roman Polanski's *Rosemary's Baby* (1968), filmed in The Dakota apartment building on Central Park West, cast New York as the focal point of an apocalyptic nightmare. Nowhere else are visions of darkness and violence quite as convincingly portrayed. In the 1930s it was King Kong who scared New York, scaling the Empire State Building to the shrieks of horrified moviegoers. The city saw the dawn of a new Ice Age due to sudden climate changes in *The Day After Tomorrow* (2004), with stark imagery such as the Statue of Liberty entombed in ice.

Times have changed dramatically since the terrorist attacks of September 11, 2001. In the aftermath of the tragedy, Hollywood producers tried to avoid committing anything that might remind audiences of the terrible disaster to film. Scenes in *Spider-Man* (2002) showing the superhero played by Tobey Maguire spinning his web between the Twin Towers were edited out before the film could be released. Director Spike Lee was among the first to respond to 9/11 with an intimate look at how deeply wounded and yet optimistic the city was in the memorable movie *25th Hour* (2002).

Breakfast at Tiffany's

1. Tiffany, 727 Fifth Avenue at the corner of 57th Street
2. Holly's townhouse, 169 East 71st Street
3. Central Park, Conservatory Pond, at 72nd Street
4. Central Park, Naumburg Bandshell
5. New York Public Library, Fifth Avenue at 42nd Street

The French Connection

6. NYPD Drug Enforcement Department (now the Police Museum), 100 Old Slip Street at the corner of South Street
7. Former Westbury Hotel, 15 East 69th Street
8. Grand Central subway station
9. 2271 Stillwell Avenue, Brooklyn
10. 62nd Street station, Brooklyn
11. Ward's Island at the foot of the Triborough Bridge

Taxi Driver

12. Collins Bar (formerly the Show and Tell), 735 Eighth Avenue at West 46th Street
13. Hilton Theatre, 213 West 42nd Street
14. Variety Theater, 110–112 Third Avenue at 13th Street
15. Doorway, 204 East 13th Street
16. Apartment house, 226 East 13th Street
17. Columbus Circle

Manhattan

18. Woody Allen's former apartment, Central Park East at 75th Street
19. Elaine's, 1703 Second Avenue
20. Guggenheim Museum, 1071 Fifth Avenue at East 89th Street
21. Museum of Modern Art, 11 West 53rd Street
22. Riverview Terrace on Sutton Square at East 58th Street
23. Dean & DeLuca, 560 Broadway at Prince Street
24. Rizzoli bookstore, 31 West 57th Street
25. Bloomingdale's, East 59th Street at Lexington Avenue
26. American Museum of Natural History, Central Park West at 79th Street

When Harry Met Sally ...

27. Washington Square
28. La Guardia Airport, Queens
29. Shakespeare & Co., Broadway and West 81st Street (closed)
30. Boathouse Restaurant, Central Park, East 74th Street and Park Drive North
31. Metropolitan Museum, 1000 Fifth Avenue at 82nd Street
32. Katz's Delicatessen, 205 East Houston Street
33. Puck Building, 295 Lafayette Street

25th Hour

34. Waterfront promenade, Brooklyn Heights
35. Carl Schurz Park, 79th to 90th Streets, benches on the East River
36. Monty's apartment, 154 East 89th Street, between Lexington and Third Avenue
37. Kitty Kiernan's, 9715 Third Avenue, Bay Ridge, Brooklyn
38. City College of New York, Convent Avenue at 138th Street
39. Ground Zero
40. Double Happiness Bar, 173 Mott Street, corner of Broome Street
41. Jane Street Theatre, 113 Jane Street

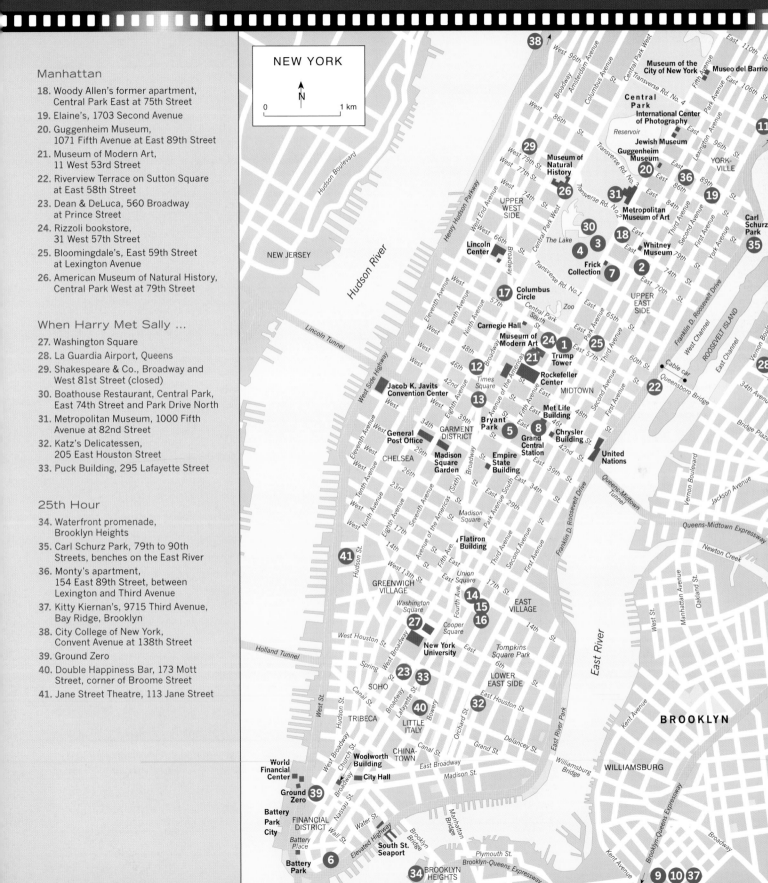

BREAKFAST AT TIFFANY'S

Director	Blake Edwards
Starring	Audrey Hepburn, George Peppard, Patricia Neal, Buddy Ebsen, Mickey Rooney, José Luis de Villalonga
USA, 1961	

No other character in film personifies New York City quite as charmingly as Holly Golightly (Audrey Hepburn), a capricious party girl with a mysterious past. Critics have dismissed Blake Edwards's idealized view of life in the early sixties as "remarkably inauthentic," and yet to film buffs and Hepburn fans, glamorous Holly is the very embodiment of that swinging era in Manhattan. Her irreverent antics – from setting a party guest's hat on fire with her foot-long cigarette holder to using a fire escape to sidestep a pushy suitor – ought to be evidence enough. Her mix of high style and high jinx became her hallmark. Who else could step into the street in a little black dress and a hat the size of a wagon wheel, and hail a cab with a whistle shrill enough to make your toes curl – and still exude such inimitable charm?

The opening scene in *Breakfast at Tiffany's* is iconic: Holly strolls down Fifth Avenue at the crack of dawn wearing an evening gown, and, sipping coffee from a paper cup, admires the window display at the famed jeweler **Tiffany, 727 Fifth Avenue at the corner of 57th Street.** Although the "city that never sleeps" appears tranquil, shooting the scene was anything but. The number of curious onlookers was a nuisance to Hepburn, whose popularity with fans had long been established since her breakthrough role as Princess Ann in *Roman Holiday* (1953). That Soviet Premier Nikita Khrushchev was in town put the crew under enormous pressure to finish the scene and clear the area as quickly as possible. Police wanted New York's flashiest boulevard to be open for traffic by 7:30 a.m. at the latest.

Top: **Breakfast in style: After a night on the town, Holly Golightly (Audrey Hepburn) sips her coffee in front of Tiffany's shop windows. The famous jeweler** (below) **is located on Fifth Avenue.**

Left: **What can you get at Tiffany's for ten dollars? Paul (George Peppard) hopes to buy Holly a trinket at her favorite boutique.**

After the unforgettable first encounter at Tiffany's, audiences see Holly through the eyes of Paul Varjak (George Peppard), a fledgling writer who moves into a brownstone on the Upper East Side. Paul falls for his pretty neighbor, a party girl who accepts $50 from her suitors "for the powder room," who is always on the lookout for a rich husband, and who doesn't find anything wrong with delivering encoded messages to a jailed mobster. Her sparsely furnished apartment shared with an alley cat becomes the social nexus for Hollywood agents, millionaires, and models, who indulge in round-the-clock revelry night after night. Interiors were shot in the studio, including the winning scenes in which Holly plays the guitar on her fire escape and sings "Moon River." Henry Mancini composed the heart-rending ballad especially for Hepburn, and with lyricist Johnny Mercer was awarded an Oscar for it.

No fire escapes adorn the residences in this upscale neighborhood, but Holly's townhouse at **169 East 71st Street** does, in fact, exist. The green-and-white awnings are gone, but little else has changed on this quiet, tree-lined street since the 1960s. Doc Golightly (Buddy Ebsen), the man from Holly's past, waits patiently in front of Holly's place and eventually tails Paul to Central Park. After they pass **Conservatory Pond at 72nd Street**, where New Yorkers still sail their model sailboats, they take a bench in front of the **Naumburg Bandshell** and discuss Holly's mysterious history. Once Holly has bid a final farewell to Doc, she and Paul spend a memorable day in the city, daring each other to try out things they have never done before: Holly takes him to the hallowed halls of Tiffany, while he shows her the **New York Public Library** on **Fifth Avenue at 42nd Street**. The far more provocative novella ends on a different note, but in the film, the bittersweet romance finds a happy conclusion after some confusion in the pouring rain.

The inimitable Holly Golightly was the brainchild of the equally idiosyncratic novelist Truman Capote. Just like his pet character, Capote had fled the conservative South to start a new, more exciting life in New York City, a story touchingly chron-

Film producers, South American millionaires, and society ladies hold raucous parties at Holly's apartment at 169 East 71st Street.

icled in Bennett Miller's *Capote* (2005), a film for which lead actor Philip Seymour Hoffman won an Oscar. Audrey Hepburn so perfectly embodies the fragile mix of childlike naiveté, feminine cunning, and insouciance that it is almost impossible to imagine that Capote had originally wanted Marilyn Monroe for the part – he thought Hepburn was entirely the wrong choice. Monroe refused the part due to the character's moral misconduct, a hard argument to swallow given her role as a sex bomb in *The Seven Year Itch* (1955). That Billy Wilder's comedy had a few things in common with *Breakfast at Tiffany's* was no coincidence: George Axelrod penned that screenplay, too, a story of two tenants in a New York apartment house and the sparks that fly between them.

THE FRENCH CONNECTION

Director	William Friedkin
Starring	Gene Hackman, Roy Scheider, Fernando Rey, Tony Lo Bianco, Marcel Bozzuffi, Frédéric de Pasquale

USA, 1971

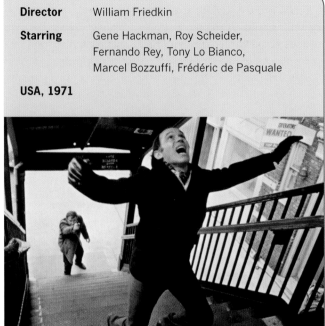

In the early 1960s, two New York cops made history with the biggest drug bust ever on American soil. The spectacular events leading to the breakup of an American-French drug cartel – the eponymous "French Connection" – prompted Robin Moore to write a novel that, in turn, inspired William Friedkin's blockbuster film. *The French Connection* remains a classic of its genre, a crime thriller whose gritty realism is underscored by dozens of filming locations throughout New York City. Highlights include one of the most spectacular car chases in movie history, and Gene Hackman in possibly his best role ever, a performance that garnered him an Oscar for his portrayal of a brutal policeman. The movie also received Academy Awards for Best Film and Best Director.

Hackman's hardboiled character, Jimmy "Popeye" Doyle, may be one of the most unlikable cops in film history. Yet he manages to capture the audience's imagination and compassion. In the opening scenes, Doyle and his more level-headed partner, Buddy Russo (Roy Scheider), chase a small-time drug dealer through a seedy section of Bedford-Stuyvesant in Brooklyn. When they nab him in an empty lot, Doyle hammers him with vicious threats and excessive force to get a confession. It's clear from the start that Popeye lives to be a cop, but for all his passion, he's also a reckless, hot-blooded, vulgar son of a gun who is unhealthily obsessed with hunting down the bad guys.

Doyle always follows his instincts, even after leaving work at the **NYPD Drug Enforcement Department, 100 Old Slip Street at the corner of South Street,** now the **Police Museum.** One evening Doyle spots small-time gangster Sal Boca (Tony Lo Bianco) celebrating with suspicious-looking businessmen, and immediately senses that something's up. Just for kicks, he and his partner trail Boca all night long. In the early morning hours they follow him from the Lower East Side to his little newspaper shop in Brooklyn, an innocent-seeming front for drug deals. Doyle has a hunch that something big is about to go down, but his boss – real cop Eddie Egan, the inspiration for the Doyle character – will permit him to continue his investigation only in the company of two FBI agents. Doyle is disgusted, and initially the trio meet with little success, losing their target when they follow Boca across the **Brooklyn Bridge** into Manhattan.

After a dramatic chase, Detective Doyle hunts down contract killer Nicoli (Marcel Bozzuffi) at the 62nd Street station in Brooklyn.

Boca turns out to be a small fish anyway: The mastermind behind the planned drug deal is Alain Charnier (Fernando Rey), whom the cops nickname "Frog One," a suave Frenchman who resides at the former **Westbury Hotel, 15 East 69th Street.** The two policemen follow their "French connection" through Manhattan, spending most of their time waiting and freezing their tails off in the cold. Doyle stays on Charnier's heels, but the clever criminal manages to shake him at the **Grand Central subway station.** He hires hit man Pierre Nicoli (Marcel Bozzuffi) to take the pesky cop out. The sniper ambushes Doyle on the roof of his house at **2271 Stillwell Avenue,** a grim housing project in Bensonhurst, Brooklyn.

Nicoli narrowly misses his target and flees into the nearby elevated train at **Bay 50th Street station.** While Nicoli, a.k.a. "Frog Two," seizes control of the train, Popeye confiscates a car and pursues the killer from the streets below, careering by twenty-six blocks and eight subway stations across the south of Brooklyn until the dramatic finale at the **62nd Street station.** The two-level, high-speed chase is considered one of the best in film history. The producers had already wowed audiences with high-speed car chase scenes a few years earlier with the San Francisco cop thriller *Bullitt* (1968), but *The French Connection* raised the bar. These days such filming conditions would be unthinkable. The crew shot the scenes of vehicles driving at reckless speeds without permits, without rerouting traffic, and without warning shop owners and passersby.

A warehouse on **Ward's Island** at the foot of the Triborough Bridge is the site of the final showdown, a confrontation with a surprise finale that leaves viewers with a bitter aftertaste. What

A grim Popeye Doyle (Gene Hackman) seals off Ward's Island.

makes *The French Connection* so intriguing is the cat-and-mouse game between cops and drug dealers, equally as frustrating as it is exciting. Just like the cops, the audience is kept in the dark for the entirety of the film, a narrative technique that lends the story a realistic, almost documentary, aspect and maintains the high level of tension from start to end. In the excellent sequel *French Connection II* (1975), director John Frankenheimer took Popeye Doyle to France, where he tracks down the elusive drug dealer on his home turf in Marseille.

Left: **Today the NYPD narcotics department serves as the police museum.**
Right: **Doyle races along New Utrecht Avenue at breakneck speed, following the killer in the elevated train above him.**

TAXI DRIVER

Director   Martin Scorsese

Starring   Robert De Niro, Cybill Shepherd, Jodie Foster, Harvey Keitel, Peter Boyle

USA, 1976

New York in the seventies had an explosive, even frightening side, and films like *Taxi Driver* contributed to its fearsome reputation as the crime capital of the United States. The city was teetering on the brink of financial collapse, trash piled up on the sidewalks, thousands of the homeless and mentally ill roamed the streets, and prostitution and the drug trade ran rampant in neighborhoods like the East Village. A few years after exploring New York's dark side with Robert De Niro in *Mean Streets* (1973), Martin Scorsese returned the same actor to the perilous skyscraper canyons of the Big Apple to lend *Taxi Driver* a hard edge. New York has changed dramatically in the three decades that have passed since filming took place. Urban renewal has been so extensive that visitors find it almost impossible to identify locations from the film such as Columbus Circle, now gleaming with its new shopping and dining complex, and the once sleazy quarter around Times Square, long since gentrified to become a popular tourist destination.

Taxi Driver brings the bad old days of the city back in haunting detail. Young Vietnam veteran Travis Bickle (Robert De Niro) is a lonesome anti-hero in the urban jungle, a man so plagued by insomnia that he takes a job as a cab driver at the taxi depot on 57th Street at 11th Avenue. The dispatch center was torn down several years ago, and a modern glass-and-steel office tower has risen in its place. Long gone, too, is the Belmore Cafeteria, the popular cabbie hangout at the corner of Park Avenue and 28th Street where a taciturn Travis sips coffee and listens to his fellow drivers' hair-raising tales.

While Travis is unfazed by having to drive through dangerous neighborhoods like Brooklyn, the Bronx, or Harlem, he is disgusted by the crime he witnesses on his nightly trips. Like a prophet of doom, he predicts that "someday a real rain will come and wash all this scum off the streets." Ironically, Travis cannot resist the pull of the seedy streets either, especially the X-rated movie theater and peep show milieu by Times Square. Hungry for human contact, he tries in vain to strike up a conversation with a cute concessionaire – De Niro's future wife, Diahnne Abbott – at the hole-in-the-wall porn flick theater **Show and Tell** on **735 Eighth Avenue at West 46th Street.** Today the location houses

At night Travis (Robert De Niro) drives his taxi to the run-down area around Times Square. Today glittering neon ads and billboard tickers reporting the latest stock market news have replaced seedy adult movie theaters.

Fourteen-year-old Jodie Foster was nominated for an Oscar for her role as the child prostitute Iris. Here she waits for customers in a doorway at the corner of 13th Street and Third Avenue.

When Betsy refuses to return his calls, Travis's hatred of the New York underworld rages out of control, and his transformation into an avenging angel begins. He focuses his attentions on a teenage prostitute named Iris (Jodie Foster), making it his mission to save her from the sinful morass of the city. His vigil takes him to the area around 13th Street in the East Village. The neighborhood looks much as it did in the seventies despite its having become a sought-after residential neighborhood in the meantime, now devoid of drug dealers and prostitutes. One night, Iris attempts to elude her sleazy pimp "Sport" (Harvey Keitel) and hops into Travis's cab in front of the **Variety Theater, 110-112 Third Avenue at 13th Street** – today a respectable Off-Broadway playhouse. Just around the corner, at the doorway of **204 East 13th Street,** Sport is waiting for customers for his "girls." Just a few houses down the street, and virtually unchanged since filming, is a trio of typical New York apartment houses. The middle address, **226 East 13th Street,** is where Iris works in the movie, and the scene of the big showdown.

Armed to the teeth, dressed in army fatigues, and with his hair shaved into a Mohawk, the way soldiers in Vietnam wore it when sent on dangerous missions, Travis attempts to assassinate Senator Palantine at a political rally on **Columbus Circle.** Afterwards he sets off to the East Village to rescue Iris from the clutches of her pimp; the bloodbath that follows is not for the faint at heart. Scorsese even had to tone down the colors in post-production to assure nothing higher than an R rating for his apocalyptic film noir.

A backdrop that has hardly changed since the seventies: 13th Street, where Sport (Harvey Keitel) and Travis have a heated argument.

the elegant **Collins Bar,** a hangout that merits a mention in the Zagat dining guide for New York City.

Travis reckons that things are finally going his way when he spots the phlegmatic career woman Betsy (Cybill Shepherd) – in his eyes a tow-headed angel strolling amid the misery of the seething metropolis. The two couldn't be more different: He's a brooding loner with no real place in society, while she is an ambitious, idealistic campaign organizer toiling for presidential candidate Senator Palantine. Still, Betsy is flattered when Travis shows up at the campaign headquarters at Broadway and 63rd Street and asks her out. They go for a cup of joe at Child's Coffee Shop, a New York institution that closed its doors years ago. Their second date goes horribly wrong when Travis takes her to an adult movie theater. Betsy storms out of the turn-of-the-century **Lyric Theater at 213 West 42nd Street,** a stand-in for the porn cinema that today is the posh **Hilton Theatre,** a venue for Broadway musicals.

MANHATTAN

Director   Woody Allen

Starring   Woody Allen, Diane Keaton, Michael Murphy, Mariel Hemingway, Meryl Streep

USA, 1979

The city that never sleeps: Mary and Isaac talk until dawn on a bench by the Queensboro Bridge.

Of all the declarations of love that Woody Allen has made to his city, *Manhattan* is the most passionate. In the overture to this black-and-white ode to the Big Apple, the camera sweeps across New York City to the music of George Gershwin's *Rhapsody in Blue,* capturing visual impressions from the Staten Island Ferry all the way over to Yankee Stadium in the Bronx: The audience is treated to shots of Broadway, Fifth Avenue, Washington Square, the Guggenheim and the Metropolitan Museum of Art, Lincoln Center and Radio City Music Hall, Sotheby's and Gucci, joggers in Central Park and harried denizens of the city hurrying down the street. In the background Allen is heard testing the opening sentence of a novel: "Chapter One. He adored New York City."

It doesn't work. Allen discards each renewed effort to sum up his love for the city in a few, well-chosen words, until finally he declares, "New York was his town, and it always would be." The camera comes to rest on a panorama of Central Park, a shot taken from the terrace of the townhouse where Allen then resided on **Fifth Avenue** at **Central Park East at 75th Street.** As the *Rhapsody* nears its crescendo, fireworks explode over the skyline, a fitting tribute to Allen's hometown and urban muse. The stage is now set for a comedy of errors about love, life, and a hilariously neurotic group of friends in New York City.

At the center of this group is Isaac Davis (Woody Allen), a man in the throes of a midlife crisis who takes up dating a seventeen-year-old named Tracy (Mariel Hemingway). He quits his job as a television writer to finally pen his novel, only to learn that his ex-wife Jill (Meryl Streep in one of her first film roles) also has plans to publish. Her book, entitled *Marriage, Divorce, and Selfhood,* will be about the failure of their marriage, and promises to reveal her husband's foibles in excruciating detail. No one seems to have much success with relationships in this loopy group of New Yorkers. Even Isaac's best friend, Yale (Michael Murphy), is unhappily married and having an affair with outré journalist Mary (Diane Keaton).

The friends meet up in trendy eateries such as **Elaine's** at **1703 Second Avenue –** long known as a favorite Upper East Side haunt of Allen's in real life, too – where Isaac introduces young Tracy to his friends. The city's museums also serve as a backdrop to their lively and at times heated discussions on art and life, and as stages for acting out shifts in their love lives. Mary voices her opinions on art at the **Guggenheim Museum,** much to Isaac's irritation, but when they run into one another again at a private viewing at the **Museum of Modern Art,** they discover a mutual attraction. Can things get any more complicated than falling for your best friend's mistress? Isaac and Mary share the romantic view from a bench at **Riverview Terrace on Sutton Square** in the early morning hours and watch the **Queensboro Bridge** emerge from the fog, a cinematic image that has since become a symbol of New York. A new day dawns and two people, as unlikely as the match may seem, are falling in love.

Dark clouds form when Isaac (Woody Allen) and Mary (Diane Keaton) go for a paddle on the lake in Central Park.

Where the *Manhattan*ites shop, eat, and drink is a tour of the city in itself. The feisty intellectuals gather at the gourmet grocery temple **Dean & DeLuca** at **560 Broadway at Prince Street** in SoHo, at the **Rizzoli** bookstore at **31 West 57th Street,** in the perfume department of **Bloomingdale's, East 59th Street at Lexington Avenue,** for an opera performance at the **Met,** and at the **Russian Tea Room,** which sadly closed its legendary salons a few years ago. The perennially stressed-out New Yorkers take breathers in the leafy oasis of **Central Park,** where Isaac plays baseball with his little son, both of them wearing T-shirts printed with the heartbreakingly funny logo "Divorced Fathers & Sons Allstars." The Park is also where Tracy manages to talk the cynical Isaac into taking a romantic moonlit jaunt in a carriage, and where Isaac and Mary get caught in a thunderstorm and flee to the Hayden Planetarium of the **American Museum of Natural History, Central Park West at 79th Street.** "When I made *Manhattan*," Allen reminisced years later to the European press, "I was very selective. I showed a view of the city as I would like to have it, and as it can be today when you take the trouble of walking down the right streets." Accompanied by the music of Gershwin, this romantic vision of New York provides a gentle counterbalance to the story's emotional chaos.

Isaac finds the young Tracy (Mariel Hemingway) fascinating and takes her shopping downtown at Dean & DeLuca's.

New York landmarks like the Guggenheim Museum form a cultured backdrop for Woody Allen's tangled love story.

WHEN HARRY MET SALLY ...

Director	Rob Reiner
Starring	Billy Crystal, Meg Ryan, Carrie Fisher, Bruno Kirby
USA, 1989	

"Men and women can never be friends because the sex thing always gets in the way." When Harry Burns (Billy Crystal) meets Sally Albright (Meg Ryan) for the first time, she denounces his philosophy of friendship and love as childish and irritating. By the end of the car trip they share from the University of Chicago to New York City in 1977, the two recent graduates can't stand one another, and neither expects to see the other again. "That's too bad," says Sally, although she clearly doesn't mean it. "You are the only person I knew in New York." With that the unlikely couple shake hands and part ways in front of the landmark triumphal arch in **Washington Square.** When years later, contrary to Harry's theory, they become close friends, the audience of course wants to know whether Harry and Sally can maintain a platonic relationship, or whether they will end up falling in love after all.

Several years after their first encounter, Harry and Sally bump into one another again at New York's **La Guardia Airport.** They meet for the third time in a bookstore – "Someone is staring at you in Personal Growth," whispers Sally's friend Marie

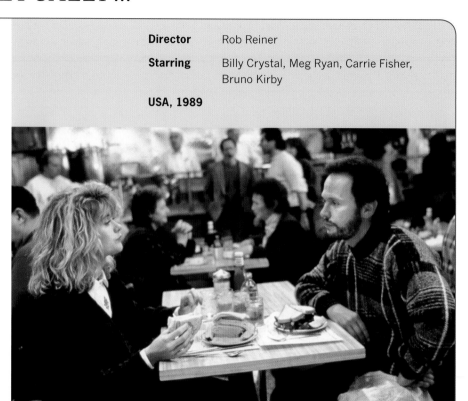

Harry (Billy Crystal) discovers that he still has a lot to learn about women at Katz's.

(Carrie Fisher) – before they finally agree to go out for coffee. These scenes were shot at **Shakespeare & Co.** at the corner of **Broadway and West 81st Street,** a literary institution on the Upper West Side that closed in 1996 when it could no longer compete with the newly opened Barnes & Noble Superstore around the corner. Nora Ephron, who wrote the screenplay for *When Harry Met Sally,* used these very events as the background for another New York romantic comedy, *You've Got Mail* (1998), starring Meg Ryan as the owner of a small children's bookstore and Tom Hanks as her romantic interest and rival as the owner of a large discount booksellers – just around the corner.

Before Harry and Sally even become friends, a miserable Harry tells his pal Jess (Bruno Kirby) at a New York Giants football game that his wife has just left him. Meanwhile, Sally casually mentions to her friends over lunch at the lakeside **Boathouse Restaurant in Central Park** that she has split from her longtime boyfriend Joe, prompting Marie to pull out her Rolodex of eligible bachelors. Single life in New York is no cakewalk, especially when the goal is to find that one in a million who could be "the one." Sally consoles herself with the thought that in Harry she has found a friend to share everything with.

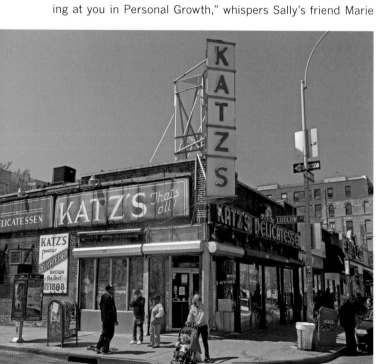

"I'll have what she's having." The hilarious scene in *When Harry Met Sally* has made the deli on the Lower East Side world-famous.

But is it friendship, or something more? Harry and Sally goof off at the Egyptian Temple of Dendur in the **Metropolitan Museum,** take long walks through Central Park, and even buy a Christmas tree together. They tell each other about their secret dreams, and even have a go at clearing up the classic misunderstandings between men and women. In the movie's most memorable

After a long car trip, Harry and Sally part ways in front of the triumphal arch in Washington Square, a popular place to hang out for students from nearby New York University.

scene, Sally lets loose with a stage-ready orgasm in a crowded restaurant to teach Harry a lesson about women's theatrical abilities in bed. According to screenwriter and New York native Nora Ephron, the orgasm scene was entirely Meg Ryan's idea. The older woman who then tells the waitress, "I'll have what she's having," is Estelle Reiner, the director's mother. Until this day a sign proclaiming, "You are sitting where Harry met Sally" embellishes the table at **Katz's Delicatessen** on **205 East Houston Street,** New York's oldest deli.

Director Rob Reiner and writer Nora Ephron drew heavily on their own memories and experiences for the script. With plenty of witty dialogue and two main characters as neurotic as they are endearing, the romantic comedy quickly found its way into moviegoers' hearts. Ephron had already made a name for herself in the movies as the co-writer of *Silkwood* (1983), a drama nominated for five Oscars including Best Writing, and as the author of the novel and screenplay *Heartburn* (1986). Film critic Roger Ebert of the *Chicago Sun-Times* praised the script of *When Harry Met Sally* as clever but also warm, noting that "it's only occasionally that the humor is paid for at the expense

Friends or lovers? The question is finally settled at a New Year's party in the **Puck Building.**

of credibility – as in a hilarious but unconvincing scene where Sally sits in a crowded restaurant and demonstrates how to fake an orgasm." The deli scene immediately achieved cult status even though *The New York Times* had disparaged the movie as a sitcom version of a Woody Allen film. That Reiner actually meant to pay homage to Allen is apparent not only from similarities in the plotline – the relationships among New Yorkers who seem to talk incessantly about love, sex, and death – but also from details such as the black-and-white opening credits, music by George Gershwin, and semi-documentary interview sequences sprinkled throughout the film.

Even the final scene is reminiscent of *Manhattan* (1979) when Allen recognizes too late that he loves his ex-girlfriend and dashes through the streets of New York to declare his passion. On New Year's Eve, Harry wanders the streets of the city by himself while Sally attends a party with Marie in the ballroom of the **Puck Building** at **295 Lafayette Street** in SoHo. When Harry gets to Washington Square, he recalls how he and Sally parted here twelve years ago, and suddenly he realizes that she is the love of his life. Accompanied by Sinatra's "It Had to Be You" – Diane Keaton's song in Allen's *Annie Hall* (1977) – he sprints through the deserted streets of the city, arriving at the Puck Building at the stroke of midnight, just in time to ring in the New Year by showing Sally how he feels.

25TH HOUR

Director Spike Lee

Starring Edward Norton, Philip Seymour Hoffman, Barry Pepper, Rosario Dawson, Anna Paquin, Brian Cox, Tony Siragusa

USA, 2002

Saying goodbye to New York: Monty (Ed Norton) in Carl Schurz Park.

No director has captured the mood of post-9/11 New York City better than Spike Lee. The Brooklyn-bred, NYU-educated director made his name in the eighties as part of a new wave of self-confident African-American filmmakers who critiqued social prejudices on the silver screen. Brimming with sensitivity and wit, his debut flick *She's Gotta Have It* (1986) about a woman and her three lovers posed a feisty challenge to traditional mores. But it was his breakthrough film, the tragicomic *Do the Right Thing* (1989), that opened America's eyes to issues it would rather have avoided. The tale of African and Italian Americans living in Brooklyn and the conflicts smoldering between them is portrayed humorously and intelligently, even when tensions boil over one sweltering summer day. Lee faces racial conflict in American society head on, as evidenced in the black-and-white love story *Jungle Fever* (1991) and in his biopic about radical civil rights activist *Malcolm X* (1992). Little wonder that, along with Woody Allen and Martin Scorsese, Spike Lee is considered one of New York's most influential filmmakers, and the right man to reflect the tragic events of September 11, 2001.

For Lee it was a logical step to paint a very personal portrait of his wounded hometown a year after the terrorist attacks that destroyed the World Trade Center and shook America to its core. In the opening credits, the glowing columns of the **Tribute in Light** loom dramatically in the night sky, a visual cue that this will be no run-of-the-mill film. As the first cinematic work to address post-9/11 New York directly, *25th Hour* was bound to be a milestone, both cinematically and culturally, and the film's early focus on the temporary *Tribute in Light* memorial anchored it in the right time frame. For an entire month, in March 2002, eighty-eight searchlights installed about a block away from Ground Zero projected two tall, narrow beams of light into the sky over Lower Manhattan each night in memory of the twin towers that once stood on that site. Mexican cinematographer Rodrigo Prieto, who also did the camerawork for *Amores Perros* (2000) and *8 Mile* (2002), captured the beams on film from the **Promenade** in **Brooklyn Heights,** training his camera on the sky until the lights were extinguished at the stroke of midnight.

Monty celebrates his final evening of freedom with Naturelle (Rosario Dawson) and his friends. Right: **Spike Lee's movie about New York in the aftermath of September 11 opens with images of the "Tribute in Light," two beams of light shining where the World Trade Center once stood.**

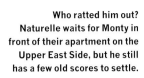

Spike Lee's story parallels the deep sense of change that pervaded the city in late 2001. As New York struggles to return to a kind of normalcy, Monty Brogan (Edward Norton) is forced to bid farewell to the city and the people he loves. He faces a seven-year jail term for dealing drugs and has only twenty-four precious hours of freedom left. A melancholy Monty sits on a bench in **Carl Schurz Park** at First Avenue between 79th to 90th Streets and stares across the **East River.** He wanders through the streets of New York with his trusty dog, saying goodbye and settling old scores. Monty maintains his composure despite a date with the penitentiary and an unsettling suspicion that gnaws at him: Who betrayed him to the police? It had to have been someone close to him. Could it have been his girlfriend Naturelle (Rosario Dawson)? She waits impatiently for Monty on the steps in front of their apartment house at **154 East 89th Street, between Lexington and Third Avenue** on the Upper East Side, and the tension slowly builds.

Naturelle and Monty's father (Brian Cox), a retired firefighter, are devastated by the impending jail sentence, but in all the years leading up to his arrest they had never once questioned the source of the cash financing his – and their – lavish lifestyle. At **Brogan's,** the Irish pub Monty bought for his dad, father and son talk about events to come. The camera pauses at a shrine commemorating the firemen of Rescue 5 on Staten Island who perished in the September 11 rescue operations. The shrine was

Who ratted him out? Naturelle waits for Monty in front of their apartment on the Upper East Side, but he still has a few old scores to settle.

Monty's best friends wonder what will become of him. Frank (Barry Pepper), a phlegmatic stock broker, and Jacob (Philip Seymour Hoffman), a bumbling teacher at the fictitious private Coventry Preparatory School (in real life the **City College of New York, Convent Avenue at 138th Street** in Harlem) ponder Monty's future over a bottle of beer in Frank's apartment near Wall Street. When they peer out the window, a yawning crater abruptly opens up below them – **Ground Zero.** Afterwards they meet Naturelle and Monty for one last night on the town at the **Double Happiness Bar, 173 Mott Street at the corner of Broome Street,** and move on later to the fictitious nightclub, Bridge. The run-down **Jane Street Theatre, 113 Jane Street,** a venue rarely used for plays anymore, was transformed into the hip hangout for the club scenes. When the eventful night draws to a close, Monty, Frank, and Jacob find themselves back where Monty's day began: in **Carl Schurz Park.** Monty surprises his friends by asking one last big favor, while his father offers a tempting way out. For Monty, and for those closest to him, the first sixty minutes of the next day – the 25th hour – become an hour of decision.

real, but the scenes were not filmed on Staten Island: **Kitty Kiernan's** at **9715 Third Avenue** in **Bay Ridge,** an Irish neighborhood in Brooklyn, stood in for the pub. Monty faces himself in the bathroom mirror, and in one of the movie's most moving scenes, he releases a flood of pent-up anger and tension. In the tirade that follows, he curses all New Yorkers, from the Pakistani cab drivers to the gays in Chelsea, the Russians in Brighton Beach, and the rich, face-lifted ladies on the Upper East Side. In short, he blasts what makes New York so beloved and unusual, its eclectic mix of people. Despite the profanity that Monty passionately hurls at his fellow New Yorkers, it is clear that ultimately he is angry with himself for screwing up his life.

It wasn't long after September 11 that New Yorkers began demonstrating their solidarity by wearing T-shirts and buttons that added "More than ever" to the classic motto "I ♥ New York." This strength of feeling pervades *25th Hour* from beginning to end, with Spike Lee paying tribute to his beloved hometown during its most difficult times. "I just had to do it," he later stated to the press. "I think we had to somehow reflect how New York was different. The majority of my films have been involved with New York and this is another New York story, a different New York, but still New York."

11

PARIS

CITY OF LOVE, CITY OF FILM

"We'll always have Paris." Humphrey Bogart delivered his legendary line to Ingrid Bergman as a tribute to their love affair on the banks of the Seine before it all went wrong in *Casablanca* (1942). Cinéastes could use the same words to describe a milestone in film history: We'll always have Paris at the Grand Café at 14 Boulevard des Capucines on December 28, 1895, when "going to the movies" was born. Cinema's debut in the City of Light was a cultural and technological breakthrough that the world would never forget.

What worried French film pioneers most those days was Thomas Edison's Kinetoscope, a peepshow device for watching films, which had arrived in Paris in 1894. The Lumière brothers of Lyon thought they could surpass the American technology and chose the basement of the Grand Café as the venue for their demonstration. For the price of one franc, patrons were treated to ten short films, snippets from real life such as *La Sortie des usines Lumière* (*Workers Leaving the Lumière Factory*) and *Arrivée d'un train à la Ciotat* (*A Train Arriving at a Station*). For the very first time ever, films were projected onto a "big" screen before a paying audience. Some claim that the Latham brothers in New York actually beat the Lumières to the punch, showing boxing films in the Big Apple as early as May 1895. Whatever the case, history thanks the Lumières for their groundbreaking feat.

Louis-Jean and Auguste Lumière, scions of a photographic equipment-producing family, were also the first to master film distribution. They sent projectionists to major capitals the world over to corner the market in providing films to paying audiences.

Edison's success soon made the Lumières' efforts obsolete, and a new movie mogul took their place in Paris. Charles Pathé would capture a third of the world's silent movie market by 1908 with popular films based on history or literature. Big-name directors Ferdinand Zecca and Albert Capellani thrilled viewers with hits such as *Quo Vadis?* (1902) and *The Hunchback of Notre Dame* (1911), respectively. As of 1913 film production took off in the golden hills surrounding Los Angeles, and Paris was all but forgotten – except as a romantic notion to be recreated time and again on the silver screen.

But what an excellent notion it was. *An American in Paris* (1951) was director Vincente Minnelli's singing and dancing tribute to the City of Light, starring Gene Kelly as an aspiring painter who falls in love with the wrong gal. Minnelli's *Gigi* (1958) with Paris native Maurice Chevalier crooning "Thank Heaven for Little Girls" was of the same charming ilk, with a few real locations thrown in for an authentic effect. Two Audrey Hepburn films, *Funny Face* (1957) and *Paris When It Sizzles* (1964), use Paris as a stylish stage for flirtation, much in the fashion of ro-

Vincente Minnelli's musical *An American in Paris* starring Gene Kelly and Leslie Caron inspired a penchant for Paris in the early 1950s.

mantic comedies *The Accidental Tourist* (1988) starring William Hurt, *Forget Paris* (1995) with Billy Crystal and Debra Winger, and *Le Divorce* (2003) starring Kate Hudson and Naomi Watts.

Paris as a postcard backdrop is nice, but what of the real Paris as a major location in big films? Jean-Pierre Melville features Paris in his masterful *Le Samouraï* (1967), a thriller starring Alain Delon that dashes too quickly through the city – especially in the famous metro scenes – to leave a lasting impression of the place. In Bernardo Bertolucci's *Last Tango in Paris* (1972), Marlon Brando conducts an affair with a young Frenchwoman in a Paris apartment, but little of the city itself is seen in the film. In a similar fashion, Luc Besson's cult film *Subway* (1985) starring Isabelle Adjani and Christopher Lambert is played out in the underground transit system, too subterranean to truly evoke the atmosphere of the city itself. It was inevitable that James Bond would at least flirt with the city: Roger Moore chases a death-defying Grace Jones up the Eiffel Tower in *A View to a Kill* (1985), yet he never settles in the city long enough to make the relationship truly memorable. The same may be said of Martin Scorsese's *The Age of Innocence* (1993), scenes from which were filmed in Paris, and *Moulin Rouge!* (2001), an update of John Huston's 1952 flick featuring Zsa Zsa Gabor and Paris's red-light milieu, this time with Nicole Kidman in the starring role but shot on elaborate sets at Fox Studios in Sydney.

While many films have employed Paris as a background flourish, others have been committed to the city heart and soul. One of the best was made just a few years after *Funny Face*, but was entirely different in tone and technique. Auteur filmmaker Jean-Luc Godard's convention-smashing *À bout de souffle* (*Breathless*, 1959) transformed the audience's view of Paris from a glitzy backdrop dotted with props like Notre Dame and the Eiffel Tower into a workaday city brimming with compli-

The Lumière brothers made cinema history in the "City of Light."

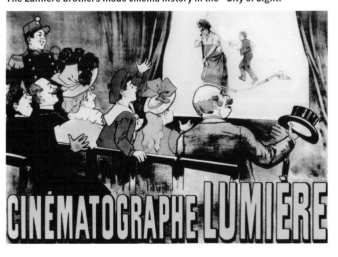

cated dames and caustic criminals. Godard's innovative camera work and quirky sense of drama brought the life of the young and aimless into sharp focus, much as Federico Fellini did in the contemporaneous *La Dolce Vita* (1960). It was no coincidence: Both films were part of a distinctive "new wave," or *nouvelle vague*, in film that swept across Europe.

An heir to this anti-establishment tradition, Leos Carax spent a fortune to hold a mirror to Paris with real-life locations and later life-size sets in *Les Amants du Pont-Neuf* (*The Lovers on the Bridge*, 1991) starring Parisienne Juliette Binoche as an artist losing her eyesight. Pomp and excess frame the frivolous and tragic affairs central to *Dangerous Liaisons* (1988), a visual celebration of the 18th century played out in grand châteaux at the city's edge. In the same year, director Roman Polanski thrilled audiences with *Frantic*, a practically forgotten but riveting film that stars Harrison Ford and shows Paris in a harrowing light. Darling *Amélie* (2001) takes her audience on a rich visual tour of Montmartre and beyond, a surreal tale of love found in life's little things that brought the first flush of fame to French actress Audrey Tautou, star of Ron Howard's *The Da Vinci Code* (2006). While the film based upon Dan Brown's popular novel fell short of critics' expectations, it did shine the spotlight on several famous Paris locations: the Louvre, the Church of St-Sulpice, where scary Silas slays a nun, the Hôtel de Païva at 28 Place St-Georges, which stands in as the American Embassy, the legendary Ritz hotel, and the pretty Château de Villette, home to Robert Langdon's (Tom Hanks) friend Sir Leigh Teabing (Ian McKellen) on the city's outskirts.

La Pyramide Inversée at the Louvre, an important location in
The Da Vinci Code **(2006) starring Tom Hanks and Audrey Tautou.**

Breathless

1. Former Pam-Pam café and the Oberon building on the Champs-Elysées
2. George V métro station
3. Normandie Cinema, 116 bis on the Champs-Elysées
4. Hôtel Les Rives de Notre Dame (formerly the Hôtel de Suède), 15 Quai Saint-Michel
5. Former editorial offices of the International Herald Tribune, 21 Rue de Berri
6. Place de la Concorde
7. Café Le Select and Café Le Cosmos (now the Lotus Café), Boulevard du Montparnasse 99 and 101
8. Apartment at 11 Rue Campagne Première
9. Intersection of Rue Campagne Première and Boulevard Raspail

Dangerous Liaisons

10. Château de Champs sur Marne, 15 miles (26 kilometers) east of Paris
11. Château Maisons-Laffitte, 13 miles (21 kilometers) northwest of Paris
12. Théâtre Montansier at the palace of Versailles, 13 miles (21 kilometers) southwest of Paris

The Lovers on the Bridge

13. Pont-Neuf
14. Musée du Louvre
15. Pont-Neuf métro
16. Samaritaine shopping halls

The Fabulous Destiny of Amélie Poulain

17. Canal St-Martin, Rue des Récollets
18. Café des Deux Moulins, 15 Rue Lepic at Rue Cauchois
19. Lamarck-Caulaincourt métro
20. Brasserie Le Carrousel, 56 Rue des Trois Frères
21. Boulevard de Clichy, Pigalle
22. Foire du Trône and the *train fantôme* in the Bois de Vincennes park
23. Carrousel on Place St-Pierre and the basilica of Sacré-Coeur
24. Au Clown de la République, Boulevard St-Martin 11
25. Gare de l'Est railroad station

PARIS

0 250 m

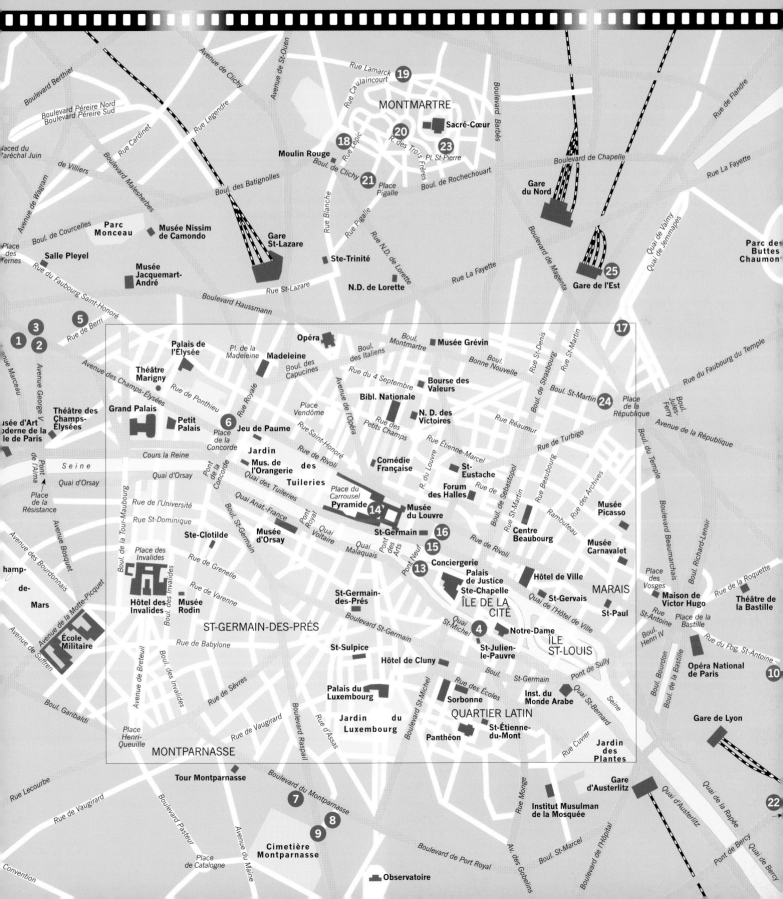

Rue Lamarck
19
MONTMARTRE
Sacré-Cœur
20
23
Pl. St-Pierre
18
Moulin Rouge
Boul. de Clichy
Rue Lepic
R. des Trois Frères
21
Place
Pigalle
Boul. de Rochechouart

Boulevard Berthier
Boulevard Péreire Nord
Boulevard Péreire Sud
Avenue de Clichy
Avenue de St-Ouen
Rue Legendre
Rue Caulaincourt

Boulevard Barbès
Boulevard de Chapelle
Gare
du Nord
Rue de Flandre
Rue La Fayette

Place du
Maréchal Juin
de Villiers
Rue Cardinet
Rue du Faubourg Saint-Honoré
Boulevard Malesherbes
Boul. des Batignolles
Rue Blanche
Rue Pigalle
Rue N.D. de Lorette
Rue La Fayette

Parc
Monceau
Musée Nissim
de Camondo
Gare
St-Lazare
Ste-Trinité
N.D. de Lorette

Avenue de Wagram
Boul. de Courcelles
Place
des Ternes
Salle Pleyel
Musée
Jacquemart-
André
Rue St-Lazare
Boulevard Haussmann

Boulevard de Magenta
Gare de l'Est
25

Quai de Valmy
Quai de Jemmapes

Parc des
Buttes
Chaumont

17

Rue de Berri
5
1 3
2
Rue du Faubourg Saint-Honoré
Avenue Marceau
Avenue George V
Avenue des Champs-Élysées

Palais de
l'Élysée
Théâtre
Marigny
Grand Palais
Petit Palais
Rue de Ponthieu
Rue Royale

Opéra
Madeleine
Pl. de la
Madeleine
Boul. des
Capucines
Boul.
Montmartre
Musée Grévin
Boul.
des Italiens
Boul.
Bonne Nouvelle
Rue St-Denis
Rue St-Martin

24
Place de la
République
Rue du Faubourg du Temple
Boul. Jules-Ferry
Avenue de la République

Théâtre des
Champs-
Élysées
Musée d'Art
moderne de la
Ville de Paris
Avenue de New York
Pont de
l'Alma
Place de la
Résistance
Seine
Cours la Reine
Quai d'Orsay
6
Jeu de Paume
Place de
la Concorde
Jardin
Mus. de
l'Orangerie
des
Tuileries
Place de la
Concorde
Rue Saint-Honoré
Place
Vendôme
Avenue de l'Opéra
Rue du 4 Septembre
Bibl. Nationale
Rue des
Petits Champs
Bourse des
Valeurs
N. D. des
Victoires
Rue Réaumur
Boul. de Strasbourg
Boul. St-Martin
Avenue de la République

Rue de l'Université
Rue St-Dominique
Boul. St-Germain
Quai Anat.-France
Quai des Tuileries
Rue de Rivoli
Comédie
Française
Rue Étienne-Marcel
St-
Eustache
Rue du Louvre
Rue de Turbigo
Rue de Turbigo
Musée
Picasso
Boulevard Beaumarchais
Boulevard Richard-Lenoir

Ste-Clotilde
Musée
d'Orsay
Boul. de la Tour-Maubourg
Rue de Grenelle
Rue St-Germain
Pont
Royal
Pont
de la
Concorde
Place du
Carrousel
Pyramide
14
Musée
du Louvre
St-Germain
16
15
Forum
des Halles
Rue de Rivoli
Boul. de Sébastopol
Rue St-Martin
Rue Beaubourg
Rambuteau
Centre
Beaubourg
Rue des Archives
Musée
Carnavalet
Place
des
Vosges
Maison de
Victor Hugo

Hôtel des
Invalides
Place des
Invalides
Rue de Varenne
Musée
Rodin
Rue de Grenelle
Boul. des Invalides
Pont
Neuf
13
Conciergerie
Palais
de Justice
Ste-Chapelle
ÎLE DE LA
CITÉ
Hôtel de Ville
St-Gervais
Quai de l'Hôtel de Ville
St-Paul
MARAIS
Place de la
Bastille
Théâtre de
la Bastille

champ-
de-
Mars
Avenue de la Motte-Picquet
École
Militaire
Avenue de Suffren
Boul. Garibaldi
Rue de Sèvres
Avenue de Breteuil
Rue de Babylone
ST-GERMAIN-DES-PRÉS
St-Germain-
des-Prés
Boulevard St-Germain
St-Sulpice
Hôtel de Cluny
Palais du
Luxembourg
Jardin   du
Luxembourg
Rue de Vaugirard
Boulevard Raspail
Rue d'Assas
Rue des Écoles
Sorbonne
QUARTIER LATIN
St-Étienne-
du-Mont
Panthéon
St-Julien-
le-Pauvre
4
Notre-Dame
ÎLE
ST-LOUIS
Pont de Sully
Boul.
St-Germain
Inst. du
Monde Arabe
Quai St-Bernard
Rue Cuvier
Jardin
des
Plantes

Quai
St-Michel
Boulevard St-Michel

Boul.
Henri IV
Quai de la Rapée

Boul. Bourdon
Boul. de la Bastille
Opéra National
de Paris
Rue du Fbg. St-Antoine
Rue de la Roquette
10
Gare de Lyon

Tour Montparnasse
7
8
9
Cimetière
Montparnasse
MONTPARNASSE
Boulevard du Montparnasse
Boulevard Pasteur
Rue de Vaugirard
Rue Lecourbe
Place
de Catalogne
Convention
Avenue du Maine
Place
Henri-
Queuille
Rue Monge
Institut Musulman
de la Mosquée
Boulevard St-Marcel
Boulevard de Port Royal
Av. des Gobelins
Boulevard de l'Hôpital
Gare
d'Austerlitz
Quai d'Austerlitz
Quai de la Rapée
22
Pont de Bercy
Quai de Bercy

Observatoire

BREATHLESS

À bout de souffle

Director	Jean-Luc Godard
Starring	Jean-Paul Belmondo, Jean Seberg, Liliane David, Daniel Boulanger

France, 1959

I make movies to keep myself busy. If I had the strength, I'd do nothing." A delight to existentialists, director Jean-Luc Godard parodies himself in *Every Man for Himself* (1980), trotting out the sneering French sense of irony that inspired his first and most critically acclaimed film, *À bout de souffle* (*Breathless*, 1959). At twenty-nine, Paris-born Godard, one of a circle of likeminded writers at *Les cahiers du cinéma* magazine, turned the world of film upside down with fresh techniques in directing and editing showcased in this surprise box-office hit. Along with his friend François Truffaut, he is considered the godfather of experimental filmmaking.

Lighter cameras, faster film stock and better, more flexible ways to record sound made it easy for Godard to shoot on location, a trademark of the

Con man Michel (Jean-Paul Belmondo) and the lovely Patricia (Jean Seberg), a nice American girl. Or not?

French New Wave. The movement rejected polished, studio-produced flicks, instituting the use of jump cuts, hand-held cameras, long tracking shots and ad-libbed dialogue that would inspire Quentin Tarantino's breakthrough *Reservoir Dogs* (1992). Godard was not only a revolutionary, but a reactionary as well: In *Breathless*, petty criminal Michel (Jean-Paul Belmondo) makes repeated references to the detective dramas of the 1940s, in particular *The Maltese Falcon* (1941) starring Humphrey Bogart, mugging in front of movie posters and rubbing his thumb across his lips. Does Godard want film to progress as an art form, or rather to return to a lost golden age?

What plays out in the streets of Paris employs elements of film noir to forge a remarkable cinematic sign of the times. Michel Poiccard is a small-time crook on the run from the law when he catches up with American-in-Paris Patricia Franchini (Jean Seberg). The blonde is busily hawking the *New York Herald Tribune* in front of the former **Pam-Pam café** and the **Oberon building** just short of the Arc de Triomphe on the **Champs-Elysées.** That Michel is a cad is clear: He killed a cop in cold blood after stealing a car in Marseille. His only concern now is to collect the cash owed to him for previous crimes and to convince Patricia to run away with him to Rome. He presumes he'll be discovered instantly as star material once he gets to the Cine-città film studios. After giving the law the slip, he emerges from the **George V métro station** and poses in front of publicity shots of Bogart at the **Normandie Cinema** at **116 bis** on the **Champs-Elysées,** today side by side with the **Lido** movie house.

Patricia is willing to fall for the image, or so it seems. In the extended bedroom scene at her apartment, filmed in **Room 12** of the **Hôtel de Suède**, now **Hôtel Les Rives de Notre Dame** at **15 Quai Saint-Michel,** the pixie-like ingénue traverses an emotional spectrum most audiences would expect of the helpless heroine.

From gushing affection to the despair of a suspected pregnancy, the viewer is seduced into casting Patricia as a good girl gone wrong. Her flat, with its cheap reproductions of works by Picasso and Renoir, and her aspirations, to study at the Sorbonne, heighten her angelic appeal. That she sleeps with Michel is of course not her fault – who could resist his deep tan, his lithe, muscled torso, his animal magnetism? That she also publicly romances the journalist Van Doude for writing assignments at the now defunct Pergola Café on the Champs-Elysées raises eyebrows, but her confrontation with police over Michel's where-abouts at the former **Tribune offices at 21 Rue de Berri** – a scene that includes Godard himself in a cameo role as an informer – confirms her devotion to him.

The chase that ensues takes the couple across the landmark **Place de la Concorde** at night. Amid the sparkling lights of one of Paris's most romantic vistas, Patricia finally declares her love to Michel. Slowly unraveling

throughout the film, the self-assured con artist has shed his cool exterior to become startlingly vulnerable. His last bout with cool is in front of the legendary bar-cafés **Le Select** and **Le Cosmos** (now the **Lotus Café**) at **Boulevard du Montparnasse 99** and **101**, respectively. Could it be that he is truly in love with Patricia, and that she is in fact toying with him, instead of the other

way round? An unexpected betrayal leaves Michel with few options. He flees the apartment at **11 Rue Campagne Première** and collapses at the intersection of **Rue Campagne Première** and **Boulevard Raspail** with only enough breath left in him to tell her how he really feels. While the film's finale left many viewers cold, critics hailed it as the ultimate expression of New Wave cool.

The Champs-Elysées, a famous location in film history. Michel and Patricia meet up on the grand avenue as she hawks newspapers. Typical corner cafés and cinemas like the Normandie and the Lido (above) **are the stage on which their love affair plays out.**

THE LOVERS ON THE BRIDGE

Les Amants du Pont-Neuf

Director Leos Carax

Starring Juliette Binoche, Denis Lavant,
Klaus-Michael Grüber, Daniel Buain,
Marion Stalens

France, 1991

Alex (Denis Lavant) swallows fire as a busker on the streets of Paris.

Below and right: **Michèle (Juliette Binoche) and Alex find love despite all odds on Paris's oldest bridge across the Seine, the Pont-Neuf.**

Little known outside of France, but a byword for romance in Paris for Europeans, *Les Amants du Pont-Neuf* (*The Lovers on the Bridge*) should have been youthful director Leos Carax's career-making movie. His first feature, *Boy Meets Girl* (1984), wowed critics at the 1984 Cannes film festival, presaging more success with *Bad Blood* (1986). Like *Blade Runner* (1982) ten years earlier, *Lovers* flopped at its long-awaited debut in 1991, but has delighted a devoted following ever since. Carax is widely acclaimed as heir to Jean-Luc Godard, but his cinema has none of the New Wave cool of that legendary director's debut film *À bout de souffle* (*Breathless*, 1959). Instead, the film is wildly emotive, riding the rollercoaster of Juliette Binoche and Denis Lavant's performances as two vagrants rejecting life but still finding love on the oldest bridge in Paris.

The City of Light is gearing up for the 1989 bicentennial of the French Revolution when Michèle (Juliette Binoche) curls up to sleep amid the scaffolding on the **Pont-Neuf.** The famous

crossing over the River Seine is closed for repairs, and has become home to two bums, young Alex (Denis Lavant) and hoary old Hans (Klaus-Michael Grüber). Both are addicted to drugs and neither is much attuned to reality. The arrival of a woman on the bridge is at once a ray of hope and a cause for despair. Alex adores her – she is his chance at love. Hans hates her, if only for the memories of a dead wife she conjures up. But Michèle has her own problems: She was once an artist, but her eyesight is fading and soon she will be blind. Her boyfriend abandoned her, she ran away from a solid, middle-class home, and now her only refuge is a bottle of cheap red wine.

Puppy-like, Alex follows her wherever she goes. He even draws the motivation to find work – as a fire-breather for pennies in the street – from her presence. Their love affair is at once tender and ridiculous, with memorable scenes such as Binoche waterskiing on the Seine under a shower of fireworks during the bicentennial celebrations, the pair rolling drunk by oversized bottles, and unlikely lovemaking on the beach. A former watchman, Hans sneaks Michèle into the **Louvre** at night to view the works of the Old Masters. She hopes these will be the images that will stay with her when she goes blind.

Alex's affection slowly turns to obsession. Posters of the missing girl appear in the **Pont-Neuf métro,** and the message they bear – that Michèle's eyesight could be saved with a new operation – fails to move him. His terror of being left alone drives him to burn the posters and attack the man hanging them. By a freak accident, he kills him. Alex's fear that Michèle could return to her ex-boyfriend transforms the gentle dope into a raging thug. Despite his efforts to keep the information from her, Michèle hears of her parents' attempts to find her and of a possible cure. She disappears; Alex goes to prison. Neither expects ever to hear from the other again.

A year later, her sight restored, Michèle visits Alex in jail and they agree to meet on Pont-Neuf to celebrate New Year's Eve once he is released. Little does Alex suspect that Michèle has begun a new life, one that may not include him. The snowy rendezvous leads to a dream-like ending on a barge. The scenes are reminiscent of Jean Vigo's 1934 film classic *L'Atalante*, a love story that was one of director Carax's inspirations.

Had the film been a box-office hit, the epic production might have been worth the expense. *Lovers* was plagued with problems from the outset. Carax obtained permission to film on the real Pont-Neuf, but, because star Denis Lavant seriously injured himself, shooting was postponed for an entire year. With the real thing no longer available, Carax moved the cast and crew down to the south of France near Montpellier where the bridge and the facades of the **Samaritaine shopping halls** behind it were recreated on a grand scale. With the mammoth sets, costs soared astronomically. Upon completion, *Lovers* had earned the notoriety of being the most expensive French film ever made.

Michèle steals into the Louvre at night to view the works of the Old Masters before she loses her eyesight in the hope that the images will stay with her when she's blind. With its countless masterpieces spanning numerous eras, the museum's collection is one of the treasure troves of the world.

DANGEROUS LIAISONS

Director	Stephen Frears
Starring	Glenn Close, John Malkovich, Michelle Pfeiffer, Swoosie Kurtz, Uma Thurman, Keanu Reeves

USA/UK, 1988

"Why do you suppose we only feel compelled to chase the ones who run away?" The Vicomte de Valmont's view of love in 18th-century France sums up this costume drama based on the pre-Revolutionary novel *Les Liaisons Dangereuses* by Choderlos de Laclos. The book beloved of Marie Antoinette has been adapted multiple times for the silver screen, including Milos Forman's ill-fated *Valmont* (1989) starring Colin Firth and Annette Bening, released a year after *Dangerous Liaisons*. Christopher Hampton first adapted the epistolary tale of nobility being naughty for the stage. It was a hit in London's West End and on Broadway before he revamped it for the silver screen. Director Stephen Frears of *My Beautiful Laundrette* (1985) cult fame looked to Renaissance and Baroque country estates on the outskirts of Paris to conjure the decadence of an age that found "social justice" under Robespierre and the razor-sharp scrutiny of Madame Guillotine.

Losing one's head to love and revenge is the theme of the story set in 1788. The wicked Marquise de Merteuil (Glenn Close) summons the Vicomte de Valmont (John Malkovich), a former lover, to make him an indecent proposal: He should deflower Cécile de Volanges (Uma Thurman) just before the convent-trained virgin weds the Marquise's despised ex-husband. The powdered, preening, smug Vicomte, notorious for his amorous conquests, declines with a yawn: The task is too simple. He has his reputation to consider, and besides, he has already set himself a far greater challenge. He will seduce the lovely Madame de Tourvel (Michelle Pfeiffer), a married woman and self-righteous holy-roller, but he wants her to believe in the sanctity of marriage even as she succumbs to his designs. Standing like a queen above the grand stair of the **Château de Champs sur Marne,** 15 miles (26 kilometers) east of Paris, the Marquise sweetens the pot: If he can bring her proof, written proof, that he has bedded Madame de Tourvel, she will condescend to spend a night of passion with him.

Valmont's first encounters with his pretty prey at his aunt's château, the Renaissance pile of **Château Maisons-Laffitte,** 13 miles (21 kilometers) northwest of Paris, are fruitless, thanks to an unknown "friend" who has spread warnings of his ill repute. A little research reveals the informant to be none other than

Fetching prey: Michelle Pfeiffer is the feisty Madame de Tourvel, the woman who must resist seduction in the lush formal gardens of Château Champs sur Marne (right).

The Marquise (Glenn Close) and Valmont (John Malkovich) plan their elaborate intrigue. She makes an indecent proposal on the stairs at Château Champs sur Marne (left). The salons of this grand house (below) serve as a stately backdrop for the drama based on an 18th-century novel. The memorable scene in which Cécile (Uma Thurman) slips Valmont the key to her bedroom takes place on the grand stair at Château Maisons-Laffitte.

Madame de Volanges (Swoosie Kurtz), mother of the chaste Cécile. Outraged, Valmont takes up the Marquise's challenge with a vengeance, and the chase is on. The filmmakers seamlessly added the oval salon, stuccoed drawing rooms, and sprawling **gardens** at Champs sur Marne as an extension to Valmont's aunt's estate. In the meantime, the Marquise has been orchestrating a love affair between Cécile and music instructor Chevalier Danceny (Keanu Reeves). The sensitive young man weeps openly at the opera, filmed at the **Théâtre Montansier** at the palace of **Versailles,** also just outside the city. The venue, 13 miles (21 kilometers) southwest of Paris, is where the Marquise is served her just desserts at the movie's close, a denouement involving Valmont and Madame de Tourvel that restores some faith, miraculously, in human decency.

Given the extended sexual tension between their characters, few fans were surprised at reports that John Malkovich and Michelle Pfeiffer fell in love on the set, an affair that allegedly wrecked the actor's first marriage. The on-screen intensity translated into instant success for the film, catapulting the erstwhile couple as well as Uma Thurman and Keanu Reeves up the Hollywood A list – despite Reeves's inexplicable choice of *Bill & Ted's Excellent Adventure* (1989) as his next role. Versatile Glenn Close was already a hot ticket, especially for her unforgettable part in *Fatal Attraction* (1987). Her phlegmatic performance as a hard-hearted aristocrat confirmed her staying power. She and Pfeiffer both took nominations, but the Oscars went to Christopher Hampton for Best Adapted Screenplay, and to the three designers who guaranteed the period piece's atmosphere and authenticity: to Stuart Craig and Gérard James for Art Direction and Set Direction, respectively, and to James Acheson for Costume Design.

THE FABULOUS DESTINY OF AMÉLIE POULAIN

Le Fabuleux destin d'Amélie Poulain

Director   Jean-Pierre Jeunet

Starring   Audrey Tautou, Mathieu Kassovitz, Rufus, Urbain Cancelier, Serge Merlin, Jamel Debbouze

France, 2001

Crème brûlée and Nino (Mathieu Kassovitz) sweeten Amélie's (Audrey Tautou) workdays at the Café des Deux Moulins.

Bob-cut beauty Audrey Tautou as *Amélie* and artists' quarter Montmartre take center stage in this kaleidoscopic comedy about small pleasures and big meanings in workaday Paris. Hepburnesque, precocious Tautou won the hearts and minds of millions at home, with the film taking four French César awards and five Oscar nominations, including Best Foreign Language Film. No wonder Ron Howard picked her to star alongside Tom Hanks in *The Da Vinci Code* (2006).

Hollywood's thumbs-up to the film was but an echo of the passionate cult following in Europe: Jacques Chirac insisted that director Jean-Pierre Jeunet attend a private screening with him in the presidential Palais de l'Elysée amid critical acclaim that *Amélie* had opened a fresh, new, life-affirming chapter in French cultural patrimony. Sweetly underscored by Yann Tiersen's retro-chic soundtrack, real estate values in the location-rich 18th Arrondissement skyrocketed on the strength of the movie's picture-postcard imagery, what *The New York Times* Paris bureau chief Elaine Sciolino termed the "Amélie Poulainization" of the down-at-heel quarter of Montmartre.

Given the story's obvious charms, it is no surprise that all Paris went wild for it. Twenty-three-year-old Amélie Poulain (Audrey Tautou) lives a lonely life of skipping stones on the **Canal St-Martin** and waiting on oddball regulars at the **Café des Deux Moulins, 15 Rue Lepic** at Rue Cauchois. Everything changes when she discovers a box of forgotten mementos hidden in

her apartment. A vow to find its owner becomes a crusade of kindness amid the cobblestone streets, corner bars, and colorful shops of Montmartre, a hilly neighborhood and the highest point in Paris long famous as the haunt of such painters as Van Gogh, Renoir, and Cézanne. Painfully shy and hesitant to leap headlong into life, she decides to pursue a campaign of aiding others instead. With her help, a blind man "sees" fruit stands and bakeries in psychedelic colors while en route to the **Lamarck-Caulaincourt métro.** More poignantly, Amélie makes the mean fruit-and-vegetable store owner Collignon (Urbain Cancelier) pay for his cruelty to his hapless Algerian assistant, Lucien (Jamel Debbouze) who tends the shop at **56 Rue des Trois Frères,** now the **Brasserie Le Carrousel.**

Karma-like, Amélie's expressions of love come full circle. A strange set of coincidences causes a curious album of passport photos kept by sex shop clerk Nino (Mathieu Kassovitz) to fall into her hands. Her wholehearted attempt to return it takes her to his various and sundry places of employment: Palace Video on the Boulevard de Clichy in neon-lit **Pigalle,** and the ghostly *train fantôme* at **Foire du Trône,** Chenille des Carpates in the **Bois de Vincennes** park. A romantic game of telephone tag on the terraces between the Victorian carrousel on **Place St-Pierre** and the domed basilica of **Sacré-Coeur** set off an elaborate game of hide and seek: Amélie buys a Zorro costume at **Au Clown de la République** at **Boulevard St-Martin 11,** and leaves enigmatic messages for Nino at the photo automats of the **Gare de l'Est** railroad station. Her reticence fuels a desire to remain anonymous despite the dizzying feeling of falling head over heels in love – an emotion she confesses to the physically frail artist Raymond Dufayel (Serge Merlin). Will Amélie have the courage to live life through her own adventures, or will she hide in the vicarious joy she brings to others?

Jean-Pierre Jeunet may have had a similar crisis in 1997 when he left France for Hollywood to direct *Alien: Resurrection* (1997) starring Sigourney Weaver and Winona Ryder. It was then that he decided to film his next project at home, in the neighborhood of Montmartre where he had lived since the seventies. The hillside community just beyond the city limits is no longer a refuge of cheap rents, but it is still a creative oasis – although

Amélie finds her Zorro costume at Au Clown de la République and uses her disguise to draw Nino into a romantic game of hide and seek.

Montmartre and Sacré-Coeur figure large in this surreal romantic comedy.

it appears a bit too tidy in *Amélie*, as graffiti and rubbish were digitally removed in the editing. Some critics pooh-poohed the film's Euro Disney effect, but tourists fell in love, combing the streets of Montmartre to look for locations and relive the film's magic. Shooting took place here over three weeks in 2000, and the cheery, unassuming Café des Deux Moulins is now a pilgrimage site, albeit minus its tobacco stand. An eponymous crème brûlée tops the menu in honor of the heroine's love of cracking the caramelized crust with the tip of her spoon. Real-life grocer-turned-restaurateur Ali Mdoughy happily shows tourists his album of photos from the filming, and welcomes the tide of springtime tourist Euros to the Brasserie Le Carrousel.

Amélie's father won't leave Paris, but his garden dwarf mysteriously travels the globe and sends him postcards from abroad. Who could be behind this strange occurrence?

12

PRAGUE

OLD-WORLD CHARM IN CENTRAL EUROPE

As a movie location, Prague is the unchallenged master of metamorphosis, a veritable chameleon among world cities. Whether filmmakers seek a pretty backdrop immersed in old-world charm or a major metropolis like London or Vienna revived from a bygone era, they're likely to find it among the cobblestone alleyways and stuccoed palaces of Prague's Old Town. Unlike Berlin, Budapest, or Warsaw, Prague and the grand architecture of the Austro-Hungarian "Danube monarchy" survived World War II largely intact. The city's lack of funds for urban development during the Cold War would be a boon for filmmakers decades later.

In Prague, buildings in a striking array of styles stand side by side as if preserved in a time capsule, gracefully spanning the Middle Ages to the eras of the Baroque and Art Nouveau. Almost every mode of European architecture since the 11th century is represented here, and with the help of set designers, the city can exude the atmosphere of almost any European city at any point in the last thousand years. Milos Forman told reporter Henry Kamm of *The New York Times* of his delight in finding a city so utterly flexible for filmmaking. "Prague is absolutely ideal. On all the squares and streets you can turn the camera 360 degrees and have to change nothing." Under the Czech dissident's direction, Prague would become the perfect stand-in for 18th-century Vienna for *Amadeus* (1984).

To Forman, Prague in the eighties was what it had always been: a beautifully preserved European city. It wasn't until the collapse of the Soviet Union and the opening of the Eastern Bloc in the mid-nineties, however, that Prague would suddenly become a mecca for foreign filmmakers. They flocked to what they considered the "Hollywood of the East," starting a film-business gold rush in the genteel neighborhoods along the Vltava River. A city rich in film history, Prague had attracted directors from abroad before. As early as 1913 Paul Wegener, a pioneer of German silent movies, filmed *The Student of Prague* in the Bohemian capital, the Faustian fable of a penniless student based on a short story by Edgar Allan Poe.

Czech filmmakers made the most of Prague in cinema's early days, too. Renowned local director Gustav Machatý shocked audiences with *Seduction* in 1929, a film that revealed Prague in all its Art Deco splendor and caused a stir with a scandalous nude scene. Machatý featured his hometown again in *From Saturday to Sunday* (1931), the story of two secretaries who want more out of life than their meager salaries. Controversy struck again when Vienna-born actress Hedy Kiesler bared all in *Ecstasy* (1932). The memorable performance grabbed the attention of studio bosses in California and helped launch Kiesler's Hollywood career as the brunette beauty Hedy Lamarr. Barrandov Studios opened its doors in a suburb southwest of Prague that same year: Milos Havel, uncle of the poet and future Czech president Václav Havel, founded the legendary studio complex, an Eastern European dream factory that was soon churning out up to eighty films annually.

The Czech film industry was largely closed to the West under the Communist regime and suffered greatly from a lack of funds and the grim realities of censorship. When restrictions were eased somewhat in the early 1960s, the "new wave" in film-

Theresa Russell and Jeremy Irons on the Charles Bridge in Steven Soderbergh's *Kafka* (top). Directors return time and again to use the beautifully preserved architecture of Prague's Old Town as a backdrop in historical films.

A view of the Tyn Church on the Old Town Hall Square.

making that had caused a creative uproar in other European countries swept through Czechoslovakia, too. The trend encouraged some of the country's most innovative filmmakers, and directors such as Milos Forman, Jirí Menzel, and Ján Kadár shaped a short golden era of new Czech film. This heyday ended prematurely in 1968 with the Soviet invasion. Isolated behind the Iron Curtain, the Czech film industry was forced to eke out a meager existence.

Not surprisingly, Prague held great appeal for the international filmmaking community right after communism collapsed, with its numerous experienced film technicians, skilled set builders, and affordable special effects technicians. Making a film in Prague cost a small fraction of what it did in Western Europe or the United States. Barrandov Studios was inundated with interest from international film companies; cameramen and directors flew in to shoot in the streets and palaces of the city.

Steven Soderbergh became the first big Western director to train the cameras on Prague after the Communist collapse with his 1991 cinematic portrait of *Kafka*. Jeremy Irons was cast in the leading role as the city's most famous poet, with beautiful black-and-white shots of the Malá Strana quarter offering audiences an unforgettably romantic impression of the city. After *Amadeus* and *Kafka*, *Immortal Beloved* (1994) with Gary Oldman

as Ludwig van Beethoven presented yet another biopic on an artist from a bygone era filmed on location in Prague. Only with *Mission: Impossible* (1996) was modern Prague discovered as an intriguing setting for a fast-paced spy thriller. *xXx* (2002), a tongue-in-cheek action film starring Vin Diesel, made full use of classic Prague locations, even staging an improbable high-speed car chase through the narrow alleys of the Old Town.

More recently, Prague has hosted adventure films such as *The League of Extraordinary Gentlemen* (2003) and *Van Helsing* (2004), filmed on location as well as at Barrandov Studios. Time and again, picturesque original locations and state-of-the-art studio support have proven irresistible to the international filmmaking milieu. *Shanghai Knights* (2003) director David Dobkin requested a life-size copy of London's Big Ben to be built in the studios, despite its towering 320-foot (nearly 100-meter) height. No order was too tall for Barrandov's set architects, however, who delivered the structure exactly as requested.

The local film industry has benefited greatly from its recent successes, as well. *Kolya* (1996), Jan Sverák's bittersweet comedy about a confirmed bachelor who suddenly becomes the sole parent of a little Russian boy, won an Oscar for Best Foreign Language Film, giving Czech filmmakers a much-appreciated boost to their self-esteem. *Everything Is Illuminated* (2005), the cinematic version of Jonathan Safran Foer's popular novel, was also filmed in and around Prague, putting the Czech capital and the gorgeous landscapes outside the city squarely in the spotlight. As the rest of Eastern Europe opens up to the West, though, Prague may find that its new-found success in filmmaking is a fleeting phenomenon. Despite the city's popularity over the last decade, countries such as Bulgaria and Romania are learning to lure the film industry with pristine film locations that are even less expensive than those in the Czech Republic.

Prague boasts more than 180 bridges, including fifteen major crossings of the Vltava. The charming comedy *Kolya* (right) is set in modern Prague.

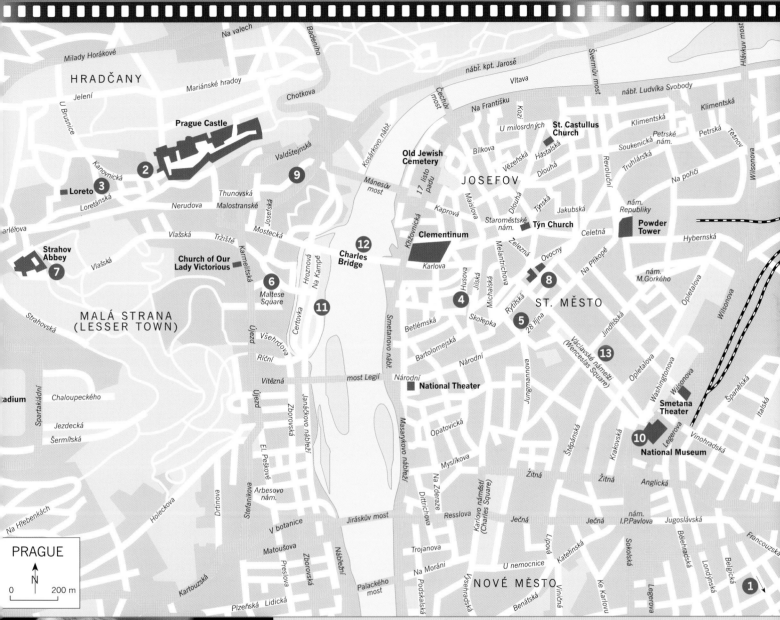

Amadeus

1. Archbishop's Castle of Kromeriz in Moravia, 168 miles (270 km) east of Prague
2. Gryspek Palace, Hradcany Square
3. Mozart's house, Hradcany Square 7
4. St. Giles's Church, Husova 8
5. Salieri residence, Palace of the Maltese Knights, (currently the Embassy of Malta), Perlová 1
6. Maltese Square
7. Theological Hall of the library at Strahov Abbey
8. Tyl Theater
9. Gardens before the Salla Terrena of the Wallenstein Palace

Mission: Impossible

10. National Museum, Václavské náměstí 68, Wencelas Square
11. Liechtenstein Palais on Kampa Island in the Vltava River
12. Charles Bridge
13. Hotel Europa, Václavské náměstí 25, Wencelas Square

AMADEUS

Director	Milos Forman
Starring	F. Murray Abraham, Tom Hulce, Elizabeth Berridge, Simon Callow, Roy Dotrice, Jeffrey Jones

USA, 1984

Who could have guessed that late 18th-century Vienna still existed in Prague? Milos Forman discovered the ideal location for his historical epic *Amadeus* in the charming capital of the Czech Republic. Given Forman's history, it was the last place anyone expected him to look. No one – least of all the Czech director himself – thought he would ever film in his homeland again. After the Soviet takeover of Czechoslovakia in 1968, Forman defected to the West and was granted U.S. citizenship. The Czech authorities punished him by routinely rejecting every visa application he made to visit. Understandably, Prague did not top Forman's list when he started the search for a suitable backdrop to *Amadeus*, but neither Vienna, Salzburg, nor Budapest would do. Only Prague fit the bill for the film that would win a grand total of eight Academy Awards, including Best Picture and Best Director.

The Czech capital was neither too modern to frame a story set in the 1700s nor too expensive for the filmmaker's purposes. Visually, it was as though time had stood still in the quaint metropolis on the banks of the Vltava: With its magnificent palaces, churches, and narrow cobblestone alleys, the city behind the Iron Curtain had exactly what Forman and his production designers were looking for. The streets and squares of the picturesque **Lesser Town** (Malá Strana) and the **Hradcany district** below Prague Castle set an architecturally attractive stage for actors in period costume. For the Czech government, the production would become a key source of foreign currency. Its importance would garner the former political refugee a visa as well as permission to film in Prague's most beautiful palaces.

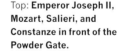

Top: **Emperor Joseph II, Mozart, Salieri, and Constanze in front of the Powder Gate.**

Two worlds meet at Hradcany Square: the emperor's Gryspek Palace (left) **and Mozart's modest little house** (right).

The library at Strahov Abbey.

In *Amadeus*, playwright and screenwriter Peter Shaffer tells the story of the rise and fall of Wolfgang Amadeus Mozart (Tom Hulce) through the eyes of his greatest rival, the imperial composer Antonio Salieri (F. Murray Abraham). Salieri is the most important musician at the court of the Austrian emperor, and is not amused when he is suddenly eclipsed by the arrival of the twenty-five-year-old musical genius. That Mozart manages to steal the favor of their patron, Joseph II (Jeffrey Jones), is one thing. What deeply offends Salieri, though, is that the young musician – so obviously blessed with divine talent – is a boastful scoundrel and a "giggling, dirty-minded creature." Overwhelmed by the beauty of Mozart's music and convinced of his own mediocrity, Salieri embarks on a mission to destroy his archrival's career.

Salieri first meets the budding genius during a concert Mozart gives at the residence of the archbishop of Salzburg, scenes filmed in the opulent Baroque halls of the **Archbishop's Castle of Kromeriz** in Moravia. Mozart's fame spreads across Europe, and Emperor Joseph II invites the young prodigy to perform for him in Vienna. In the film, the emperor resides in the **Gryspek Palace,** a 16th-century palais on **Hradcany Square** that currently serves as the residence and offices of the archbishop of Prague. All of the props used were priceless museum pieces, from the sovereign's golden throne to the luxuriant tapestries adorning the walls – even including the very piano that Mozart plays.

Hradcany Square is also the location of the charming little house at **Number 7** where Mozart and Constanze live after they are wed at **St. Giles's Church** (Kostel svatého Jiljí) at **Husova 8.** In contrast with Mozart's humble home, Salieri lives at the bleak but bombastic **Palace of the Maltese Knights, Perlová 1,** now the Embassy of Malta. Until 1989, the palace housed a museum for musical instruments, its historic harpsichords adding atmosphere to an already ideal stand-in for the resentful composer's abode. **Maltese Square** (Maltézské náměstí) also appears in the movie as the setting of a lively market scene. Salieri spins his web of intrigue in the **Theological Hall** of the library at **Strahov Abbey,** the very institution whose famous organ Mozart is alleged to have played during a visit in 1787.

Despite the level of access granted the director, not every historic building was instantly accessible to the film crew. Forman's greatest coup was to persuade the authorities to allow him to film in the **Tyl Theater.** The venue has remained

Mozart (Tom Hulce) conducts the premiere of *Don Giovanni* at the Tyl Theater.

virtually unchanged for more than two centuries, and famously hosted the premiere of Mozart's *Don Giovanni* on October 29, 1787. Naturally, Forman wanted the Tyl to host the opera performances so central to the movie. Constructed entirely of wood, the building erected in 1783 is among the very last of its kind: Practically all other such structures have succumbed to fire.

Considering the hazards, it is little wonder that the theater initially balked at the idea of allowing Forman access, especially after he announced that he would be using period lighting – meaning candles. Forty firemen kept watch over the building during the shoot, their eyes glued to eleven chandeliers holding a total of 6,000 candles. A special steel structure rested on the roof so that not a single nail had to be driven into the historic fabric of the building to hang the monumental chandeliers.

The verdant **gardens** before the Salla Terrena of the **Wallenstein Palace** served as the site of an open-air concert for the emperor at which Mozart conducts one of his piano concertos. The only set that had to be specially constructed for the production was Emanuel Schikaneder's wooden folk theater, rebuilt from scratch at Prague's Barrandov Studios for the scenes in which Mozart watches a parody of his *Magic Flute*. At the end of this lively tale, Salieri regrets that his sinister intrigues have contributed to the downfall a musical genius. By the time he realizes his mistake, it's too late: Mozart dies alone and impoverished, a towering genius reduced to ruin.

MISSION: IMPOSSIBLE

Director	Brian De Palma
Starring	Tom Cruise, Jon Voight, Emmanuelle Béart, Henry Czerny, Jean Reno, Ving Rhames, Kristin Scott Thomas, Vanessa Redgrave

USA, 1996

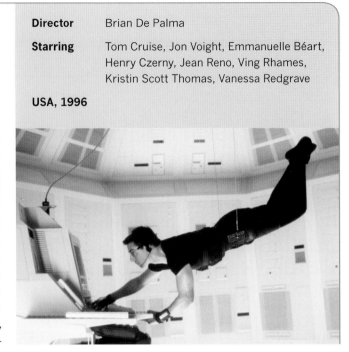

Just as the thaw in global politics had begun to melt the icy fronts of the Cold War, director Brian De Palma resolved to adapt the era's most famous spy television series to the big screen. The location he chose for the movie was Prague, one of the blossoming cities of the former Eastern Bloc, a city rapidly gaining in stature as a center of international filmmaking. When De Palma and his film crew arrived in the spring of 1995, they were among the first to bring a major foreign production to the Czech capital. This time Prague would be far more than a charming backdrop or a stand-in for a different city, as in *Amadeus* (1984). The movie's success at the box office paved the way for more action flicks to be shot in the streets of Prague, films such as the stunt-packed *xXx* (2002), starring muscle-bound marauder Vin Diesel, and *Shanghai Knights* (2003), with Jackie Chan and Owen Wilson in the lead roles.

Just like the eponymous TV series, which ran on American television between 1966 and 1973, the movie opens with a message for Jim Phelps (Jon Voight), head of a team of special agents from the "Impossible Missions Force." The video communiqué self-destructs just seconds after delivering an "impossible" assignment: A secret list revealing the names of all IMF agents operating around the world is about to be stolen and sold on the black market. Phelps and his team must prevent the transaction – with the aid, of course, of the sort of high-tech gadgetry that has been part of every special agent's repertoire since novelist and former British Naval Intelligence officer Ian Fleming created James Bond.

The agents prepare for their dangerous mission in Prague.

Incognito, Phelps and his team infiltrate the American Embassy in Prague during a fancy reception. The real-life embassy is located in a pretty townhouse just off of Petrín Park at Trziste 15, a setting that filmmakers may have found too boring for the movie. Instead they filmed in the ornate entrance hall of the **National Museum,** a lavishly-turned-out neo-Renaissance pile at **Václavské námestí 68** that dominates one end of the historic square. On the museum's grand staircase, agents Sarah Davies (Kristin Scott Thomas), dressed as an embassy staffer, and Ethan Hunt (Tom Cruise), masquerading as an American senator, mingle with the guests as the rest of the team takes

Arms dealer Max (Vanessa Redgrave) secretly resides at the opulent Art Nouveau premises of the Hotel Europa on Wenceslas Square.

up positions behind the scenes. For exterior shots, De Palma's crew once again traded in the real embassy for a statelier venue: the **Liechtenstein Palais** on **Kampa Island** in the Vltava, the river that flows through the center of Prague.

Initially all goes according to plan, but the tide turns unexpectedly with a series of fast-paced events. Phelps takes a bullet on the **Charles Bridge** and tumbles into the dark waters of the Vltava, and the perilous mission teeters on the verge of failure – just half an hour into the movie. With his team effectively wiped out, Hunt suddenly finds himself on his own and utterly unsure of whom to trust. He puts in a call to a CIA contact, Eugene Kittridge (Henry Czerny), who happens to be in Prague, a coincidence Hunt reckons is too unlikely to swallow. Hunt suspects a trap, and against his better judgment he agrees to a rendezvous. They decide to meet at the upscale eatery Akvarium, a fictitious restaurant constructed at Pinewood Studios outside London complete with a dramatic, neon-lit glass front and vast lobster tanks. Hunt escapes the ill-fated appointment after a massive explosion and sprints across the real **Václavské Náměstí Boulevard** to safety.

The CIA thinks Hunt is the mole in their midst. To clear his name, he starts investigating the conspiracy against him and makes contact with a mysterious arms dealer named Max. Max turns out to be an enterprising businesswoman (Vanessa Redgrave) who is willing to pay several million dollars for the coveted list revealing the secret agents' names. Max's stylish pied-à-terre is the **Hotel Europa** at **Václavské náměstí 25**, an Art Nouveau gem on Wenceslas Square with a magnificent sky-lit, wrought-iron staircase. Hunt's "mission: impossible" begins to fully live up to its name once he leaves Prague and heads for CIA headquarters in Langley, Virginia, where he plans to break into the main computer. The surprising grand finale on a high-speed train between London and Paris is a miniature masterpiece of stunt work and special effects, filmed not in and around the Channel Tunnel, but in Scotland outside of Dumfries.

Agent Sarah (Kristin Scott Thomas) at the reception in the embassy, filmed in the entrance hall of the National Museum (bottom right).

The agents suddenly become the hunted ones near the Liechtenstein Palais on an island in the Vltava.

In the television series, battle lines are clearly drawn: The IMF team fights criminal cartels and dictators as a closely knit unit. The movie, in contrast, deliberately blurs the distinctions between good and evil. Anyone could be the enemy, and the tension and paranoia that Hunt feels as a discredited agent have a riveting effect on the audience. "*Mission: Impossible* is an action thriller, but we wanted to make it different," Cruise said after the film's release. "One of the reasons it's so hard to make a spy movie these days is that there is no Cold War. The obvious villains have changed." Prague's fog-filled streets and historic palaces helped audiences to accept the plot's premise by providing an Eastern European location that appeared exotic to American audiences, and that could easily be cast as the stomping ground of unscrupulous spies and heartless mercenaries. The two sequels (2000 and 2006) continued the successful formula of star power, a suspenseful plot with multiple twists, and exotic locations.

ROME

Piazza del Popolo, with its twin churches, is popular for its chic cafés that double as front-row seats for watching the comings and goings on the square.

ALL ROADS LEAD TO CINECITTÀ

In Rome's love affair with film, all roads to lead to Cinecittà. Divas Sophia Loren and Gina Lollobrigida, directors Vittorio De Sica, Bernardo Bertolucci, Roberto Rossellini, Luchino Visconti, and of course Federico Fellini with long-time actor-friend Marcello Mastroianni – all the stars flocked to the sprawling studios on the outskirts of Rome to build Italy's celluloid empire. A myth-making laboratory from its beginnings in the 1930s, Cinecittà had a knack for making legends out of the men and women who worked there, and a reputation for producing outstanding dramas and comedies. It also gave Rome a new role in international pop culture: Fans came to see the Roman Forum and the Sistine Chapel, but also to have their photos taken before famous locations from the silver screen.

Rome may not have been built in twenty-four hours, but Cinecittà took only 475 days to complete. Between January 1936 and April 1937 Carlo Roncoroni constructed the complex on Via Tuscolana southeast of the city. This was Mussolini's brainchild: The "City of Cinema" would be fascism's answer to Hollywood. At almost 150 acres (sixty hectares) it was vaster than the Vatican. With parades and confetti, Il Duce himself threw open the doors on April 28, 1937, "so that Italy could spread the glory of Roman culture more quickly to the rest of the world." The dictator was on set to watch his sons Vittorio and Bruno produce dramas such as *Scipio Africanus* (1937) as well as operas, thrillers, romances, and a handful of propaganda flicks. Luckily, Vittorio Mussolini proved to be more than a puppet of his father's regime. He called together the era's great cinéastes, making Fellini and Rossellini part of a milieu that would guarantee Italian filmmaking a brilliant future.

In the 1950s Cinecittà came into its own as "Hollywood on the Tiber," and, thanks to a few key films, Rome became a popular movie location. Foreign directors were lured by dramatic skylines and exotic backdrops, as well as cheap labor and a good exchange rate. American Mervyn Le Roy was first with *Quo Vadis?* (1950), a love story of ancient Rome. The movie revived Italy's earliest film tradition, the historical epic, a genre established with Filoteo Alberini's *The Capture of Rome* (1905) and Arturo Ambrosio's *The Last Days of Pompeii* (1908), and perfected in William Wyler's 1959 remake of *Ben-Hur*. For Rome's reputation in Hollywood circles, *Quo Vadis?* was a milestone: Stars took accounts of luxurious hotels, fashionable lunches, and late-night parties in the Via Veneto district back with them to the glittering hills of southern California.

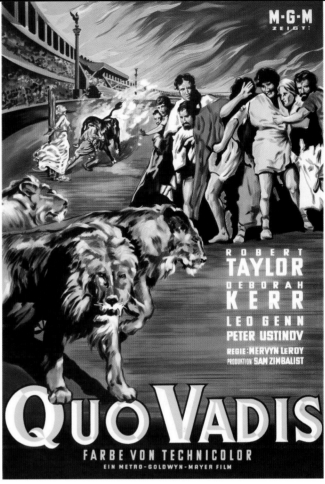

M·G·M ZEIGT:

ROBERT **TAYLOR**
DEBORAH **KERR**
LEO GENN
PETER USTINOV
REGIE: **MERVYN LEROY**
PRODUKTION: **SAM ZIMBALIST**

QUO VADIS
FARBE VON TECHNICOLOR
EIN METRO-GOLDWYN-MAYER FILM

Ancient Rome was the inspiration for countless costume films such as the fifties classics *Quo Vadis?* and *Ben-Hur*.

Below: **Another black-and-white classic in Rome: the Fiat Cinquecento.**

135

Wyler's cast and crew were eager to see the Eternal City and live the good life while filming *Roman Holiday* (1953). Audrey Hepburn's American movie debut as a hooky-playing princess earned her an Oscar and the adoration of a generation, and her whirlwind romance on a Vespa still has tourists searching for Gregory Peck's flat on artsy Via Margutta.

Federico Fellini put Via Veneto's high society in the spotlight in *La Dolce Vita* (1960), and with Walter Santesso as Paparazzo, he gave the world a new moniker for pesky tabloid photographers. Blond bombshell Anita Ekberg's unforgettable scene in the Trevi Fountain is as iconic in Europe as Marilyn Monroe's floating skirt in *The Seven Year Itch* (1955). By no means on a par with these films, but pleasantly kitschy, is *Three Coins in the Fountain* (1954), the story of three American secretaries who toss coins into the Trevi Fountain in the hopes of meeting the men of their dreams. The golden era of the big Italian directors brought Rome a lot of big-screen exposure, even if the major movies such as Vittorio De Sica's *Stazione Termini* (1953), Pier

Paolo Pasolini's *Accattone* (1961), and Fellini's *Roma* (1972) failed to reach broad international audiences. Luckily, these classics can be enjoyed on videocassette or DVD.

The Talented Mr. Ripley (1999) saw director Anthony Minghella looking back in time for cliché images of post-war Italy, while Ridley Scott's blockbuster *Gladiator* (2000) took history into the future, reinventing the genre of the historic epic with a high-tech twist that seemed to revive ancient Rome. Meanwhile, Cinecittà is busily attracting filmmakers from home and abroad to its famed studios. Martin Scorsese and his production designer Dante Ferretti chose the studio complex in Rome to recreate the alleys and houses of Manhattan in the 1860s for the epic *Gangs of New York* (2002).

Left: **The mightiest dome in ancient Rome has fascinated visitors ever since the Roman Emperor Hadrian (117-138) rebuilt the Pantheon in the second century A.D.** Above: **Tiny workshops such as this busily restore the décor in churches and private apartments in Rome.**

ROME

N

0 — 250 m

Tevere

Villa

Borghese

Museo e Galleria Borghese

Ponte del Risorgimento

Sta. Maria del Popolo

① Piazza del Popolo

Sta. Maria in Montesanto

Sta. Maria dei Miracoli

Corso d'Italia

⑦

Piazza dei Quiriti

Piazza della Libertà

Ponte Reg. Margherita

Via Cola di Rienzo

Via G. Belli

L. in Augusta

Via di Ripetta

Via del Corso

Monte Pincio

Viale della Trinità dei Monti

③

Villa Medici

⑯

Via Vitt. Veneto

Via Boncompagni   Via Calabria

⑲

Gesù e Maria

Via della Croce

Piazza di Spagna

SS. Trinità dei Monti

Spanish Steps

Sta. Maria della Vittoria

Via L. Bissolati

Via XX Settembre

Via Crescenzio

Piazza Cavour

Ponte Cavour

Augustus Mausoleum

⑤

V. Tomacelli

Via Condotti

Via due Macelli

Via Sistina

Palazzo Barberini

②

Terme di Diocleziano

Via Cernaia

㉔

Castel S. Angelo

⑭

L. Prati

L. Marzio

Palazzo Borghese

Via del Corso

Galleria Colonna

Via del Tritone

Fontana di Trevi

Palazzo del Quirinale

S. Carlo alle Quattro Fontane

S. Bernardo

Piazza della Repubblica

Opera

Piazza Barberini

Ponte S. Angelo

Ponte Vitt. Em. II

L. Castello

L. Tor di Nona

Museo Napoleonico

S. Agostino

Via dei Coronari

Sta. Maria de la Pace

㉕

Sta. Maria dell'Anima

㉒

Palazzo Madama

S. Ignazio

Pantheon

⑥

Piazza Colonna

SS. Apostoli

S. Andrea al Quirinale

Via del Quirinale

Via Nazionale

Sta. Pudenziana

Piazza dell'Esquilino

Via A. De Pretis

Via del Viminale

S. Agnese

Piazza Navona

Sta. Maria sopra Minerva

Galleria Doria Pamphili

Palazzo Colonna

⑮

Chiesa Nuova

Museo di Roma

S. Girolamo della Carità

Campo de' Fiori

S. Andrea della

Il Gesù

⑧

⑨

Piazza Venezia

⑩

Fori Imperiali

Via Cavour

Via del Corso

L. del Sangallo

Via Giulia

Via Arenula

Monumento a Vitt. Emanuele II

⑪

Sta. Maria in Aracoeli

Via Cavour

S. Pietro in Vincoli

Villa Farnesina

Piazza Farnese

Palazzo Farnese

㉖

S. Carlo ai Catinari

Teatro di Marcello

Via del Teatro di Marcello

Campidoglio

⑫

Forum Romanum

Via Labicana

S. Clemente

Palazzo Corsini Galleria Nazionale d'Arte Antica

L. dei Vallati

GHETTO

L. de' Cenci

Isola Tiberina

Colosseum

⑦

Arco di Constantino

Monte Esquilino

L. della Farnesina

Palazzo Spada

Ponte Garibaldi

L. d. Anguillara

Arco de Jano

④

Monte Palatino

SS. Giovanni e Paolo

SS. Quattro Coronati

Via Claudia

Via G. Garibaldi

⓪

Sta. Maria in Trastevere

Piazza di Sta. Maria in Trastevere

S. Crisogono

Sta. Maria in Cosmedin

Piazza Bocca della Verità

⑬

Tiber

Circus Maximus (Circo Massimo)

Via del Circo Massimo

Via di San Gregorio

S. Gregorio Magno

Villa Celimontana

Monte Celio

S. Stefano Rotondo

S. Pietro in Montorio

Sta. Cecilia in Trastevere

Viale Trastevere

Sta. Sabina

Monte Aventino

Sta. Prisca

Viale Aventino

Viale delle Terme di Caracalla

TRASTEVERE

Viale Glorioso

Ponte Sublicio

Via Portuense

Tevere

Piazza Cavalieri di Malta

Via A. Galvani

Pyramid of Cestius

Piazza di Porta S. Paolo

Viale d. Campo Boario

㉓

Terme di Caracalla

Viale G. Baccelli

⑳

Roman Holiday

1. Pincio Hill
2. Palazzo Barberini, Via Barberini 18
3. Joe Bradley's apartment, Via Margutta 51
4. Arch of Septimius Severus on the Roman Forum
5. Spanish Steps
6. Via della Stampiera 85, across from the Trevi Fountain
7. Colosseum
8. Church of Il Gesù
9. Piazza Venezia
10. Trajan's Forum
11. Monument to Vittorio Emanuele
12. Campidoglio
13. Church of Santa Maria in Cosmedin with the Bocca della Verità
14. Castel Sant'Angelo
15. Palazzo Colonna, Piazza SS. Apostoli 66

La Dolce Vita

16. Via Veneto between Via Boncompagni and Porta Pinciana
17. Odescalshi Palace of Bassano di Sutri, 37 miles (60 kilometers) northwest of Rome
18. Trevi Fountain (see point 6)
19. Excelsior Hotel, Via Veneto 125
20. Studio 5, Cinecittà, Via Tuscolana 1055
21. Fregene, 24 miles (40 kilometers) west of Rome

The Talented Mr. Ripley

22. Piazza Navona, Fountain of the Four Rivers
23. Caffè Latino, Via di Monte Testaccio 96
24. St. Regis Grand Hotel, Via Vittorio Emanuele Orlando 3
25. Palazzo Taverna, Via Monte Giordano 36
26. Turtle Fountain, Piazza Mattei
27. Spanish Steps (see point 5)

ROMAN HOLIDAY

Director	William Wyler
Starring	Audrey Hepburn, Gregory Peck, Eddie Albert, Hartley Power, Paolo Carlini
USA, 1953	

G od kissed the face of Audrey Hepburn, and there she was." When Billy Wilder cast the doe-eyed ingénue as *Sabrina* (1954), she had just won fans the world over with her American movie debut in William Wyler's *Roman Holiday*. The modern-day tale of a princess coming of age made the newly discovered twenty-three-year-old a star. It also raised the profile of the Italian capital, bringing sorely needed tourist and film industry dollars to a metropolis toiling to recover from the economic ravages of World War II. Hepburn's Oscar-winning performance gave the Forum, the Spanish Steps, and the city's charming cafés and piazzas a fresh presence in popular culture. The effect was by no means accidental: Opening credits bill the love story as "filmed on location in Rome," and the film delivers an entertaining tour of the Eternal City.

Crowds of bystanders followed the crews and actors around the atmospheric streets and piazzas of the Centro Storico for six months starting in May 1952, all eager for a glimpse of Hollywood at work. Few scenes were recorded at Cinecittà studios on the edge of town as the old neighborhoods with terrace views of the skyline, quaint markets, and quirky characters lent the story a backdrop brimming with romantic élan. The artists' quarter at **Pincio Hill** known from Grand Tour times as the "English ghetto" is the center of a Cinderella story in reverse: Young

A Vespa tour through the streets of Rome: Ann and Joe zip past the Colosseum.

Princess Ann, abroad on a global goodwill tour, buckles under the weight of her duties. Balls, receptions, speeches, parades – the pressure of public life drives the budding royal to tears and inspires a spontaneous decision to run away. She flees her posh accommodations, represented by the grand exteriors of the **Palazzo Barberini** at **Via Barberini 18,** now the National Gallery of Ancient Art. Incognito as Anya Smith, she meets Gregory Peck,

The Church of Santa Maria in Cosmedin and the Bocca della Verità or "mouth of truth" play a memorable role in the unforgettable love story between a reporter and a princess that would catapult Audrey Hepburn to international stardom.

a.k.a. reporter Joe Bradley, at the **Forum,** and he grudgingly gives her a place to sleep in his flat at **Via Margutta 51.** The next day he recognizes her face in the papers and, ever the conniving newsman, promises his editor an exclusive interview complete with celebrity photographs.

Despite his paparazzo ambitions, Bradley falls head over heels in love. From their first encounter by the **Arch of Septimius Severus** on the **Roman Forum,** to her daring haircut at **Via della Stampiera 85** by the **Trevi Fountain** and ice cream on the **Spanish Steps,** Hepburn's elfin charms are as irresistible and ubiquitous as the great landmarks of Rome. A visit to the **Colosseum** kicks off a whirlwind tour of the city on Italy's most typical mode of transport, the motor scooter. With press photographer Irving Radovich (Eddie Albert) in tow, the two speed their Vespa past the **Church of Il Gesù, Piazza Venezia, Trajan's Forum,** the **monument to Vittorio Emanuele,** and Michelangelo's **Campidoglio,** formerly Rome's town hall.

After reckless driving garners them a brush with the law, the scene shifts to the **Church of Santa Maria in Cosmedin** and the **Bocca della Verità,** or "mouth of truth." The scene in which Joe pretends to lose his hand after inserting it in the ancient drain cover decorated with the face of a river god was not originally in the script. Audrey's charming reaction, what Peck called "a magical combination of high chic and high spirits," persuaded Wyler to edit it in to the film. After a night of dancing and fistfights on a river barge by **Castel Sant'Angelo,** Anya and Joe fall hopelessly in love. Whether they flaunt royal convention and stay together remains a mystery until the press conference in the ornate Great Hall of **Palazzo Colonna** at **Piazza SS. Apostoli 66,** home to one of the city's outstanding collections of art, whose main entrance is on the Via della Pilotta.

Hepburn was stunned by the film's overwhelming success. "Heaven help me live up to all this," she wrote of her overnight rise to stardom and the media frenzy surrounding her. The slender actress known for her grace and captivating sense of humor would have no trouble on that count: her next four major feature films, *Sabrina* (1954), *Funny Face* (1957), *Love in the Afternoon* (1957), and *The Nun's Story* (1959) were box-office gold. Hepburn would make some thirty movies in her lifetime as well as becoming a major figure in global charity campaigns, working as a special ambassador for the United Nations' UNICEF children's fund. The center of an ancient empire and burial place of emperors and poets always kept a place in its heart for the little ballerina from Brussels who would define an age and immortalize Givenchy's inspired "Audrey" style as Holly Golightly in *Breakfast at Tiffany's* (1961). On the day she died in 1993, admirers placed bouquets of flowers on the banks of the Tiber by Castel Sant'Angelo. It was the very spot where a princess had danced with the man she loved in a film that lent Rome a new claim to fame.

A verdant side street close to the Spanish Steps and shoppy Via Condotti: Via Margutta and the famous apartment Number 51 lent a homey backdrop for the royal runaway (Audrey Hepburn) and reporter Joe Bradley (Gregory Peck) to get better acquainted.

LA DOLCE VITA

Director	Federico Fellini
Starring	Marcello Mastroianni, Anita Ekberg, Anouk Aimée, Yvonne Furneaux, Magali Noël, Alain Cuny, Annibale Ninchi, Walter Santesso
Italy, 1960	

Life imitating art imitating life – where else does the age-old maxim get a better run for its money than in Federico Fellini's *La Dolce Vita*, a three-hour epic that holds a mirror to the sweet life of the rich and famous in postwar Rome? Marcello Mastroianni is gossip columnist Marcello Rubini, a man whose aspirations to become a "real writer" are lost in the glittering cafés and discos of **Via Veneto.** He and Paparazzo (Walter Santesso), namesake of the modern celebrity photographer, chase movie stars, industrial big shots, and local nobility up and down the celebrity catwalk between **Via Boncompagni** and **Porta Pinciana** for the tabloid press. Documentary-style scenes of bourgeois excess at parties and orgies shocked the nation but fascinated the world, earning Fellini the wrath of the Church and the moneyed classes at home, but acclaim from critics and audiences abroad and the coveted Golden Palm at the Cannes film festival.

Via Veneto needed no introduction in 1960. The grand, sloping boulevard built in the 19th century had become a mini Champs-Elysées by the 1950s, bustling with exclusive boutiques, luxury hotels, and flashy sidewalk hangouts like Rosati's, Café de Paris, and Doney's. For Fellini it was the nexus of a hedonistic universe: It is here that Marcello picks up Maddalena (Anouk Aimée), a wealthy housewife, courts Sylvia (Anita Ekberg), a Hollywood starlet, treats his father (Annibale Ninchi) to fun with a French dancing girl, and joins the bored nobility

How could the renowned Fontana di Trevi become even more famous? Sexy Swedish bombshell Anita Ekberg made it possible when she waded into the colossal fountain as the uninhibited starlet Sylvia, transforming the stone-cold monument into a romantic location.

Via Veneto had it all at the beginning of the sixties, and that was more than enough for gossip columnist Marcello Rubini (Marcello Mastroianni) and the original Paparazzo (Walter Santesso). Among its attractions: film stars, exclusive hotels like the Excelsior (right) – pied-à-terre to movie star Sylvia – bored and beautiful housewives like Maddalena (Anouk Aimée, driving, far right), and nonstop nightlife.

heading off to the **Odescalshi Palace** of **Bassano di Sutri,** 37 miles (60 kilometers) to the northwest, for an all-night blow-out party. Fellini's random episodes of hedonism contrast with carefully selected Catholic references to show the lawless Babylon Rome had become: helicopters flying a statue of Jesus to the Vatican, a fake miracle, and the death of Marcello's intellectual and spiritual beacon, Steiner (Alain Cuny). *"La Dolce Vita* takes the temperature of an ailing society," said Fellini, "a society that has every appearance of running a fever."

Filming began on location in Rome in the spring of 1959. The city granted permission to shoot on Via Veneto between 2 a.m. and 6 a.m., and, bureaucratic complications aside, things went off without a hitch. Former Miss Universe contestant Anita Ekberg waded into the baroque **Trevi Fountain** in an evening dress and, due to chilly March temperatures, rubber hip boots, creating one of cinema's immortal scenes, later recreated at Cinecittà studios. After the frolic in the fountain, Anita's beau decks rival Marcello outside the **Excelsior Hotel,** whose proud cupolas are still a landmark at **Via Veneto 125.** Despite the awkward hour, onlookers mobbed the scene to watch Maddalena drive Marcello down Via Veneto, hindering the motorcade of actors and camera crew and infuriating Fellini. He insisted that the rest of the city shots take place at **Cinecittà** at **Via Tuscolana 1055,** southeast of the city center. Production costs soared as designer Piero Gherardi rebuilt the famous boulevard in **Studio 5,** a replica so exact that the only thing missing was the upward slope of the street.

Marcello and Sylvia face the omnipresent celebrity press after a night on the town.

As with much of Fellini's work, *La Dolce Vita* is autobiographical. Originally a small-town boy from the Adriatic resort town of Rimini, Fellini himself had roamed Via Veneto scraping together a living as a caricaturist and reporter. Shots at the end of the film in the seaside settlement of **Fregene,** 24 miles (40 kilometers) west of Rome, may have been reminiscent of his childhood home. By the time he befriended celebrity photographer Tazio Secchiaroli, he was a well-known director in his mid-thirties, riding high on Oscar-winning successes such as *La Strada* (1954) and *Cabiria* (1957), and looking for the next big thing. Legend has it that Secchiaroli found it for him one hot summer night in 1958. That evening the photographer snapped the deposed King of Egypt flipping over his table at an outdoor café, Ava Gardner dancing flamenco at a bar, and blond bombshell Anita Ekberg slapping her drunken husband at a nightclub. The scuffles that ensued brought Secchiaroli lucrative material and Fellini the brilliant idea to capture postwar Rome as sin city for the big screen. Little did the photographer know that the world would remember him not as Sophia Loren's favorite portraitist, but as the model for the original paparazzo, a dubious honor at best. Fellini would fare significantly better, living up to his famous credo that "you exist only in what you do." His subsequent films, such as *8½* (1963), *Satyricon* (1969), and *Amarcord* (1973), are recognized still as classics of Italian cinema. His work was a direct reflection of his dynamic view of the world: "There is no end. There is no beginning. There is only the infinite passion of life."

THE TALENTED MR. RIPLEY

Director   Anthony Minghella

Starring   Matt Damon, Jude Law, Gwyneth Paltrow,
Cate Blanchett, Philip Seymour Hoffman

USA, 1999

Anthony Minghella's masterful adaptation of Patricia Highsmith's 1955 novel is an ode to Italy's most stunning locations. French heartthrob Alain Delon starred in *Plein Soleil* in 1960, giving the first filming of the Ripley affair its undeniable sex appeal. Minghella trawled 20th-century visual history for fresh sources of inspiration to enliven his take on the first of five pulp thrillers devoted to con man Tom Ripley.

The director of *The English Patient* (1996) scanned photographs by Henri Cartier-Bresson as well as Fellini flicks *I Vitelloni* (1953) and *La Dolce Vita* (1960) for cliché images of beautiful young Italians living a leisured life. He found the perfect backdrop to his vision in the Eternal City. As the film's locations go, the isles of Ischia and Procida by Naples offer the most picturesque locations, and Venice the most dramatic – with St. Mark's Square and the view of the plague church, Santa Maria della Salute, from the balcony of the Europa e Regina Hotel – but it is Rome, with its wild youth, romantic nights, and crumbling monuments set to the jazz of Charlie "Bird" Parker, that best captures the spirit of the film.

Matt Damon is Tom Ripley, a toilet attendant who by chance meets a shipping magnate in New York City of the late 1950s. The millionaire mistakes him for a school pal of prodigal son Dickie Greenleaf (Jude Law), and begs him to travel abroad to bring the heir to the family fortune home. Tom goes along with

Tom Ripley envies Dickie and Marge's leisured lifestyle.

The strange friendship between Tom Ripley (Matt Damon) and shipping heir Dickie Greenleaf (Jude Law) turns into a nightmare after a fateful trip to Rome.

Tom and Dickie's girl Marge (Gwyneth Paltrow) speed by Rome's Turtle Fountain in the old Jewish quarter.

the plan until he gets a taste of the good life in Italy. Mixing martinis, sailing the Bay of Naples, and jamming in jazz clubs with the stunningly handsome playboy prove to be too much fun. Once he's moved in with Dickie in fictional Mongibello, filmed on the pretty islands of Ischia and Procida, his only concern is how to stay. "I've come to like everything about the way you live," gushes Tom to Dickie. "It's one big love affair." Even though Dickie's winsome gal Marge (Gwyneth Paltrow) agrees, she objects to Tom's "crush" on her fiancé and wonders if he'll ever bug off back to the Big Apple.

The pals' excursion to Rome becomes a metaphor for great expectations gone awry. Dickie's old friend Freddie (Philip Seymour Hoffman, the star of the 2005 hit *Capote*) races up **Piazza Navona** in a red sports coupe to **Bernini's Fountain of the Four Rivers** at the heart of the Centro Storico. The obnoxious redhead, who has the wherewithal to live the sweet life and the instinct to identify an outsider, quickly becomes Tom's rival for Dickie's attention. Freddie easily prevails, turning on his charismatic charm to edge out the pasty pretender. Bitter over a failed friendship and, in Tom's mind, a botched love affair, Ripley leaves Rome. But memories still haunt him, like the night he crooned "Tu Vuo' Fa l'Americano" and "My Funny Valentine" with Dickie at the Neapolitan nightclub Vesuvio, a masterful scene actually filmed in Rome at **Caffè Latino, Via di Monte Testaccio 96.** Despite Dickie's promise to make it up to him with a trip to San Remo, Tom succumbs to a jealous rage once they reach the casino town not far from the French border.

Alone, Tom returns to Rome several weeks later and adopts Dickie's persona. He sets up in style at the Grand Hotel, today the refurbished **St. Regis Grand** at **Via Vittorio Emanuele Orlando 3.** Convinced he can live life as the Greenleaf heir, he takes

Left: **Meredith (Cate Blanchett) and Tom chat about life abroad on the graceful Spanish Steps. Little does the well-to-do American woman suspect that her new acquaintance is a conniving con man.**

an apartment in town. But Freddie's not so easily fooled and quizzes the landlady about Dickie's whereabouts on the stairs outside his flat – a grand space that, like the interior of the hotel suite, actually belongs to the **Palazzo Taverna,** a private residence and home of the ancient Borgia and Orsini families at **Via Monte Giordano 36,** not far from Castel Sant'Angelo. Girlfriend Marge, also beside herself with worry, joins Tom for a wild-goose chase past his ornate apartment. The exterior used is not on Piazza Gioia, the made-up square mentioned in the film's dialogue, but on **Piazza Mattei** in the old Jewish quarter instead, a square marked with the **Turtle Fountain** that Tom and Marge pass on a motor scooter.

No one can locate the Greenleaf heir, and the movie's final sequence is a brilliant exercise in sustaining suspense – as well as the film's crowning achievement in terms of location. Minghella and crew managed, against all odds, to return Rome's bustling **Piazza di Spagna** to the quieter, less touristed days of the 1950s. With only twenty-four hours to set up the shoot, the plaza before the **Spanish Steps** was transformed with new storefronts and an American Express office, which in reality is located just over 100 yards (100 meters) away. Awnings were added at the corner of fashionable **Via dei Condotti** to create the fictitious Caffè Dinelli, capriciously named for an eatery on England's Isle of Wight owned by the director's aunt. Tom had arranged for Marge to meet Dickie here, but sends his duped "girlfriend" Meredith (Cate Blanchett) instead. Mischievous Ripley watches the drama unfold from the Spanish Steps, peering over the balustrade and the **Barcaccia Fountain** as the pressure mounts. The last scenes were acted as crowds of onlookers poured onto the square from numerous points of entry and a busy underground station. The area roped off for cameras and actors diminished with each successive wave of passersby. Minghella credits First Assistant Director Steve Andrews and the hard-working Italian crew for the scenes' remarkable success.

SAN FRANCISCO

ALLURE AND INTRIGUE BY THE BAY

Just mention this West Coast metropolis, and instantly you've conjured images of the Golden Gate Bridge, cable cars, Alcatraz, and stately Victorian row houses. It's not only the Bay City's popularity as one of America's great tourist attractions that has inspired such universal familiarity, but also the role that San Francisco has played in film. Movies such as *The Maltese Falcon* (1941), *Vertigo* (1958), *Bullitt* (1968), and *Dirty Harry* (1971) have helped to forge a strong cinematic impression of the "City by the Bay" in popular culture.

In the grand scheme of things, San Francisco is a relatively young city. Missionaries dedicated the original city center to Saint Francis of Assisi in 1776, and in 1782 built Mission Dolores church in his honor – a mere 100 years before motion picture technology was invented. The settlement initially known as Yerba Buena would grow parallel to the film industry: In 1906, shortly after the great earthquake that destroyed the city, footage of the wreckage could be seen throughout the country in movie theaters known as nickelodeons. *The Jazz Singer* (1927), the very first feature-length film with spoken dialogue, was partly filmed in a San Francisco jazz club. The enormous success of such "talkies" would end the era of silent film.

Perhaps the most visible tribute to San Francisco's love affair with film is the Castro Theatre, a movie palace built in 1922 in a flamboyant neo-Spanish Baroque style and featuring a mighty Wurlitzer organ. Although multiplex cinemas have long since marginalized such small movie houses, this living landmark still pays tribute to the glory days of ornate film palaces. Around the time it was built, Austrian-born director Erich von Stroheim filmed his cinematic feat *Greed* (1924) entirely on location in San Francisco. For the first time ever, a "real" interior – in a Victorian house at the corner of Hayes and Laguna Streets – was used for filming instead of one created on a set. Even today the city remains at the forefront of modern film technology. George Lucas's production and special effects company has opened a vast studio in historic Presidio Park, close to the Golden Gate Bridge. Animated films such as *Shrek* (2001) and *Finding Nemo* (2003) made in the Bay Area studios of Pixar and PDI/Dream-Works are unequaled in technological sophistication.

Next to New York, the hilly "city by the bay" is generally considered America's most European metropolis.

The city's fascinating history has also delivered a plethora of material for films, touching on the first Spanish missionaries of the late 1700s, the gold rush of 1849, the 1906 quake, the flower-power era of the late sixties, and the dot-com boom of the nineties. Almost all the historical eras of the city may be encountered in film, from the lawless bordellos and rowdy gambling houses of director Howard Hawks's *Barbary Coast* (1935) to the tale of a computer animator in *Dopamine* (2003). The city's famously steep hills have inspired directors to choreograph daredevil chase scenes, such as those in the breakneck police thriller *Bullitt* (1968), a flick that, for many fans, remains the quintessential San Francisco film.

For all its popularity in film, San Francisco presents directors with a few challenges, as well: parking is tight, and the tortuously steep streets become a logistical nightmare when trailers and equipment have to be rolled in and placed so they are convenient to the filming but at the same time out of camera range. And despite its renown, S.F. is small as major cities go. Three-quarters of a million people live on a densely populated peninsula – no wonder filmmakers get flack from residents when they arrive. Neighborhoods such as North Beach and Russian Hill – favorites with directors – do not always welcome cast and crew with open arms when their streets are blocked off for days, or even weeks, during filming.

Architectural landmarks such as the Golden Gate Bridge and the Transamerica Pyramid make it easy for filmmakers to use San Francisco as a location, or merely a backdrop – with the help of a few well-chosen beauty shots. Television series will often use scenes of the famous bridge or cable cars to locate a show in the Bay City, filming the rest more cheaply in Canada. Even classic films such as *The Maltese Falcon,* starring Humphrey Bogart as detective Sam Spade – a flick that in the minds of Americans and Europeans alike is synonymous with San Francisco – was, with the exception of a few shots in the very beginning, filmed almost entirely in the studio.

San Francisco's instant recognizability and geographic location make it a top candidate for catastrophe films. The 1906 quake that razed the city was accompanied by unprecedented media interest and helped establish the metropolis as the foremost urban stage for disaster. *Old San Francisco* (1927) showcased the seamy underworld of the Barbary Coast, culminating with the fall of the city to a great earthquake. A giant radioactive octopus makes short work of San Francisco in special-effects

Above: **Humphrey Bogart as detective Sam Spade in the 1941 film noir classic** *The Maltese Falcon.* Right: **Alcatraz and the Transamerica skyscraper.**

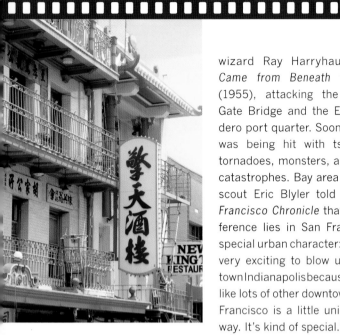

wizard Ray Harryhausen's *It Came from Beneath the Sea* (1955), attacking the Golden Gate Bridge and the Embarcadero port quarter. Soon the city was being hit with tsunamis, tornadoes, monsters, and other catastrophes. Bay area location scout Eric Blyler told the *San Francisco Chronicle* that the difference lies in San Francisco's special urban character: "It's not very exciting to blow up downtown Indianapolis because it looks like lots of other downtowns. San Francisco is a little unique that way. It's kind of special."

While certain facets of the city pop up in films time and again, others are largely ignored, or get their fifteen minutes of fame in independent films. The fog that cloaks the city in summer and allegedly inspired Mark Twain to the say that "the coldest winter I ever spent was a summer in San Francisco" rarely makes an appearance in films. An exception may be *House of Sand and Fog* (2003) starring Ben Kingsley and Jennifer Connelly. San Francisco's renowned ethnic variety is also strangely missing, its large Asian population and the Latino center in the Mission District somehow invisible. Indie films such as *Cherish* (2002), *Haiku Tunnel* (2001), and *Dopamine* are exceptions, showing sides of the city less well known to non-residents but thoroughly familiar and even clichéd to those who live there. Hollywood's version of San Francisco is a perennially sunny city, where unsuspecting Caucasians ride around on cable cars whenever the famous trolleys are not being hunted down by hulking monsters or carried out to sea by a tidal wave.

"Frisco" is a city of distinctive neighborhoods, from Chinatown (above) **with its dim-sum eateries to the colorful Castro district with its historic movie theaters and gay flair.**

Vertigo

1. Ernie's Restaurant, 847 Montgomery Street (closed)
2. Brocklebank Apartments, 1000 Mason Street, Nob Hill
3. Mission Dolores Cemetery, 324 Dolores Street at the corner of 16th Street
4. Palace of the Legion of Honor, Lincoln Park
5. Presidio Park, Fort Point at the foot of the Golden Gate Bridge
6. 17-Mile Drive near Monterey, 112 miles (180 km) south of San Francisco
7. Mission San Juan Bautista, 90 miles (145 km) south of San Francisco
8. York Hotel, 940 Sutter Street, rooms 501 and 502

Bullitt

9. Bullitt's apartment, 1153 Taylor Street
10. Chalmers's villa, 2700 Vallejo Street at the corner of Divisadero in Pacific Heights
11. San Francisco General Hospital, 1001 Potrero Avenue
12. Bimbo's 365 music club, 1025 Columbus Avenue
13. Taylor Street between Vallejo and Filbert
14. Marina Boulevard
15. McLaren Park
16. Gas station on Guadalupe Canyon Parkway in Daly City
17. San Francisco International Airport

Dirty Harry

18. Bank of America, 555 California Street
19. Chinatown Hilton, 750 Kearny Street
20. Saints Peter and Paul Cathedral, Washington Square
21. Forest Hill subway station
22. Mission Dolores Park
23. Aquatic Park near Fisherman's Wharf
24. Mount Davidson
25. Kezar Stadium in Golden Gate Park (demolished)
26. Roaring 20s strip club, 552 Broadway
27. Sir Francis Drake Boulevard, Marin County
28. Larkspur Landing Shopping Center, Marin County

The Rock

29. Alcatraz
30. Fairmont Hotel, 950 Mason Street at the corner of California Street
31. New Russian Hill Market, 1198 Pacific Avenue
32. Candlestick Park, stadium of the San Francisco 49ers

Mrs. Doubtfire

33. The Hillards' house, 2640 Steiner Street at the corner of Broadway in Pacific Heights
34. Daniel's apartment, 520-522A Green Street at the corner of Bannam Street, North Beach
35. Bridges Restaurant, 44 Church Street, Danville, 30 miles (50 km) east of San Francisco
36. Crissy Field

SAN FRANCISCO

27 28

Golden Gate Bridge

↑ Alcatraz

29

Fort Point

5

Golden Gate
National
Recreation Area

101

Golden Gate Promenade 36

PRESIDIO

Lincoln Boulevard

Mason St.

Palace of Fine Arts
Exploratorium

Richardson Ave.

Marina Boulevard

Beach St.

Golden Gate National
Recreation Area

14

MARINA

Lombard St.

Greenwich St.

Union St.

10 Vallejo St. 33
Broadway

PACIFIC
HEIGHTS

Jackson St.

Washington St.

Alta
Plaza

Sacramento St.

California St.

West Pacific Avenue

Jackson St.

Sacramento St.

Lake St.

Pine St.

California St.

RICHMOND

Clement St.

Geary Boulevard

Anza St.

Cabrillo St.

Balboa St.

Fulton St.

Asian Art
Museum

M. H. De Young
Memorial

Golden Gate Park

California
Academy of
Sciences

Stadium

25

HAIGHT-ASHBURY

Lincoln Way

Irving St.

Kirkham St.

BUENA VISTA

Quintara St.

FOREST HILL

Taraval St.

6 7

24 ↓

National Maritime Museum

Fort Mason Center

Bay St.

Francisco St.

Chestnut St.

Laguna St.

Webster St.

Green St.

Steiner St.

Broderick St.

Divisadero St.

Scott St.

Pine St.

Sutter St.

Post St.

Geary Boulevard

O'Farrell St.

Turk St.

Baker St.

Masonic Avenue

Fulton St.

Panhandle

Fell St.

Oak St.

Scott St.

Haight St.

Buena
Vista
Park

Frederick St.

17th St.

18th St.

Douglas St.

Twin
Peaks

Portola Drive

21

Aquatic
Park

23

The Cannery

Ghirardelli
Square

NORTH
BEACH

Greenwich St.

Filbert St.

Franklin St.

Gough St.

Van Ness Avenue

Polk St.

Larkin St.

Hyde St.

Leavenworth St.

Jones St.

Taylor St.

Mason St.

Powell St.

Stockton St.

Grant Ave.

Kearny St.

Columbus Ave.

Fisherman's
Wharf

Jefferson St.

North Point St.

12

13

31

NOB HILL

9 2
30

8

Clay St.

Pine St.

Bush St.

Sutter St.

Geary St.

O'Farrell St.

Ellis St.

Post St.

Lafayette
Park

Haas-
Lilienthal
House

Japan Center

WESTERN ADDITION

Ellis St.

Webster St.

Alamo
Square

HAYES
VALLEY

Laguna St.

Gough St.

Market St.

101

City Hall

Opera House

Main Public Library

Civic
Center

Civic Auditorium

MISSION

Mission
Dolores

3

22

16th St.

17th St.

Church St.

Dolores St.

Mission St.

South Van Ness Avenue

Valencia St.

18th St.

25th St.

27th St.

28th St.

Castro St.

Telegraph Hill

Pier 39

North Point St.

Lombard St.

Battery St.

Montgomery St.

Embarcadero St.

20

34
26

CHINA-
TOWN

1

Tin How
Temple

19

Chinese
Historical
Society

18

Wells Fargo
History Museum

Union
Square

Sheraton Palace Hotel

San Francisco
Center

FINANCIAL
DISTRICT

TENDERLOIN

SOMA

Ansel Adams
Center

Market St.

Howard St.

Folsom St.

Bryant St.

9th St.

7th St.

5th St.

4th St.

3rd St.

2nd St.

China Basin

Embarcadero
Center

Ferry Bldg.

Justin
Herman
Plaza

San Francisco
Museum of
Modern Art

80

35

San Francisco-Oakland
Bay Bridge

San Francisco Bay

280

Potrero Avenue

POTRERO

23rd St.

18th St.

11

101

15 16 17 ↓

32

VERTIGO

Director Alfred Hitchcock

Starring James Stewart, Kim Novak,
Barbara Bel Geddes, Tom Helmore

USA, 1958

Master filmmaker Alfred Hitchcock once said that "San Francisco would be a good location for a murder mystery." And while *Vertigo*'s murder doesn't actually take place in the city, San Francisco's role in the film looms almost as large as that of the actors. Hitchcock used the Victorian architecture, the fog, and the Spanish heritage that permeate the Bay City to conjure an atmosphere of intrigue in which the film's protagonists quite literally lose themselves. The debut of the painstakingly restored film in 1996 was a hit with press and public alike – quite unlike the premiere of the original in 1958, which the critics received with much more skepticism.

Scottie Ferguson (James Stewart) is forced to retire from the police force when an increasingly strong sense of dizziness associated with a fear of heights begins to interfere with his work. Knowing Ferguson has time on his hands, Gavin Elster (Tom Helmore), an old school friend, asks him to employ his detective skills on his behalf: Scottie is to shadow Gavin's wife, Madeleine (Kim Novak). The woman appears to be losing her mind: She is convinced that the ghost of her great-grandmother is following her, and her husband fears that she will, like her ancestor, attempt to take her own life. Scottie sees Madeleine for the first time at **Ernie's**, a restaurant at **847 Montgomery Street** that was a local favorite until it closed in 1995. Hitchcock ordered the

eatery to be recreated down to the finest detail in the studio, and even had food from Ernie's flown in.

The route that Scottie takes as he shadows Madeleine could double as a tour of San Francisco's famous sights. It starts at the Elsters' apartment in the exclusive **Brocklebank Apartments** at **1000 Mason Street** in Nob Hill, across from the Fairmont Hotel. Madeleine visits her great-grandmother Carlotta's grave at the **Mission Dolores Cemetery** at **324 Dolores Street** at the corner of

Scottie (James Stewart) follows Madeleine (Kim Novak, top) all over San Francisco, from the Palace of the Legion of Honor (left) to Fort Point at the foot of the Golden Gate Bridge (above).

Scottie's vertigo finally gets the better of him at Mission San Juan Bautista 90 miles (145 kilometers) south of the city – with tragic consequences.

some 90 miles (145 kilometers) south of S.F., is an important state landmark. And although all the mission scenes were filmed on location, the bell tower is a product of Hollywood ingenuity. Shortly before filming commenced, the church's tower had to be demolished due to its alarming state of disrepair. Scale models and matte paintings stood in for the missing tower.

With Madeleine's death, Scottie plunges into a crisis. He takes long, rambling walks through the city to visit the places they used to go together. Near Union Square he spots a young woman, Judy Barton (Kim Novak), who looks almost exactly like Madeleine and tails her to her room in the **Empire Hotel** at **940 Sutter Street.** The auberge is now known as the **York Hotel,** but **Rooms 501 and 502,** which served as models for studio sets used during filming, are exactly the same today as they were back then. Scottie talks the brunette look-alike into joining him for dinner at Ernie's. Obsessed with the idea of having found Madeleine again in Judy, he convinces her to change her appearance so that she looks even more like the dead woman, all the while ignoring her resistance to the idea. When the transformation is complete, Scottie begins to suspect the worst: that Judy may have been the decoy in a sophisticated conspiracy to commit murder, and that he was duped into playing an unwitting part in the crime. He drives Judy to Mission Bautista and forces her to climb the stairs of the bell tower, where he accuses her of being an accomplice to a killing. The bells begin to toll ominously as the film hurtles towards its shocking conclusion.

16th Street, a location famous for its church, the oldest building in the city. From there the detective follows her to **Lincoln Park** and the **Palace of the Legion of Honor,** an art museum where Madeleine goes to view a painting of her great-grandmother. The near absence of any other people underscores the dreamlike quality of these silent sequences. At **Fort Point** in **Presidio Park** at the foot of the **Golden Gate Bridge,** Madeleine jumps into the Bay in an apparent suicide attempt. Scottie saves her, and at the same time discovers that he's head over heels in love with the enigmatic schizophrenic.

On the third day, Scottie and Madeleine leave the city and drive south. Their first kiss takes place on a cliff battered by rough surf on **17-Mile Drive** near **Monterey,** the famous coastal loop 112 miles (180 kilometers) south of San Francisco. In the hope that Madeleine can be cured of her recurring nightmares at an old Spanish abbey, they drive on to **Mission San Juan Bautista.** Their arrival at the sanctuary the next day takes a tragic turn: Scottie watches helplessly as Madeleine falls to her death from the bell tower. The mission, founded in 1797 and located

Scottie insists that Judy transform herself into Madeleine. In the background is the landmark Coit Tower.

BULLITT

Director	Peter Yates
Starring	Steve McQueen, Robert Vaughn, Jacqueline Bisset, Don Gordon, Robert Duvall, Simon Oakland, Norman Fell
USA, 1968	

Chase scenes are to police thrillers as one-liners are to comedies: part of the standard repertoire. Too often they're employed in a last-ditch effort to give a weak film a shot in the arm. With its muddled plot and now legendary car chase, *Bullitt* could be classed in this category. But two factors elevate this cop tale to celluloid legend: the quintessentially cool Steve McQueen as Lieutenant Frank Bullitt, and the movie's convincing realism. Filmed entirely on location in San Francisco, director Peter Yates made outstanding use of the city's notoriously hilly topography. What's more, the flick raised the Ford Mustang, McQueen's car, to cult status, and in honor of his sartorial chic, plainclothes policemen in the Bay City began to wear turtleneck sweaters instead of regulation shirt and tie. Subsequent films such as *Dirty Harry* (1971) attest to *Bullitt*'s influence in establishing S.F. as a location of choice for police thrillers.

The film's strong visual realism comes across in the opening scenes as a hung-over Lieutenant Frank Bullitt (Steve McQueen) opens the door of his apartment at **1153 Taylor Street** for his partner Delgetti (Don Gordon). The building looks so much the same today that you practically expect to see Bullitt perusing the freezer case in the store across the street. The contrast with the world of the rich and the famous inhabited by career politician Chalmers (Robert Vaughn), couldn't be greater. Chalmers's Bay-view villa stands proudly in Pacific Heights at **2700 Vallejo Street** at the corner of **Divisadero,** a residential area still preferred by high society. Chalmers gives Bullitt an important assignment: to keep watch over Johnny Ross (Pat Renella), a star witness in an upcoming trial against the Mafia.

Steve McQueen as Bullitt, a Mustang-driving cop whose reputation spanned the globe.

Ross takes a shotgun blast from an assassin as he opens the door to his room at the fictitious Hotel Daniels, in reality the Kennedy Hotel on Embarcadero, one of many buildings razed in the 1989 earthquake that rocked the city. The witness is rushed to the **San Francisco General Hospital at 1001 Potrero Avenue** – director Peter Yates drafted staff nurses and doctors to play themselves in their own working environment to ensure that day-in-the-life scenes at this major city hospital would appear credible. Johnny Ross dies that same night, and Bullitt secretly arranges for his body to be taken to the municipal morgue so

The posh villa in Pacific Heights that bad-guy Chalmers (Robert Vaughn) calls home. Bullitt buys a paper at the intersection of Clay and Taylor Streets.

Chalmers won't learn of the latest developments and take him off the case. Determined to collar the bad guys, and with the aid of a taxi driver, Bullitt tries to trace Ross's footsteps on the day of the hit, but the killers are already on the cop's tail.

Any attempt to recreate the legendary car chase that ensues is hampered by the magic of moviemaking. The route was pieced together with utter disregard for the real topography of San Francisco. The high-speed pursuit kicks off in the east of the city, but switches suddenly to North Beach, where the camera catches the landmark music club **Bimbo's 365** at **1025 Columbus Avenue** as the drivers take a sharp curve over Columbus Avenue. The most riveting phase of the chase – when the cars fly off of the crests of steep hills – was shot on **Taylor Street between Vallejo and Filbert.** Inadvertent comic relief comes in the form of a VW beetle that pops up time and again during these spliced-together sequences.

The chase moves seamlessly to **Marina Boulevard,** a thoroughfare that also makes appearances in *Mrs. Doubtfire* (1993) and *Dirty Harry* (1971). The action hops from the Marina over to **McLaren Park,** back in the east of the city, and ends in a fiery explosion at a **gas station** on **Guadalupe Canyon Parkway** in **Daly City.** Despite the incongruous nature of the locations, and the quick shifts from one to the next, the audience is treated to a fairly exact impression of what it is like to drive in San Francisco: Streets really can be so absurdly steep that driving them, even at normal speeds, is nothing if not an adventure. Clever cinematography may be credited with the chase scenes' realism: A hand-held camera filmed the scenes through the windshield while the camera car, nicknamed the "Bullittmobile," tailed the cars at speeds of up to 110 mph (180 kph).

The Mafia hit men are killed during the chase, but Bullitt's troubles are far from over. Still in the line of fire, politically at least, he faces the threat from above that he'll be taken off the case. With a little extra time to clear up what actually happened, Bullitt discovers that Johnny Ross is still alive. The man killed at the hotel was not the Mafia informant, but a decoy. Ross decides to make a run for it and books a flight to London. Bullitt tries to arrest him at **San Francisco International Airport,** chasing him across the runway and back into the terminal, where the film comes to a heart-stopping conclusion.

The wild car chases through the hilly streets of San Francisco have made this otherwise conventional cop flick into a cult classic.

DIRTY HARRY

Director Don Siegel

Starring Clint Eastwood, Harry Guardino, Reni Santoni, Andrew Robinson, John Larch, John Mitchum, John Vernon

USA, 1971

Left: **The Bank of America skyscraper, where the sniper Scorpio draws a bead on his first victim.** Right: **Clint Eastwood became a legend as hard-as-nails cop Harry Callahan, here poised for action on Mount Davidson.** Below: **Scorpio evades the long arm of the law at Saints Peter and Paul Cathedral.**

In the early seventies, San Francisco was a hippie mecca still fully under the spell of the Age of Aquarius. But it was also the home of über-cop Dirty Harry, a man who was anything but a flower child. When the movie made its debut, Harry's war on a serial killer and a justice system that, in his view, protected criminals at the cost of victims was decried by critics as too right-leaning. Nevertheless, it was a huge box-office hit. *Dirty Harry* is based on the real-life case of the "Zodiac Killer," a murderer who terrorized San Francisco in the late sixties and who was never brought to justice. Alongside stunning aerial shots of the Bay City, it was Inspector Harry Callahan's cool ways and tough-guy quips that thrilled audiences and became the hallmark of the successful *Dirty Harry* series.

The film opens with a cold-blooded murder: A sniper known as Scorpio (Andy Robinson) takes aim from the roof of the **Bank of America,** a skyscraper that was still under construction at **555 California Street.** A woman swimming in the rooftop pool

Given no other choice, Dirty Harry takes the law into his own hands.

of the **Chinatown Hilton, 750 Kearny Street,** is shot, and plainclothes policeman Harry Callahan (Clint Eastwood) is called in to take the case. His first meeting with the mayor (John Vernon) annoys the dyed-in-the-wool cop notorious for unconventional but highly effective methods of law enforcement – it's clear that politics and bureaucracy are going to be major hurdles to catching the killer. For Callahan, there's practically no worse news. No one is as focused as he is when it comes to doing his job, and to him, politics has nothing to do with the fight for justice. Always on duty and unacquainted with what it means to have a private life, he prefers to work alone. His partners typically end up badly wounded or simply quit the force.

The hunt for Scorpio takes "Dirty Harry" all over the city. The first murder took place in the Financial District, and a second is narrowly avoided in North Beach thanks to aerial surveillance of the neighborhood where Scorpio lies in wait near **Saints Peter and Paul Cathedral** on **Washington Square** – a church that also served as the temple of Jerusalem in Cecil B. DeMille's *The Ten Commandments* (1923). Despite a massive police search, Scorpio escapes and murders a boy in Potrero Hill. When he takes a young girl hostage, the mayor caves in to his demands for ransom and sends Callahan to deliver the cash. Scorpio forces the hardboiled cop to crisscross the city on what seems like a wild-goose chase: from a phone booth in the Marina to the **Forest Hill underground station,** then on to **Mission Dolores Park** and the **Aquatic Park** near Fisherman's Wharf, and from there to the top of **Mount Davidson,** the city's highest peak – a distance of some 15 miles (25 kilometers) in total.

After the handoff, Scorpio reveals his plan to kill the hostage anyway. A fight ensues, and the wounded sniper makes his getaway. Callahan corners him in the since demolished **Kezar Stadium** in **Golden Gate Park** and forces him to reveal the hostage's location. But the girl is already dead, and it looks like Scorpio will evade the long arm of the law after all: Callahan's arrest involved an illegal search that violated police procedures, so the murderer is set to get off scot-free.

Callahan takes the situation to heart and decides to make catching Scorpio his life's mission. He follows the murderer into Chinatown and the **Roaring 20s** strip club at **552 Broadway.** Scorpio tries to shake him by hiring a thug to stage an attack on himself, and then pins the blame for the assault on the hard-charging cop. Harry is officially taken off the case – not exactly a boon to the citizens of San Francisco, as Scorpio's next move is to kidnap a school bus full of kids. Callahan is summoned to the mayor's office to help, but this time he refuses to deliver the ransom, a move that in his mind would equate to giving in. Instead, he does things his way. When the school bus turns onto **Sir Francis Drake Boulevard** in Marin County, Scorpio spies Callahan standing on an old railway viaduct and panics. He stops the bus near a cement factory – today the **Larkspur Landing Shopping Center** – and runs. After a chase through the factory, Scorpio takes a boy hostage, but now there's no escape. In classic Dirty Harry style, Callahan takes the law into his own hands to see that justice is finally served.

The concrete block of the Chinatown Hilton, the scene of a terrible crime, stands to the right of the Transamerica Pyramid.

MRS. DOUBTFIRE

Director   Chris Columbus

Starring   Robin Williams, Sally Field, Pierce Brosnan, Harvey Fierstein, Polly Holliday

USA, 1993

Men in skirts are always good for a laugh in the movies: Just consider the cross-dressing shenanigans that defined films such as *Some Like It Hot* (1959), *Tootsie* (1982), and *The Adventures of Priscilla, Queen of the Desert* (1994). Robin Williams got the chance to discover his feminine side in *Mrs. Doubtfire*: After four hours in the make-up artist's chair, the comedian's gender-bending transformation was allegedly so perfect that he could even stroll across the studio lot with not as much as a glance in his direction. His double role as fun-loving father and sharp-tongued nanny won Williams a Golden Globe, and the film was honored as the best comedy of the year. The three make-up artists who conjured up Mrs. Doubtfire during filming were honored at the Academy Awards with golden statuettes for their outstanding work.

Robin Williams plays Daniel Hillard, a periodically employed actor who lends his voice to cartoon characters. While his on-again, off-again job as a voice-over artist is less than ideal, he seems blessed with the perfect family: His wife, Miranda (Sally Field), is a successful interior designer, their three kids are as cute as can be, and they live in a pretty Victorian house at **2640 Steiner Street, corner of Broadway,** in the exclusive Pacific Heights neighborhood of San Francisco. Sadly, things are not as perfect as they appear. To celebrate his son's birthday in boisterous style, Daniel transforms the house into a petting zoo with kids and animals romping wildly to hip-hop music. The party spins out of control, and Miranda comes home to chaos. When she finally puts her foot down, the dream turns into a nightmare: Miranda wants a divorce and custody of the kids. Stunned, Daniel moves out of the house and into a run-down flat at **520-522A Green Street, corner of Bannam Street,** above the Danilo Bakery in the North Beach quarter of Little Italy.

To see his kids and save his marriage to Miranda (Sally Field, top), Daniel (Robin Williams) transforms himself into the capable nanny Mrs. Doubtfire.

The divorce court allows Daniel to see his kids on the weekends, clearly not enough time for the doting dad. Since Miranda works during the day, she decides to hire a nanny to help with the household and to look after the three children. Daniel offers to do the job, but Miranda refuses, forcing him to take drastic comedic measures. With the aid of his brother (Harvey Fierstein), a gay make-up artist, he transforms himself into the kindly, old-fashioned housekeeper Mrs. Doubtfire. Miranda fails to recognize her husband when he comes to interview as a grey-haired Scottish lady with impeccable references. He, or she, gets the job. Now that Daniel is a housekeeper in his own home, his most sincere hope is to cook, vacuum, and iron his way back into his family's heart.

Everything goes according to plan until competition arrives on the scene: Miranda's old flame, the slick charmer Stu (Pierce Brosnan). Daniel uses Mrs. Doubtfire's entire repertoire of wiles to drive the pretty-boy suitor away, from dispensing grandmotherly advice to sharp retorts – but it's all in vain. Tensions mount, and a showdown becomes unavoidable at **Bridges Restaurant, 44 Church Street** in **Danville,** some 30 miles (50 kilometers) east of San Francisco. Daniel arrives at the trendy eatery as Mrs. Doubtfire to celebrate Miranda's birthday with Stu and the kids; but he also has a dinner meeting with the TV studio boss he works for to discuss an idea for a new show – at the same time and the same place. This tour de force of feverish costume changes is fated to go completely wrong, and Daniel's cover is blown. For the film's improbably rosy world, in which the kids find all of dad's jokes funny, and grinning nannies whip up gourmet meals at a moment's notice, the final scenes are a bracing reality check. Flaunting Hollywood convention, *Mrs. Doubtfire* does without a typical happy end.

Like the character of Mrs. Doubtfire, the film's version of San Francisco is also an illusion. The sun always shines, one house is more beautiful than the next, and the Bay City's famed ethnic variety is nowhere to be seen. Cable cars, the pretty North Beach quarter, a bike tour past picturesque **Crissy Field** on the bay with the Golden Gate Bridge as backdrop – this is the San Francisco of tourism brochures and postcards, attractive but somehow not fully satisfying, a bit like Robin Williams's role in the film. He's at his best and his funniest in *Mrs. Doubtfire* when he seems to be improvising, such as when he bombards a grouchy city employee with funny voices, or when he stays late at the TV studio to play with plastic dinosaurs. But for most of the film, Williams is chained to the nanny's persona, a part rather limited in scope when compared with his memorable roles in *Good Will Hunting* (1997) and *One Hour Photo* (2002).

Daniel cleans his former home, a fancy Pacific Heights villa (above), **but lives in a messy bachelor pad in modest North Beach** (left).

THE ROCK

Director	Michael Bay
Starring	Sean Connery, Nicolas Cage, Ed Harris, John Spencer, David Morse

USA, 1996

Alcatraz, the notorious high-security prison in the San Francisco Bay, a place no inmate ever managed to escape, has always loomed large in the imaginations of filmmakers. The island fortress played a central role in movies such as *Birdman of Alcatraz* (1962) with Burt Lancaster in the leading role, *Escape from Alcatraz* (1979) starring Clint Eastwood, and *Murder in the First* (1995) with Kevin Bacon and Christian Slater. *The Rock* offers an unconventional approach to the typical Alcatraz plot: Rather than prisoners trying to make a break, the protagonists are attempting to break in. And Alcatraz is no longer an operating prison, but, as in reality, one of the Bay City's most popular tourist attractions. *The Rock*'s glamorous premiere took place on the prison isle to great fanfare.

The action-packed Bruckheimer production comes alive not only through the acting talents of Sean Connery and Nicolas Cage, but also from imaginatively executed action scenes as well as stunning shots of Alcatraz and San Francisco. The plot centers on the highly decorated Vietnam vet General Hummel (Ed Harris) and his vengeful plan. An elite troop of soldiers under his command steals fifteen rockets armed with deadly nerve gas before taking a group of tourists hostage on **Alcatraz** and issuing an ultimatum: The U.S. government should fork over $100 million from a classified weapons fund as compensation to the families of soldiers killed on secret missions, or face a chemical attack on the entire San Francisco Bay area. If time runs out, the rockets will be launched from Alcatraz.

Washington reacts by dispatching FBI chemical warfare expert Stanley Goodspeed (Nicolas Cage) to San Francisco to help a team of Navy SEALs penetrate the subterranean tunnels to Alcatraz. The only man who knows the underbelly of Alcatraz like the back of his hand is John Mason (Sean Connery), a British agent who, thirty years ago, made a name for himself as the only person ever to have escaped the island prison. Since then Mason has been jailed without the benefit of a trial in a high-security facility. He is understandably reluctant to help the FBI, and escapes from a suite in the luxurious **Fairmont Hotel** at **950 Mason Street,** at the corner of **California Street.** A chase ensues through the steep

John Mason (Sean Connery) and Stanley Goodspeed (Nicholas Cage) inside the former high-security prison on the island of Alcatraz.

streets of Russian Hill, with a cable car exploding into flames before the **New Russian Hill Market** at **1198 Pacific Avenue.** Aficionados of San Francisco may raise an eyebrow since the famous cable cars lack the gas tanks needed for such a blast – they are moved by means of steel cables located under the street. But that's Hollywood. Goodspeed finally nabs the escapee, and Mason agrees to help.

The film delivers one action-packed scene after the next in the surprisingly well-lit tunnels below Alcatraz. The soldiers are successfully ambushed by the terrorists, and Mason and Goodspeed are left to handle things on their own. Mason em-

Alcatraz, a cliff-bound island in San Francisco Bay, was used as a federal penitentiary from 1859 until 1963.

ploys his extensive combat experience to keep the enemy at bay despite numerous close calls. In the meantime, the ultimatum has timed out, and General Hummel gives in to pressure from his accomplices to fire a rocket armed with nerve gas at the fan-packed **Oakland Coliseum** (in reality it's the **San Francisco 49ers stadium, Candlestick Park**). At the very last second he steers the rocket off course, forcing it to plunge into the Bay. The other terrorists are less than pleased by developments, and

Mason flees the swank Fairmont Hotel (top and center). **A cable car explodes in front of this small market in the Russian Hill neighborhood** (right) **during the subsequent chase scenes.**

Seasoned British agent John Mason shows the FBI how to infiltrate Alcatraz undetected using a scale model of the island and its prison buildings.

seize command of the operation. Their new plan: to take the remaining armed rocket – all others have since been disarmed by Goodspeed – and wreak havoc on the city of San Francisco.

Adding pressure to an already tense situation, fighter jets are en route to Alcatraz to bomb the island, an attack that would kill not only the terrorists but Mason and Goodspeed as well. Shots of fighter jets flying under the Golden Gate Bridge were courtesy of the Blue Angels, also known as the Navy Flight Demonstration Squadron, an elite team of six U.S. Navy pilots who present their choreographed aviation prowess in shows such as October's Fleet Week in San Francisco. The island's lighthouse, specially reconstructed for the film, is the scene of the showdown as the jets close in and Goodspeed uses the few seconds he has left to defuse the last rocket and, with any luck, signal that all is well. The Spanish explorers who stopped at Alcatraz in the 18th century probably never would have imagined it as the setting for adventure. Back then, the island colonized by pelicans – *alcatraces* in Spanish – seemed useful only as a fortified lookout. The U.S. would use it as a prison until 1963; some ten years later, Alcatraz was integrated into the Golden Gate National Recreation Area.

15

SYDNEY

HOLLYWOOD DOWN UNDER

For Sydneysiders, the Emerald City has always been as cinematic as Los Angeles, Paris, or Hong Kong. The world-famous Opera House, scenic Harbour Bridge, the proud towers of the bustling Central Business District, and pretty beaches lend it an appeal that is both familiar and exotic. Yet only recently has the capital of New South Wales had its day in the cinematic sun as a hub of global film production and as a sought-after location. In 1998 Hollywood's Fox Studios opened on Sydney's outskirts, and its early box-office successes discounted fears that Australia was a fringe market, or worse – just a flash in the pan as the upcoming 2000 Summer Olympics drew major media attention. Warner Roadshow Studios also invested in Australia, erecting its vast complex an hour's flight north of Sydney. Filming Down Under promised significant cost savings over working in Hollywood. No wonder directors return to Sydney time and again.

Sydney's stunning waterfront with its landmark Opera (above) and the Harbour Bridge form a dramatic backdrop to *Mission: Impossible II* with Thandie Newton (right).

Below: **Sydney's stairway to heaven: Skyscrapers of glass and steel make for a dynamic skyline in the financial district.**

In 1999, Fox made the blockbuster film *The Matrix*, whose "generic" metropolis is anything but to the denizens of Sydney. *Dark City* (1998) preceded it, providing some of the sets for Keanu Reeves and company. Fox's *Mission: Impossible II* (2000) with Tom Cruise and Thandie Newton took advantage of its Sydney location in several key scenes, while set-centric *Moulin Rouge!* (2001), a vehicle for Australia's still rising star Nicole Kidman, *Star Wars: Episode II – Attack of the Clones* (2002), and Aussie director Phillip Noyce's *The Quiet American* (2002) were filmed primarily in the studios.

There was nothing quiet about the American who got the Australian film industry rolling in 1896. That year, the French Lumière brothers, inventors of the trailblazing Cinématographe,

sent early film technology to Australia to promote French-made cameras and films. In August the flamboyant magician Carl Hertz beat them to it. He showed the very first commercial films before U.K.-born Joseph Perry took up the charge with the Limelight Division of the Salvation Army, which traveled the continent to show movies. Like film pioneers who ventured out to the Hollywood Hills of L.A., Perry made his initial hit with a Western in 1904, followed by the world's first ever feature-length film, *The Story of the Kelly Gang*, made in Sydney in 1906. But it was not just the city that held an appeal to filmmakers: By 1912 more than thirty feature-length films had been produced in Australia, many of them "bushranging" epics pitting man against the continent's formidable, beautiful nature.

The desire to explore the magical Australian outback leapfrogged over the moribund postwar decades to the 1970s. Numerous films confronted Aboriginal themes, such as Phillip Noyce's *Backroads* (1977) and Fred Schepisi's *The Chant of Jimmie Blacksmith* (1978). A well-intended system of state support, the short-lived Australian Film Development Corporation (AFDC) and its successor, the Australian Film Commission (AFC), gave new impetus to Australian film against long-time British and American competitors. Born of these initiatives were Ken Hannam's *Sunday Too Far Away* (1975), a

hit at Cannes, and Peter Weir's mysterious *Picnic at Hanging Rock* (1975). Still, nothing could compare with the international success of George Miller's *Mad Max* (1979), the tale of road warrior Max Rockatansky (Mel Gibson) in a brutal, futuristic world – a movie made without state funding.

Money flowed into Australian filmmaking as never before, and success was widespread: *Gallipoli* (1981), *The Man from Snowy River* (1982), *Phar Lap* (1983), *Crocodile Dundee* (1986) plus its sequels, and two more *Mad Max*es (1981 and 1985) were major box-office hits in America, whose market for English-language movies was more than ten times the size of Australia's. The myth of the outback is writ large in most of these films, leaving city locations completely out in the cold.

Although films "made in Australia" were thriving, many directors still packed their bags and headed out to California. A brain drain of Australian New Wave directors occurred on a grand scale: Peter Weir, George Miller, Fred Schepisi, and Bruce Beresford sallied forth, as did Phillip Noyce, who returned to make his moving tale of Aboriginal girls on an epic journey home in *Rabbit-Proof Fence* (2002). A new generation of filmmakers quickly filled the void, producing *Strictly Ballroom* (1992), *Romper Stomper* (1992) with a young Russell Crowe, *Muriel's Wedding* (1994), *Priscilla: Queen of the Desert* (1994), *Shine* (1996), and more. Great directors such as Jane Campion, Geoffrey Wright, Jocelyn Moorhouse, P.J. Hogan, Baz Luhrmann, Rob Sitch, Stephan Elliott, and the enigmatic Alex Proyas look set to stay in Australia, a promising prospect for Ozzie filmmaking's reputation on the global cinema scene.

Victorian and modern architecture come together at the Westin Hotel on Martin Place (above), **a location in** *The Matrix*. **Filmmakers love Sydney's mix of contemporary and historic building styles.**

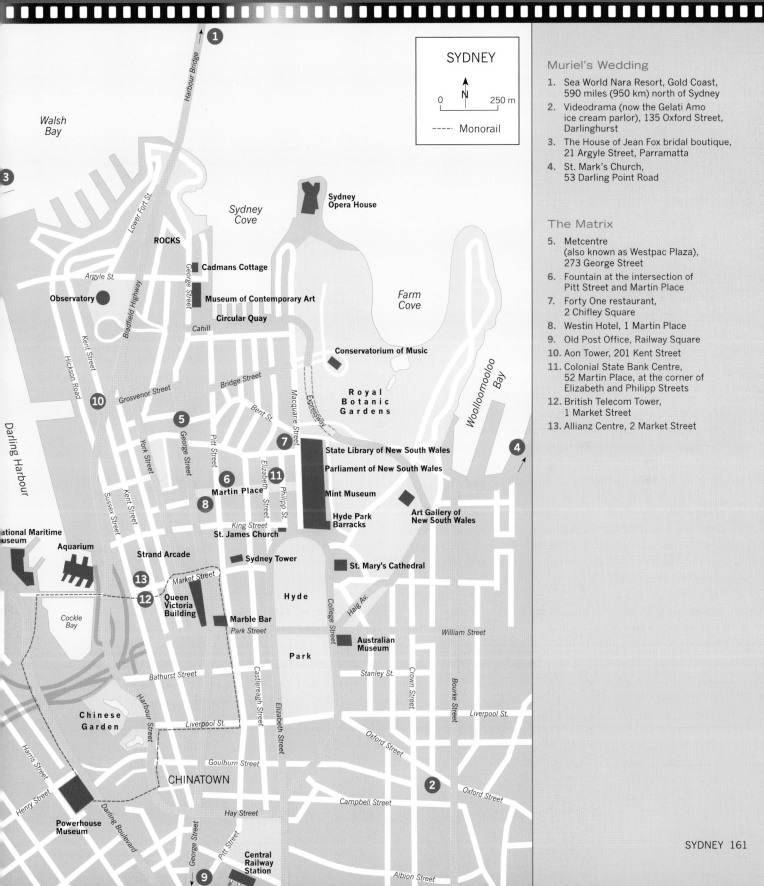

SYDNEY

0 N 250 m

----- Monorail

Walsh
Bay

Sydney
Cove

Sydney
Opera House

ROCKS

Cadmans Cottage

Farm
Cove

Museum of Contemporary Art

Circular Quay

Cahill

Observatory

Argyle St.

Lower Fort St.

George Street

Conservatorium of Music

Kent Street

Bradfield Highway

Bridge Street

Royal
Botanic
Gardens

Woolloomooloo
Bay

Grosvenor Street

Bent St.

Macquarie Street

Expressway

Darling Harbour

Hickson Road

York Street

George Street

Pitt Street

Kent Street

Sussex Street

State Library of New South Wales

Parliament of New South Wales

Elizabeth Street

Philipp St.

Mint Museum

Hyde Park
Barracks

Art Gallery of
New South Wales

Martin Place

King Street

St. James Church

National Maritime
Museum

Aquarium

Strand Arcade

Market Street

Queen
Victoria
Building

Sydney Tower

St. Mary's Cathedral

Hyde

College Street

Haig Av.

Cockle
Bay

Marble Bar

Park Street

Park

Australian
Museum

William Street

Bathurst Street

Castlereagh Street

Elizabeth Street

Stanley St.

Crown Street

Bourke Street

Liverpool St.

Chinese
Garden

Harbour Street

Liverpool St.

Goulburn Street

Oxford Street

Harris Street

CHINATOWN

Oxford Street

Powerhouse
Museum

Henry Street

Darling Boulevard

Hay Street

George Street

Pitt Street

Campbell Street

Central
Railway
Station

Albion Street

Muriel's Wedding

1. Sea World Nara Resort, Gold Coast, 590 miles (950 km) north of Sydney
2. Videodrama (now the Gelati Amo ice cream parlor), 135 Oxford Street, Darlinghurst
3. The House of Jean Fox bridal boutique, 21 Argyle Street, Parramatta
4. St. Mark's Church, 53 Darling Point Road

The Matrix

5. Metcentre (also known as Westpac Plaza), 273 George Street
6. Fountain at the intersection of Pitt Street and Martin Place
7. Forty One restaurant, 2 Chifley Square
8. Westin Hotel, 1 Martin Place
9. Old Post Office, Railway Square
10. Aon Tower, 201 Kent Street
11. Colonial State Bank Centre, 52 Martin Place, at the corner of Elizabeth and Philipp Streets
12. British Telecom Tower, 1 Market Street
13. Allianz Centre, 2 Market Street

MURIEL'S WEDDING

Director	P. J. Hogan
Starring	Toni Collette, Rachel Griffiths, Sophie Lee, Rosalind Hammond, Belinda Jarrett, Pippa Grandison, Bill Hunter

Australia, 1994

Chances are you didn't recognize Toni Collette in *The Sixth Sense* (1999) or *About a Boy* (2002) as the bumbling bride of Cinderella-story *Muriel's Wedding*. Rejected at casting as too skinny, Collette put on forty pounds in seven weeks to plump up for the part that would make her a star both in her native Australia and abroad.

It was worth the weight: P.J. Hogan's feature debut stole the show from the campy *Adventures of Priscilla, Queen of the Desert* (1994) at the Australian Film Awards, earning the leading lady Best Actress accolades and qualifying Brisbane-born Hogan for more nuptials in *My Best Friend's Wedding* (1997) with Julia Roberts. Unlike the leggy redhead, Muriel is no stereotypical pretty woman, and calls upon her adopted hometown, Sydney, to transform her life. Locations such as shops downtown on Oxford Street, the bridal boutiques of Parramatta, and a fairytale church at Darling Point provide a convincing backdrop as the city where dreams come true.

Outdated, perhaps, to a mid-nineties audience, Muriel's fantasy world revolves around getting married. Stuck out on the beaches of fictitious Porpoise Point, the odds are slim. Her family is hopelessly dysfunctional, she's frumpy, her friends are cruel and beautiful, and her greatest achievement since high school has been to fail a secretarial course. After nearly being arrested for shoplifting an outfit to wear to a wedding, Muriel flees to the sanctuary of her bedroom, her ABBA cassettes, and pin-ups from bridal magazines. She harbors dreams of being as exciting and beautiful as her so-called friends, but the harder she tries to fit in, the more she fails.

Things get worse before they get better: Muriel's good-looking pals announce that she's not invited to vacation with them because she's a loser. Opportunity knocks in the form of a blank check her mother gives her to start her on a career as a cosmetics consultant. While trailing her erstwhile friends at Hibiscus Island, in reality the **Sea World Nara Resort** on the Gold Coast, a well-known vacation destination far north of Sydney, she meets up with another member of the out crowd from high school. Rhonda (Rachel Griffiths) has transformed herself into a sexy hedonist with big-city ambitions. After a memo-

A little white lie: Muriel (Toni Collette) tells shopkeepers at The House of Jean Fox bridal boutique in Parramatta that all her wedding dreams are about to come true.

rable karaoke rendition of ABBA's "Waterloo" in the resort bar, they move to Sydney in search of fun and adventure – and eligible bachelors. The anthem by the Swedish pop group serves as a declaration of independence for the two women who, while channeling band members Agnetha Fältskog and Anni-Frid Lyngstad, assume an aura of invincibility. Viewers who followed ABBA's early days may recall that "Waterloo" was the breakthrough song that helped the quartet to win the Eurovision song contest in the early seventies, making the girls' choice of battle hymn all the more fitting.

Muriel takes a job at **Videodrama** on **135 Oxford Street** in the heart of the Darlinghurst shopping district, now home to the Gelati Amo ice cream parlor but still across the street from the **dry cleaner's** where Rhonda works. Muriel's so obsessed with watching recorded coverage of the royal wedding of Charles and Diana that she almost misses making the acquaintance of her first boyfriend while renting him a videocassette. Marriage seems no closer, but just as she gets going in the dating department Rhonda is diagnosed with a tumor in her spine and is confined to a wheelchair. Muriel pledges to help her build a new life, but secretly sojourns to **The House of Jean Fox** in **Parramatta.** The shop was located at **48 Macquarie Street** during filming, later moving to **21 Argyle Street.** Muriel fibs and tells the shopkeepers that she's to wed in a month, and that her mother is in the hospital and can't help pick out the dress. Eager to help, they take Polaroids of her in various gowns to show her ailing mom. Rhonda's accidental discovery of a secret wedding album full of snaps showing Muriel in full bridal regalia renders a sad situation even more pathetic.

Muriel's dream unexpectedly becomes a reality when she answers an ad in the paper. A South African swimmer is willing to pay an enormous sum to wed an Australian for "green card" privileges so he can compete as an Aussie in the 2000 Olympics. Athlete David Van Arckle (Daniel Lapaine) looks panic stricken as a veiled Muriel strides down the aisle of **St. Mark's Church,** a neo-gothic landmark at **53 Darling Point Road** in the eastern suburbs. Paparazzi snap shots of the couple, and Muriel ignores the sneer of distaste on her bridegroom's face as they leave the church to embark on a new life together. If a society wedding to a perfect hunk is the solution to her problems, then Muriel is the girl with all the answers.

Rhonda (Rachel Griffiths) phones her best friend from the dry cleaner's on Oxford Street where she works. Muriel is across the street at the Videodrama, busily renting tapes to prospective husbands.

Muriel gets disapproving looks from her popular school friends while on vacation at Sea World Nara Resort. The awkward wannabe is certain that a dream wedding at St. Mark's Church (bottom) will win her membership in the clique.

THE MATRIX

Directors	The Wachowski Brothers
Starring	Keanu Reeves, Laurence Fishburne, Carrie-Anne Moss, Hugo Weaving, Gloria Foster, Joe Pantoliano

USA, 1999

A combination of *Alice in Wonderland,* Plato's world of forms, the Old Testament, and Earth as an alien-controlled nightmare powered this sci-fi flick to a box-office hit in 1999. Brimming with superhero action and high-flying special effects, it comes as no surprise that the writing, directing Wachowski brothers started out as scripters for Marvel comics, birthplace of Spider-Man and the X-Men.

What raised eyebrows in the film industry was the fact that this was only the siblings' second time writing *and* directing a film after their freshman effort, *Bound* (1996). Although the story is set in the year 2199 in the Wachowskis' hometown of Chicago, filming took place in Sydney, a city in pre-2000 Olympics fever. Location manager Peter Lawless told the Australian dailies that the financial capital's glass-and-steel skyline conjured "generic America" or "metropolis anywhere," an effect tough to achieve back in the Windy City with such highly recognizable skyscraper monuments as the gargantuan Hancock Center and the Tribune Tower on the Magnificent Mile.

Clad in black leather and shades, and performing gravity-defying feats of martial arts, the cast of deliciously fit, deliriously handsome characters belongs to a renegade group of humans trying to rid the world of its malevolent machine masters. Only one thing is missing: a messiah. He appears in the unlikely Clark Kent-like character of Thomas A. Anderson (Keanu Reeves), a mild-mannered computer programmer who leads a double life as a cyber renegade named Neo – an anagram of one, as in "The One."

Exactly what he's fighting against remains unclear until he receives a phone call from shadowy resistance fighter Trinity (Carrie-Anne Moss). Her boss Morpheus (Laurence Fishburne), named for the Greco-Roman god of dreams, challenges Neo to awaken from the fog of his fake life as a human power source in a virtual world called The Matrix. Easier said than done: Matrix agents chase Neo down at the office where he works after he attempts to flee by climbing out on the ledge of the **Metcentre** (also referred to as Westpac Plaza) at **273 George Street.** The unstoppable Reeves insisted on performing the daring stunt in person.

United against the machines: Trinity (Carrie-Anne Moss) and Neo (Keanu Reeves).

Allusions to Alice falling down the rabbit hole abound as Neo makes the jump from simple energy cell to "real" human, a process akin to being flushed down a giant cosmic toilet. No matter. Revived and received as the newest member of the crew aboard Morpheus's biblically named ship, the *Nebuchadnezzar,* Neo embarks on a twofold journey to knowing himself and knowing how to annihilate the bad guy "agents" with an endless arsenal of heavy-duty weapons.

The effects are ingenious. The combat training scene featuring the distracting "Woman in Red" was filmed before the **fountain** where **Pitt Street** joins **Martin Place** in the heart of Sydney's CBD. While Neo is busy learning from Morpheus just how to become a fighting machine, his pal Cypher (Joe Pantoliano) defects to the dark side over a juicy steak at a Sydney hot spot, **Forty One** in the tower at **2 Chifley Square,** a restaurant especially beloved for its views of the harbor. Cypher eventually betrays his comrades with a sneeze as they crawl through the walls of an old mansion to elude the baddies. Chase scenes were filmed on the grand staircase at

Agent Smith (Hugo Weaving), evil personified.

the **Westin Hotel, 1 Martin Place,** an auberge ennobled by the renovated Victorian Renaissance Revival **General Post Office** that forms part of the hotel complex. Exteriors were filmed at the **Old Post Office** on **Railway Square.**

Evil Agent Smith (Hugo Weaving) and his cronies kidnap and torture Morpheus, and a showdown that is the technical highlight of the film breaks loose amid Sydney's reflective forest of glass-faced skyscrapers. Neo and Trinity commandeer a helicopter from the **Aon Tower** at **201 Kent Street** and fire rounds caught in beautiful, slow-mo detail, a scene so famous that it's called the "bullet-time sequence." Their target is the agents staked out in the **Colonial State Bank Centre** at **52 Martin Place.** Morpheus leaps to freedom, but the helicopter

crashes spectacularly against the glass facade of the **British Telecom Tower** at **1 Market Street.** Luckily, Neo lands atop the **Allianz Centre** across the way at **2 Market Street** and rescues Trinity just in the nick of time. Accidental shots of the famous Sydney Opera House and the Harbour Bridge in the background were purposely edited out of the background to preserve the city's anonymity.

The Matrix picked up four Academy Awards in technical areas such as Best Visual Effects thanks in part to the principal actors' four months of training under Hong Kong kung-fu master Yuen Wo Ping. Long-awaited sequels *Reloaded* and *Revolutions* (both 2003) did not nearly as well despite a loyal following. The video game Animatrix, which the follow-up films closely resembled in special effects and storylines, was, however, a big commercial hit.

The directors (right) chose Sydney as "metropolis anywhere," but audiences in the Australian city immediately recognized their hometown. Left: The Chifley Tower where Cypher betrays his comrades. Center: Agents chase Neo through the Metcentre. Right: The British Telecom Tower, site of the spectacular helicopter crash.

TOKYO

WHERE QUIET MEETS CHAOS

The famous cherry blossoms lend the vast city a peaceful aura every spring.

Some cities inhabit our imaginations for their grand presence in cinema: Los Angeles, turbulent in *Rebel Without a Cause*; Paris, magical in *Amélie*; and New York, Woody Allen poignant in *Manhattan* as well as Meg Ryan orgasmic in *When Harry Met Sally*. The capitals of Western culture are a familiar foil to faraway megalopolis Tokyo, with its pulsing entertainment and shopping districts, serene temples, and holy mountain, Fujiyama, rising in the distance. From Hollywood's perspective, the very foreignness of the Japanese capital limits it as a mecca for locations. At least two outstanding films are exceptions to the rule: One, *Godzilla* (1954), is more than half a century old, and the other, *Lost in Translation* (2003), is a recent box-office hit.

While utterly different, each of these films offers viewers a solid sense of place. Miniature sets may have stood in for downtown in *Godzilla*'s Tokyo, but landmarks of commerce and government are easily recognizable, especially as they succumb to the monster's mega-reptilian wrath. *Lost in Translation* adopted Tokyo's popular business and pleasure quarters as laboratories for Westerners to experience sensory overload, Japanese style. While part of the thrill for *Godzilla*'s audiences was to point out well-known neighborhoods, no one watching *Lost in Translation* could avoid a feeling of anomie, that distinctively contemporary urban panic associated with the loss of comforting social conventions that was famously captured in Edvard Munch's renowned early modernist painting *The Scream*.

Why does Tokyo frighten us? The scale alone is alarming: Some 30 million people – roughly a quarter of Japan's population – call the greater metropolitan area spreading from Tokyo Bay across the Great Kanto Plain home. This mass of civilization finds its way to work and play amid a tangle of streets notorious for lacking reliable house numbers, and seems not to mind that another seismic disaster on the scale of the Great Kanto earthquake that leveled the city in 1923 may be on its way. Everything about Japan seems ultra-foreign to American and European movie fans – the language, the history, and the

Charlotte (Scarlett Johansson) feels *Lost in Translation* amidst the chaos of the teeming metropolis.

society notorious for its strict schools and unforgiving corporate culture. Add to that Japan's role in major wars against the U.S. and Europe, and rightly or not, Tokyo makes for a credible backdrop for strangeness and alienation, especially from our xenophobic Western perspective.

Locations aside, Japan and Tokyo in particular occupy an important place in the history of film. Directors such as Eizo

Tokyo is a city of hustle and bustle, twenty-four hours a day.

Tanaka, Kensaku Suzuki, and Daisuke Ito introduced *auteur* films as an alternative to traditional dramas in the twenties and thirties, beginning the transformation of Japanese cinema from an insular industry producing period dramas, or *jidaigeki*, to an international force. Although many studios reopened in the ancient capital of Kyoto after the 1923 quake, some filmmakers found they simply could not reproduce Tokyo's daily life on sets well enough for the popular modern dramas known as *gendai-geki*, their bread and butter. European art cinema, particularly German Expressionist and French influences, found a way into Japanese culture in this time of dissatisfaction and upheaval. Censors were not happy with all of the developments, such as the social critique embedded in Kenji Mizoguchi's "tendency" films for Mukojima Studios from the 1930s forward. But new perspectives were here to stay.

War provided another hiatus, with fascist films stealing the limelight until the late forties. Legendary director Akira Kurosawa is credited with jump-starting modern Japanese cinema with *Rashomon* (1950), an action-packed epic that would win the Golden Lion in Venice the following year. It was Yasujiro Ozu of Shochiku Films who kept Tokyo before the camera, both before and after World War II, transforming the city into an allegorical backdrop for family-oriented dramas such as *The Only Son*

(1936) and *Tokyo Story* (1953); also *Late Spring* (1949) and his last film, *An Autumn Afternoon* (1962). These films may mostly be unknown to Western moviegoers. Still, the gap between East and West is slowly closing as Western filmmakers have become fascinated with the East and Eastern directors have searched out fresh impulses in the West. Movies from directors such as Nagisa Oshima (*A Secret Post-Tokyo War Story*, 1970), the late Juzo Itami (*Tampopo*, 1985), and Shohei Imamura (*Black Rain*, 1989) helped to open Japanese film to outside influences, encouraging the international dialogue pursued by directors like comedian Takeshi Kitano (*Violent Cop*, 1989) and animation master Hayao Miyazaki (*Spirited Away*, 2001) today. Miyazaki's enchanting films – such as his fantastical *Howl's Moving Castle* (2004) – have established Japanese *animé* movies in the international mainstream and in the hearts of millions of children.

Above: **Tokyo may be a modern metropolis, but it still holds tradition in high regard – as seen in this wedding ceremony at one of the city's numerous temples.**

Left: **Japanese *animé* movies have won a large following outside Japan. Hayao Miyazaki's delightful feature film *Spirited Away* about a daring little girl won Best Animated Feature at the Oscars in 2003, and was followed up by *Howl's Moving Castle*, nominated for an Academy Award in 2006.**

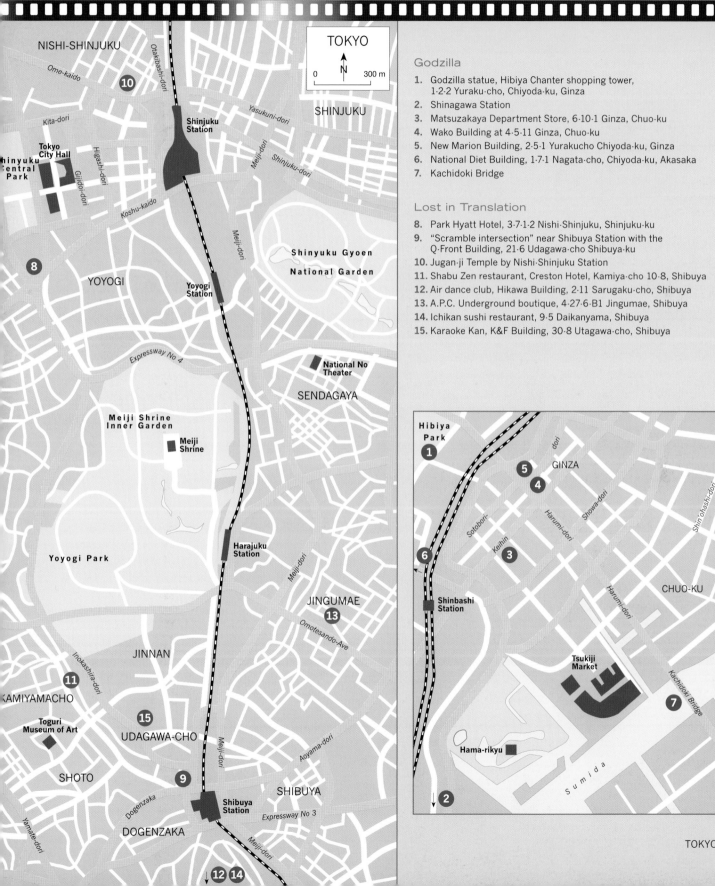

Godzilla

1. Godzilla statue, Hibiya Chanter shopping tower, 1-2-2 Yuraku-cho, Chiyoda-ku, Ginza
2. Shinagawa Station
3. Matsuzakaya Department Store, 6-10-1 Ginza, Chuo-ku
4. Wako Building at 4-5-11 Ginza, Chuo-ku
5. New Marion Building, 2-5-1 Yurakucho Chiyoda-ku, Ginza
6. National Diet Building, 1-7-1 Nagata-cho, Chiyoda-ku, Akasaka
7. Kachidoki Bridge

Lost in Translation

8. Park Hyatt Hotel, 3-7-1-2 Nishi-Shinjuku, Shinjuku-ku
9. "Scramble intersection" near Shibuya Station with the Q-Front Building, 21-6 Udagawa-cho Shibuya-ku
10. Jugan-ji Temple by Nishi-Shinjuku Station
11. Shabu Zen restaurant, Creston Hotel, Kamiya-cho 10-8, Shibuya
12. Air dance club, Hikawa Building, 2-11 Sarugaku-cho, Shibuya
13. A.P.C. Underground boutique, 4-27-6-B1 Jingumae, Shibuya
14. Ichikan sushi restaurant, 9-5 Daikanyama, Shibuya
15. Karaoke Kan, K&F Building, 30-8 Utagawa-cho, Shibuya

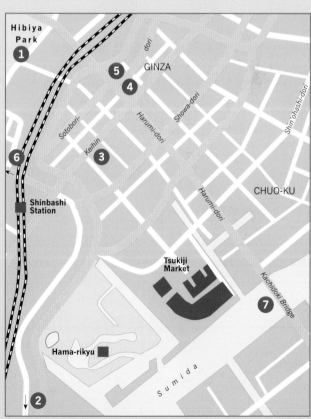

GODZILLA

Gojira

Director	Ishiro Honda
Starring	Momoko Kochi, Akihiko Hirata, Akira Takarada, Takashi Shimura
Japan, 1954	

onsters have captured the imagination of millions of moviegoers ever since *King Kong* lived up to its tagline as "the most awesome thriller of all time" in 1933. But could any of these behemoth baddies boast a social conscience on top of gnashing teeth and fiery breath? The great lizard from beneath Tokyo Bay could: *Gojira*, or *Godzilla*, as the film became known internationally, is a tale told nine years after the U.S. dropped the atomic bomb on Hiroshima and Nagasaki. This was also the year of the *Fukuryu Maru* disaster, in which the crew of a fishing boat was irradiated during America's Castle Bravo nuclear test on Bikini Atoll. With the horror of nuclear holocaust hanging in the air, producer Tomoyuki Tanaka seized the opportunity to make a political statement for peace hauntingly shot in black and white, and using miniature sets of several real locations in Tokyo.

Protégé of film legend Akira Kurosawa, director Ishiro Honda of Toho Films and co-writer Takeo Murata took Tanaka's idea and added to it an adaptation of the plot of sci-fi master Ray Harryhausen's successful *dai kaiju*, or "big monster" flick, *The Beast From 20,000 Fathoms* (1953). The love triangle between a dutiful daughter, a navy man, and a mad scientist humanized a problem that was larger than life. The 165-foot (fifty-meter) monster was a fitting allegory for nuclear holocaust, a topic so large and so horrible that it was taboo to speak of it. Honda also added a playful touch: Godzilla was the nickname given to one of Toho's overweight employees, a play on the Japanese words for gorilla and whale.

Godzilla served as a symbol for the horrors of nuclear holocaust.

Forget the U.S. version released in 1956 as *Godzilla, King of the Monsters,* featuring added scenes shot with a pre-Perry Mason Raymond Burr as narrator and boy reporter. Nothing beats the original with subtitles for the full impact of the Japanese perspective. The story opens with fear: The radio news reports that sailors by Odo Island are dying of radiation sickness. Panic grips Tokyo. Researchers rush to the Pacific isle and discover gigantic, reptilian footprints on the beach that are emitting radiation. Could it be the mythological creature Godzilla, a dinosaur-like lizard awakened from a deep, submarine sleep? Islanders flee in alarm as Big G lays waste to Odo. Paleontologist Dr. Yamane (Takashi Shimura) speculates that nuclear testing has caused a normal reptile to morph into a skyscraping beast. Even worse, the tiny island does not seem to have been enough to slake the monster's thirst for destruction – Godzilla is headed for Tokyo, the megalopolis home to millions.

The damage inflicted on recognizable scale models of real buildings made Godzilla's fifteen-minute rampage through the streets of Tokyo especially memorable. Today these locations are revered tourist sites, memorialized by a statue of *Gojira* himself located in **Ginza** in front of the **Hibiya Chanter** shopping tower at **1-2-2 Yuraku-cho, Chiyoda-ku.** Godzilla's first feat as he emerges from Tokyo Bay is to demolish a train near **Shinagawa Station,** one of Japan's oldest railway stations, opened in 1872

The Wako Building (left) and the National Diet Building (right, below the plane) are two of Tokyo's famous landmarks that fall victim to Godzilla's rage.

just south of the city. Successfully negotiating the electrified wire trap set for him by the Self-Defense Forces, Godzilla stomps into downtown, as freshly invigorated by the 100,000 volts as from a rush of adrenaline.

After crushing the **Matsuzakaya Department Store** at **6-10-1 Ginza, Chuo-ku** in the shoppy Ginza district, Godzilla bites off the bell tower of the **Wako Building** at **4-5-11 Ginza, Chuo-ku**, a beacon of Tokyo's postwar commercial boom on a major intersection with Harumi-dori. The symbolic value would not have been lost on Japanese viewers. His last stop in Ginza is the **New Marion Building (2-5-1 Yurakucho Chiyoda-ku)**. In the Akasaka district, the stately, temple-fronted **National Diet Building,** seat of the country's political power at **1-7-1 Nagata-cho, Chiyoda-ku,** suffers a similar fate before the monster takes out the **Kachidoki Bridge** on the Sumida River on its way back to the sea. Hard to believe that the special effects run by Eiji Tsuburaya depended on a man in a lizard suit: Godzilla was in fact an actor by the name of Ryosaku Takasugi dressed in an extremely heavy latex suit tromping amidst a Tokyo of ten-foot (three-meter) high skyscrapers recreated in perfect miniature detail, a thrill to viewers who lived or worked in monster-ravaged areas.

The future of Tokyo and perhaps all Japan hinges on a desperate appeal by Dr. Yamane's daughter, Emiko (Momoko Kochi), to her fiancé, the eccentric Dr. Daisuke Serizawa (Akihiko Hirata). She begs him to employ his controversial invention, the "oxygen destroyer," a device he reluctantly demonstrates in an aquarium to the rue of several pet fish. Navy frogman Hideto Ogata (Akira Takarada) falls in love with Emiko and tries hard to keep his paws off the prof's lovely daughter while hoping he can save the day. Who will get the girl? How will Godzilla be stopped?

The political statement regarding the evils of nuclear war was lost on most non-Japanese viewers, who were too mesmerized by Godzilla's might to notice. In the twenty years following the original film, fifteen more Godzilla flicks were made with co-monsters Mothra, Gigan, Megalon, and many

GODZILLA

On the set of Roland Emmerich's 1998 adaptation of *Godzilla:* As in the Japanese classic, scale models of the city play an important role in this disaster flick that showcases the destruction of New York City.

more, known to aficionados as the "first series" films. Storylines would far exceed the original Godzilla in outlandishness. In *Destroy All Monsters* (1969), the final film in this "Shiwa series," several major metropolises become imperiled: Moscow meets the wrath of Rodan, Beijing succumbs to Mothra's offspring, Godzilla takes on New York City, and Gorosaurus goes after Paris. Why? Because aliens had seized control of the monsters and ordered the destruction of the planet, much to the consternation of the U.N. The second series took off in 1985, with seven more films culminating in *Godzilla vs. Destroyer* in 1995. Special effects master Roland Emmerich's 1998 adaptation of the original movie inaugurated a third period, this time showcasing the destruction of New York City – a topic he'd revisit in his disaster flick *The Day After Tomorrow* (2004). None of these could compare, however, with the 1954 original, the second most successful Japanese film of all time next to Kurosawa's *The Seven Samurai*, released the same year.

LOST IN TRANSLATION

Director   Sofia Coppola

Starring   Bill Murray, Scarlett Johansson,
                 Giovanni Ribisi, Anna Faris, Takashi Fujii

USA, 2003

Bill Murray might have nabbed the Oscar for Best Actor for his performance in this film had Sean Penn not wowed judges with *Mystic River* the same season. And while there's no use in crying over spilt milk, many a Murray fan shed a tear for the comeback that was almost all-inclusive. His subsequent films – like *The Life Aquatic with Steve Zissou* (2004) and *Broken Flowers* (2005) – show his dry humor as a logical extension of the oddball antics he made famous in the 1970s on television's *Saturday Night Live* and with the golf goofiness of *Caddyshack* (1980). More recent comedies *Groundhog Day* (1993), *Rushmore* (1998), and *The Royal Tenenbaums* (2001), demonstrated that Murray has staying power, and that the Chicago native's comic talent strikes a universal chord.

Bob in the Diplomatic Suite at the Park Hyatt: He's in town to film a commercial for Suntory whisky, pocket a cool $2 million, and have a midlife crisis.

And while being the funny man has been his stock in trade for decades, *Lost in Translation* proves what critics have often surmised: that Murray is also a superb dramatic actor. With this in mind, Sofia Coppola's sophomore feature film after *The Virgin Suicides* (1999) made casting Murray in the lead role a prerequisite. The budding director and daughter of directing legend Francis Ford Coppola built the script around the comedian's melancholic persona juxtaposed with the neon-lit otherworldliness of Tokyo, a megalopolis that offers two touchingly despondent characters the connection of a lifetime.

Has-been movie star Bob Harris (Bill Murray) expects little of Japan's teeming capital when he arrives at the futuristic **Park Hyatt Hotel** atop a swank office building at **3-7-1-2 Nishi-Shinjuku:** His plan is to film a commercial for Suntory whisky, pocket a cool $2 million, and fly back to his wife and kids in L.A. Also staying at the Hyatt is Charlotte (Scarlett Johansson), a twenty-five-year-old Yale grad tagging along with her photographer husband, played by Giovanni Ribisi. When Bob and Charlotte meet by chance in the panoramic **New York Bar** on the **52nd floor,** their parallel crises intersect: Charlotte's paparazzo is too self-absorbed to pay her the attention she needs. Bob's twenty-five-year marriage, like his career, is on a downhill slide.

Lonely hearts' club: Charlotte (Scarlett Johansson) and Bob pass the time at the New York Bar on the fifty-second floor of the Park Hyatt.

Between the rooftop pool, crowded elevators, and dramatically lit corridors, the despondent denizens of two completely different phases of life take comfort in one another's company. Coppola casts Bob's and Charlotte's separate guest rooms at the Park Hyatt as disparate worlds, even though both spaces belong to the **Diplomatic Suite** – the bedroom and dining room, respectively. When Charlotte ventures out of the hotel alone, the city provides a convincing backdrop of loneliness and

A tiff and new culinary horizons at Shabu Zen restaurant.

alienation. She braves the rain under a translucent umbrella to take in the Times Square ambience of the famous **"scramble intersection"** by **Shibuya Station,** but even the animated dinosaur loping across the **Q-Front Building's multistory LCD screen (21-6 Udagawa-cho Shibuya-ku)** seems a bit forlorn.

The story offers many parallels to the director's life. Sofia Coppola visited Tokyo repeatedly to promote her designer clothing line in the 1990s, and develops Charlotte as a kindred spirit in the quest for the meaning of life. Charlotte visits holy places on her own – the **Jugan-ji Temple** by Nishi-Shinjuku Station near the Park Hyatt, and the Heian Shrine and Nanzenji Temple in Kyoto – but finds no consolation. It is amid the urban hubbub of Tokyo's entertainment districts, Shinjuku and Shi-

buya, that Charlotte's world sidles up to Bob's, and a few truths about life emerge despite the chaos around them.

Together they set out on a metaphorical odyssey through the bewildering jungle of Japanese nightlife, from the **Shabu Zen restaurant** in the **Creston Hotel (Kamiya-cho 10-8, Shibuya),** the dance club **Air** in the **Hikawa Building, 2-11 Sarugaku-cho,** where filmed fireworks illuminate the interior, to the fictitious strip joint filmed in the high-end couture shop **A.P.C. Underground, 4-27-6-B1 Jingumae.** At sushi bar **Ichikan, 9-5 Daikanyama,** Charlotte reveals a horribly blackened toe, and Bob unmasks the empathy he feels for a young woman stumbling through the first phases of her adult life. When Murray serenades her with Roxy Music's haunting 1982 hit "More Than This" at **Karaoke Kan,** in the **K&F Building, 30-8 Utagawa-cho,** the film's message begins to come to light: When life seems like a labyrinth full of dead ends, one meaningful connection with another person can help you find the way out.

Bob tucks Charlotte into her bed after the night on the town, and just as viewers are wondering whether romance will finally blossom, it becomes obvious that it doesn't have to. Delivered deadpan, Bob's observations on life and love are something Charlotte intuitively understands. If Murray's looks were less meaningful, the connection between Bob and Charlotte could have been seen as intergenerational camaraderie instead of the love affair the critics were hoping for.

No ordinary romance: What does the future hold for Charlotte and Bob?

VENICE

Venice is rarely seen in all of its splendor in the movies. Instead, characters tend to lose themselves between its crumbling buildings and brackish canals.

UNDER THE SPELL OF A SINKING CITY

If Venice's past were anything but long and illustrious, you could almost imagine the city as a crazy project dreamed up by a megalomaniac set designer. Constructed atop long wooden piles sunk into the lagoon, the former maritime power on the Adriatic rises improbably from the waves like a fata morgana. The urban wonder built on 116 islands is like no other city in the world. There are no cars, and canals take the place of roads. In between the ubiquitous waterways, a maze of tiny alleys and bridges and the miniature vistas of little *campi* and *piazzette* reveal Venice's true treasure, the well-proportioned palaces and churches that make up La Serenissima's architectural majesty.

Although Venice wears its epithet proudly, audiences rarely see the city depicted as a place of serenity and romance on the silver screen. The charming musical feature film *Everyone Says I Love You* (1996) is one notable exception: Woody Allen falls head over heels in love with Julia Roberts before the radiant backdrop of Venice, following her across the picturesque bridges and cobblestone alleyways on a quest to win her heart. Decades before, a schoolmarmish Katharine Hepburn succumbed to the charms of Venice and handsome hunk Rossano Brazzi in David Lean's nearly forgotten classic *Summertime* (1955). Brimming with outlandish architectural detail, thanks to Byzantine influences, the venerable city serves as an exotic setting for period pieces such as Fellini's *Casanova* (1976) and adventure flicks like Spielberg's *Indiana Jones and the Last Crusade* (1989) as well.

But it's the dark side of Venice that most directors seek to capture when filming here – the eerie magnetism of a crumbling city that is slowly and irrevocably succumbing to the sea. Many of the greatest Venice movies are based on the novels and short stories of famous authors who were fascinated with the city's perpetual state of decay. In Thomas Mann's *Death in Venice* (filmed in 1971), Daphne du Maurier's *Don't Look Now* (1973), Ian McEwan's *The Comfort of Strangers* (1990), and Henry James's *The Wings of the Dove* (1997), Venice is portrayed as a languishing beauty who casts her spells in rotting doorways and damp salons upon denizens and expatriates alike. The labyrinth of winding alleys and canals serves as a metaphor for human trials and tribulations or the twisted pathways of the mind. Death seems always to linger around the next bend. Strangers are the most likely to fall under the sway of Venice, a fact that is based in reality. Locals have been moving out of the city for decades, leaving only some 64,000 real Venetians to deal with the annual deluge of 15 million tourists.

Cinema is part of what keeps the dying city alive. Along with the carnival celebrations, one of Venice's main attractions is the Mostra Internazionale d'Arte Cinematografica film festival. Initially staged in 1932 on the terrace of the Hotel Excelsior on the barrier island known as the Lido, the gathering was originally meant to be a sideshow, a publicity event to boost the Biennale art expo. Organizers were thrilled with its unexpected success and established the film expo as a juried independent festival four years later. The Mostra has always been more attuned to political and cultural change than other big-name film festivals, making it one of the world's most lively and respected international cinematic competitions. Venice made headlines recently with the news that there is only one movie theater left in the lagoon city, the Giorgione. Given its cultural significance as the festival host, Venice faces a paradoxical situation with the demise of cinema in a city that in the sixties boasted twenty movie theaters. The extinction of movie houses in Venice is yet another sign of the inexorable decline of a great city. And yet after so many centuries of surviving despite numerous prophecies of doom, Venice refuses to give up. Filmmakers are still enraptured by its unequalled charm, returning time and again to film on location. They seem undaunted by the challenges involved even though the hurdles are significant, to say the least. Shooting a movie here means battling not only the hordes of tourists, but the authorities as well – a delicate situation since it is their official sanction that is required to film in the historic palaces.

The greatest challenge of all, however, is the water. Boats are needed to transport crew, actors, and equipment – a logistical nightmare compounded by the notorious vagaries of Venice's weather. Starting in November and extending through spring, the *acqua alta* regularly floods city squares with a foot or more of the lagoon's brackish water. No wonder that one of the latest major film productions in Venice, Shakespeare's *The Merchant of Venice* (2004), starring Al Pacino, Jeremy Irons, and Joseph Fiennes, relied on sets for many of its interior shots. And yet key scenes were still shot in Venice. Thanks to the clout of the star-studded cast, filmmakers were able to gain permission to shoot inside the Doge's Palace, one of the most important buildings in the city and a highlight of St. Mark's Square. *Merchant* was followed up by Lasse Hallström's Venetian love story *Casanova* (2005) starring *Brokeback Mountain* (2005) heartthrob Heath Ledger, also filmed on location in the lagoon city.

Shakespeare's *Merchant of Venice* with Al Pacino as Shylock, set in 16th-century Venice, was shot on location.

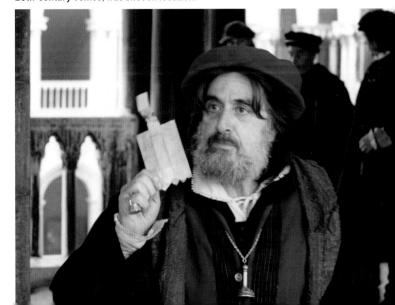

Summertime

1. Santa Lucia train station
2. Pensione Accademia, Fondamenta Bollani, Dorsoduro 1058
3. Gran Caffè Chioggia, Piazzetta San Marco
4. Antiques shop, Campo San Barnaba
5. Canal San Barnaba
6. The island of Burano

Death in Venice

7. Lido
8. Hotel des Bains, Lungomare Marconi 17
9. Alleyways of the San Marco quarter around La Fenice opera house

Don't Look Now

10. Church of San Nicolò dei Mendicoli, Dorsoduro
11. Ristorante Roma, close to the train station on the Grand Canal by Ponte Scalzi
12. Hotel La Fenice et des Artistes, San Marco 1936
13. Hotel Gabrielli Sandwirth, Riva degli Schiavoni 4110
14. Hotel Bauer (formerly the Bauer-Grünwald), Campo San Moisè
15. Palazzo Grimani

The Wings of the Dove

16. Basilica di San Marco
17. Santa Maria della Salute
18. Caffè Florian, St. Mark's Square
19. Cemetery island of San Michele
20. Palazzo Barbaro

Bread and Tulips

21. St. Mark's Square
22. Flower shop, Piazza Chiesa dei Miracoli, Cannaregio
23. Campo Due Pozzi
24. Fernando's apartment building, Campazzo San Sebastian, Santa Croce

The talented Tom Ripley (Matt Damon) enjoying the good life in Venice.

LIDO DI VENEZIA

7

Gran Viale S. M. Elisabetta

Via Sandro Gallo

Lung. G. Marconi

8

0   400 m

6

S. MICHELE

19

Canale delle Navi

Fond. della Sensa

Fond. degli Ormesini

Fond. dei Mori

Campo Madonna dell'Orto

Fond. della Misericordia

CANNAREGIO

Rio Terrà n Leonardo

Sal. Specchieri

Campo S. Stae

C. Larga

C. Tintor

Campo San Cassiano

Campo San Cassiano

Campiello

Campo Pescaria

Campo SS. Apostoli

Fond. Mendicanti

Fond. Mendicanti Nuove

S. POLO

Campo Giacomo dell'Orio

Campo S. Giacomo di Rialto

Campo S. Polo

22

Campo SS. Giovanni e Paolo

po Frari

Canal Grande

Fond. del Vin

Fond. del Carbon

Campo S. Salvator

Campo S. Lorenzo

Fond. di S. Lorenzo

Campo Confraternita

Sal. S. Giustina

15

Campo Manin

S. MARCO

Campo S. Angelo

9

12

Campo Francesco Morosini

Campo S. Zaccaria

13

Campo Bandiera e Moro

23

16

21

Piazza San Marco

18   3

Viale 22 Marzo

Molo

14

Riva   degli

Schiavoni

Riva Ca' di Dio

Fond. dell'Arsenale

CASTELLO

ISOLA DI S. PIETRO

20

17

Canal Grande

Fond. Bragadin

Fond. Ca' Bala

Fond. Zattere ai Saloni

DORSODURO

Canale di S. Marco

Riva dei Sette Martiri

Via Garibaldi

Viale Garibaldi

Fond. S. Giuseppe

Giardini Pubblici

Viale Trento

ISOLA DI S. ELENA

Viale 24 Maggio

Lido

ISOLA DI S. GIORGIO MAGGIORE

Fond. S. Giovanni

Fond. d. Zitelle

Fond. S. Giacomo

Campo Redentore

Calle dello Squero

Parco della Rimembranze

Campo Sportivo

Viale 4 Novembre

Viale Vittorio Veneto

Viale Piave

SUMMERTIME

Director	David Lean
Starring	Katharine Hepburn, Rossano Brazzi, Isa Miranda, Jane Rose, MacDonald Parke, Gaetano Autiero

UK/USA, 1955

Venice has rarely looked more radiant than in this all-but-forgotten flick starring the great Katharine Hepburn as a spinsterish secretary who fulfils her lifelong dream of traveling to Venice, where she meets the love of her life. The story is set in the mid-fifties, and the film paints an affectionate and at times ironic portrait of Americans touring Europe. Jane Hudson (Katharine Hepburn) clearly loves the city bathed in a golden light, and grows more enraptured with each new palace, church, canal, and tiny alleyway she sees. She pulls out her Super 8 camera on the *vaporetto* water bus en route from the brand-new **Stazione Ferroviaria Santa Lucia** train station to the Accademia, eager to capture every picturesque detail. The McIlhennys, a retired American couple she meets on the boat, are rather less inspired, dismissing Venice as an amusement park built on the water.

The travelers meet again at the **Pensione Fiorini,** a little auberge that welcomes visitors to Venice and serves as the meeting place for a handful of American tourists. In the quiet Dorsoduro quarter across from the San Marco quarter and St. Mark's Square, the 17th-century palazzo of Villa Maravege, or the "villa of wonders," houses two dozen rooms and still welcomes guests today as the **Pensione Accademia** at **Dorsoduro 1058** on **Fondamenta Bollani.** Just as in the movie, the leafy, flower-edged terrace with its views of a minor canal is a favorite place for guests to linger and daydream about exploring the city. It is here that Jane spends her first afternoon, happy finally to have arrived in Venice but lonely, too, as she watches all the other guests set out in pairs, leaving her all by herself.

But the city lovingly nicknamed *La Serenissima* beckons, and Jane finally marches off to see its fabled monuments on her own. She follows the chiming of the cathedral bells through the narrow alleys to **Piazza San Marco,** Venice's bustling center, and watches the people parading by from an outdoor table at the **Gran Caffè Chioggia** on the narrow part of St. Mark's Square, the **Piazzetta San Marco** just opposite the Doge's Palace. When she notices that a handsome man is watching her from the next table, she gets nervous and leaves in a rush. Rossano Brazzi's performance as Renato de Rossi in this silent scene is brilliant, especially his memorable grand entrance.

Jane (Katharine Hepburn) falls in love with Italian heartthrob Renato (Rossano Brazzi) when she spends the best week of her life in Venice. She stays at the Pensione Fiorini, the real-life Pensione Accademia.

Fate sees to it that Jane and Renato meet again as she examines a glass goblet in his **antiques shop** on **Campo San Barnaba,** the little square right next to the temple-fronted church of San Barnaba that featured in *Indiana Jones and the Last Crusade* (1989). Jane tries to stay cool and reserved, but who can resist Italian charm for long? On the next day she returns with her guide, Mauro (Gaetano Autiero), so that she can at least snap a picture of Renato's shop with her camera – and promptly falls backwards into the murky green waters of **Canal San Barnaba.** Now that she is quite literally head over heels in love, a passionate romance develops between the two. Jane and Renato enjoy carefree days of wandering through the city, meeting in St. Mark's Square in the evenings, and taking day trips to the island of **Burano** by motorboat. Jane's camera and guidebook have long been forgotten, but alas, such happiness is not meant to last. The vacation is slowly but surely drawing to an end, and the besotted American is forced to choose between her head and her heart.

Jane has the clever little tour guide Mauro (Gaetano Autiero) show her around town. On one of her excursions she discovers Renato's antiques shop, right by the bridge on the Rio di San Barnaba next to the church of the same name.

British director David Lean managed to win one of Hollywood's leading ladies for the role of Jane Hudson, a performance that garnered Katharine Hepburn an Oscar nomination. But for him Venice, too, played a lead role in the film. Aided by director of photography Jack Hildyard, he captured the magic of the lagoon city in rich Technicolor images. For all its beauty, the movie encountered bad press even before it hit the theaters, albeit undeserved. The story based on Arthur Laurents's play *The Time of the Cuckoo* was rumored to have been about an illicit love affair between a single American woman and a married Italian man, a scandalous topic in an era when the adulterous affair between the director Roberto Rossellini and actress Ingrid Bergman had incited immense public outrage in the United States.

The Venetians were more concerned that filming might disrupt tourism. Only a generous donation toward the restoration of St. Mark's cathedral and a promise to the cardinal that Hepburn would always cover her arms and legs while filming near the church could calm the troubled waters. Lean filmed on location for the first time with *Summertime*, a small film that would pave the way for major motion pictures that he would shoot in more exotic locales. Lean went to Ceylon, today's Sri Lanka, to film *The Bridge on the River Kwai* (1957), where 500 men and 35 elephants worked for eight months on a set built to look like the eponymous bridge. The director scoured the deserts of Jordan and Morocco for *Lawrence of Arabia* (1962), and the icy plains of Finland for the epic *Doctor Zhivago* (1965).

DEATH IN VENICE

Morte a Venezia

Director	Luchino Visconti
Starring	Dirk Bogarde, Björn Andresen, Silvana Mangano, Romolo Valli, Mark Burns

Italy / France, 1971

Even today, visitors associate the **Lido** with Luchino Visconti's dark masterpiece *Death in Venice*. The seaside resort situated on a slim strip of barrier island between Venice and the Adriatic Sea is no longer quite the fashionable getaway it once was, despite the best efforts of a handful of grand hotels to preserve its fin-de-siècle glamor. Still, the Lido offers something not found in Venice: an atmosphere of calm and gentility miles from the lively bustle of the lagoon city.

Only during the annual film festival and the summer holidays when tourists descend upon the isle looking for *gelato* and a stretch of sand in the sun does the Lido come to life. Not since the early 13th century has business been so good: Back then, some 30,000 Christians crowded the beaches begging the enterprising Venetians to build them ships so they could set sail for the Holy Land on the fourth crusade. After that, tranquility returned, allowing the few hundred inhabitants, mostly farmers and fishermen, to live in peace. Poets found the island's seclusion hard to resist. Both Goethe and Lord Byron are said to have wandered the lonely dunes, and Thomas Mann (1875-1955) as well. His novella *Death in Venice* serves as the basis of Visconti's screenplay.

When the author from Lübeck, Germany, traveled to Venice with his wife, Katia, in the summer of 1911, a seaside getaway for the rich and beautiful was already blossoming on the Lido. A shrewd businessman had conceived the idea of transforming the island into a summer paradise by building luxurious hotels and had made it a reality only a few years earlier. The **Hotel des Bains** at **Lungomare Marconi 17**, offering elegant and opulent

Aschenbach (Dirk Bogarde) shivers in his deck chair as he sails into Venice.

lodgings in the style of the Belle Epoque, opened its doors in 1905. Wealthy families flocked to its salons and beachfront cabanas from all over Europe, arriving with entire entourages to spend the summer enjoying the pleasant climate. During his stay, Mann met Wladyslaw Moes, a young Polish nobleman who was vacationing at the hotel with his parents and siblings. The author, who had repressed his homoerotic tendencies his entire life, was enthralled with the boy, and began writing the novella that would cause an immense uproar upon its publication in 1912. The public was shocked: The revered author of the suc-

On the beach at the Hotel des Bains: Gustav von Aschenbach can't take his eyes off young Tadzio (Björn Andresen) and is fascinated by the boy's beauty and innocence. The traditional bathing cabins, or *capanne*, are still there today.

cessful novel *Buddenbrooks* had chosen to write about a taboo topic – the (platonic) love of a man for a youth.

Visconti first met Thomas Mann in the early fifties and became closely acquainted with him. The director had already proven his talent for adapting important literary works to the silver screen with *The Leopard* (*Il Gattopardo*, 1963) and *The Stranger* (*Lo Straniero*, 1967). He and his film crew occupied the Hotel des Bains for six months in 1970, reviving all of its former glory as the epicenter of Mann's story. Visconti took pains to cast the right actors in the main roles. He chose the revered British character actor Dirk Bogarde to play the burned-out composer Gustav von Aschenbach, a man who had subjected himself to rigorous self-discipline all his life only to succumb to a new and thrilling passion. Visconti scoured Europe and held countless auditions to find the boy Aschenbach finds so spellbinding. He finally cast the bewitchingly handsome fifteen-year-old Björn Andresen as Tadzio in Stockholm.

Thomas Mann had called Venice "the most improbable city in the world," a place that should "be approached only from the high seas by ship" since "arriving in Venice from the mainland was like entering a palace through the back door." True to the novel, Aschenbach (Bogarde) travels by steamer to Venice with the intention of getting some much-needed rest. From the deck he watches the **Campanile** and the dome of the plague church **Santa Maria della Salute** emerging from the morning mist. As soon as he disembarks, things start to go wrong: A painted-up old dandy mercilessly pokes fun at him, and a shady gondolier ignores his plaintive requests to be rowed to the *vaporetto* boat station by the Doge's Palace, taking him straight across to the Lido instead.

After his unsettling arrival, Aschenbach's **Room 308** at the Hotel des Bains – with views of the Adriatic and the beach – is a peaceful refuge. In the evening, guests descend to the busy **hotel lobby** to listen to chamber music and wait for dinner to be served in the formal dining room. In the lobby, Aschenbach spies Tadzio for the very first time and is dumbstruck. The aging composer can't keep from staring at the mysteriously beautiful youth who is spending his holidays at the hotel with his sisters, his governess and his mother, a Polish countess. The next day at the **beach** Aschenbach watches him from his beach chair – the long rows of old-fashioned bathing cabanas, or *capanne*, have been preserved virtually unchanged until today.

Aschenbach's fascination with the boy turns into an obsession just as the muggy climate and sirocco winds begin to disagree with his health. Hastily he decides to leave Venice. But when he discovers that his luggage is registered incorrectly at the train station – a scene filmed not at Venice's Santa Lucia station, but at the Cinecittà studios in Rome instead – Aschenbach makes up his mind to stay after all, resigning himself to his fate in a calm, almost cheerful manner. Neither the rumors of cholera circulating in Venice nor the city's bizarre attempts to cover it up can sway him from his decision. On his quest to follow Tadzio and his family, the sweat-drenched composer stumbles through the winding **alleys of the San Marco quarter** by **La Fenice opera house** where the stench of carbolic smoke meant to drive away the epidemic hangs in the air. Tension mounts as the distraught composer starts to lose his grip on reality.

Aschenbach is trapped, overwhelmed by his feelings for Tadzio and held hostage by the smoldering beauty of a city touched by death. The story develops slowly and inevitably, with Visconti's use of dreamlike images and long shots evoking an increasingly menacing atmosphere. The tender tones of Gustav Mahler's Third and Fifth symphonies provide the perfect musical background for the film, not least because Thomas Mann, moved by reports of the dying composer, had created his hero with some of Mahler's passionate, repressive traits.

Little has changed at the Des Bains. Director Luchino Visconti discusses a scene with Dirk Bogarde in the hotel's elegant restaurant.

DON'T LOOK NOW

Director   Nicolas Roeg

Starring   Donald Sutherland, Julie Christie, Hilary Mason, Clelia Matania, Massimo Serato

Italy / UK, 1973

The works of the English novelist Daphne du Maurier were no stranger to the silver screen when director Nicolas Roeg filmed her short story *Don't Look Now* on location in Venice in the early seventies. Her suspense-filled narratives had already served as the basis for film classics such as Hitchcock's *Rebecca* (1940) and *The Birds* (1963). With well-placed jump cuts, clever montage techniques, and haunting images of the lagoon city, the directorial newcomer was poised to elevate the gloomy, poetic thriller into a classic of its genre. Roeg, a well-known cameraman, deliberately tried to show sides of Venice well beyond St. Mark's Square and outside the tourist season. His efforts paid off: The labyrinths of narrow alleys in various quarters of the city provided just the right setting for this dense, atmospheric thriller.

Laura (Julie Christie) and John Baxter (Donald Sutherland), an English couple whose daughter has recently drowned in their garden pond, retreat to wintry Venice in the hopes of putting the tragedy behind them. The change of scenery and John's job restoring a local church are supposed to provide some diversion from their terrible loss. The church, which was in fact being refurbished at the time of filming, is **San Nicolò dei Mendicoli,** a seventh-century gem tucked away in a remote, working-class neighborhood of Venice near the sprawling naval base in the Dorsoduro quarter. While John sets to work on the mosaics of San Nicolò, one of the city's oldest churches, an eerie series of murders takes place in the foggy, dark city, underscoring the couple's entrenched mood of despair.

Laura (Julie Christie) and John (Donald Sutherland) at the Ristorante Roma on the Grand Canal.

Their shared sense of foreboding grows at the **Ristorante Roma,** close to the train station on the Grand Canal by **Ponte Scalzi,** when they are approached by two elderly Scottish sisters. The blind Heather (Hilary Mason) is a medium, and claims to be in contact with the Baxters' dead daughter. While Laura finds comfort in the idea that her child is safe and well in the afterlife, John rejects the notion as pure hocus-pocus. The desperate hope of learning more leaves Laura no peace, and later she pays the sisters a visit at their boarding house. They implore her to leave Venice with her husband as soon as possible, an unsettling encounter that takes place at the **Hotel**

La Fenice et des Artistes, San Marco 1936, right next to La Fenice opera house. A ghostly silence reigns back at the Baxters' lodging, the fictitious Hotel Europa: Furniture is draped in dust covers for the winter season, and the absence of other guests creates a spooky silence. The peach-colored **Hotel Gabrielli Sandwirth** at **Riva degli Schiavoni 4110** was used for exterior shots, while interior scenes were filmed at the **Hotel Bauer** (long known as the Bauer Grünwald) at **Campo San Moisè.**

Laura leaves Venice in haste, but John stays on only to encounter a series of increasingly mysterious incidents. Scaffolding in San Nicolò inexplicably collapses, and John narrowly dodges a falling beam. A little while later he spots his wife on a boat with the two Scottish women near the Rialto Bridge – even though she is supposed to be back in England. John closes his eyes to all these warning signs, but is unable to ignore the most unsettling vision of them all: his dead daughter flitting through the alleyways of Venice in a red raincoat. When one of the Scottish women describes how much her blind sister

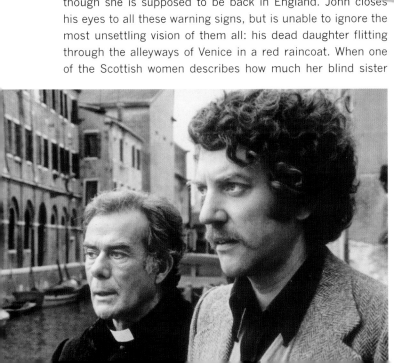

despises Venice as a dead city, John still refuses to take it as a serious warning. "She says it's like a city in aspic, left over from a dinner party and all the guests are dead or gone. It frightens her. Too many shadows." Still, despite the increasingly menacing atmosphere, John cannot resist following the vision of his daughter through the nocturnal city. In a cul-de-sac at the gates of the deserted **Palazzo Grimani** behind Ponte Novo, the movie finds resolution in a fateful encounter and a surprising finale.

John has come to Venice to restore the church of San Nicolò dei Mendicoli (top right). **He ignores the mysterious signs, some of which are life-threatening. Not even the bishop (Massimo Serato) can persuade him to leave town.**

THE WINGS OF THE DOVE

Director	Iain Softley
Starring	Helena Bonham Carter, Linus Roache, Alison Elliott, Alex Jennings, Charlotte Rampling, Elizabeth McGovern

USA/UK, 1997

Millie (Alison Elliott) has no idea that Kate (Helena Bonham Carter) is after her money.

"See Venice and die" could have been the tagline for this opulent period piece. Cinematographer Eduardo Serra captured exhilarating images of the lagoon city, offering a pretty visual paraphrase of Goethe's comment on Naples that reflects the desperate last wishes of the fatally ill American heiress Millie Theale (Alison Elliott), one of the main characters. Director Iain Softley's adaptation of Henry James's eponymous novel offers a Venice where love and death are found in equal measure, and where emotions that had been painstakingly kept in check back in England find unfettered and at times explosive expression. The movie makes such an enduring impression as a "Venice film" that it is easy to overlook the fact that much of it was actually set in London.

Following the death of her mother, Kate Croy (Helena Bonham Carter) moves in with her Aunt Maude (Charlotte Rampling), whose dearest wish is to bring young Kate out into London society and arrange for her marriage to Lord Mark (Alex Jennings), a cynical aristocrat. But Kate is in love with the penniless journalist Merton Densher (Linus Roache). When she befriends the wealthy American Millie Theale and learns that her new acquaintance is dying, she concocts a dastardly plan: to push her lover into the arms of the expiring heiress and wait until he has inherited her fortune. Then the newly wealthy journalist can offer Kate a proposal of marriage befitting her social station. The strategy would have been perfect if Merton, initially reluctant to play along, had not inadvertently fallen for Millie.

Although originally set in 1902, the director decided to push the story forward by ten years. Especially for the London scenes, the small leap in time allowed Softley to place his society characters in an exciting phase of the new century complete with the latest technological developments – cars, telephones, underground trains – elements that depict the British capital as a modern, restless, fast-paced metropolis. When the plot suddenly shifts to continental Europe, the contrast with Venice becomes acute: Here earthy golden hues take the place of cool city blues, and candles and torches underscore exotic scenes with flickering light and dramatic shadow – as when Kate, Merton, and Millie are drawn into nighttime's carnival revelry. These dreamlike sequences in particular showcase the unusual magic of Venice.

Merton, Millie, and Kate on the steps of Santa Maria della Salute.

During their initial days in town, Kate, Merton, and Millie approach the city almost reverently, marveling at the sights in the brilliant daylight. Millie defies her illness and climbs up to the open-air gallery of the **Basilica di San Marco** with the horses of the famous bronze quadriga prancing in the background as Kate and her lover stroll across **St. Mark's Square.** The merry trio stop on the steps of the great domed **Santa Maria della Salute** church for a picnic. But it's not until the friends take a nocturnal gondola ride that Venice draws them in. In one of the movie's most striking scenes, their voices echo from the facades of the houses as the iridescent light of the oil lanterns reflects off the surface of the water, and their gondolas disappear into the closeness of a small canal.

Betrayal and forbidden love put a sudden end to the trio's fun-filled frolic, and Venice changes its mien, suddenly gloomy with rain-filled streets reminiscent of film noir. Jealous Kate returns to London and sends Merton desperate missives imploring him to remain true to their original plan. When Merton spots Lord Mark at **Caffè Florian** on St. Mark's Square, he sus-

pects that the cranky aristocrat is in town to tell Millie the truth about him and Kate. Shortly after the encounter, a visibly shaken Merton carries Millie's coffin to its final resting place among the cypresses of the **cemetery island of San Michele.** With her death, the goal of the conspiracy has been realized. But can Merton really return to Kate after all that has occurred?

A charming counterpoint to the atmospheric outdoor location shots in Venice are the sequences inside Millie's Venetian palazzo. In an unusual coincidence of reality and fiction, Softley's team shot these scenes at **Palazzo Barbaro,** the grand house where Henry James allegedly wrote *The Wings of the Dove* a century earlier, and the model for the fictitious Palazzo Leporelli of his novel. American patroness Isabella Stewart Gardner, who rented the palace repeatedly, encouraged the writer to pitch camp in the library of the Gothic pile close to the Accademia Bridge on the Grand Canal. How fitting that the beautiful palace, a well-known meeting place for American artists and literary figures, would be immortalized in the screen adaptation of the novel which it is reputed to have inspired.

Director Iain Softley (right) **found the perfect setting for the film version of this tragic love triangle in the elegant salons of Palazzo Barbaro on the Grand Canal** (below), **rooms that inspired Henry James to write his novel.**

BREAD AND TULIPS

Pane e tulipani

Director	Silvio Soldini
Starring	Licia Maglietta, Bruno Ganz, Giuseppe Battiston, Antonio Catania, Marina Massironi

Italy / Switzerland, 2000

Only the lucky few find true love in Venice. The mist-filled lagoon famous for eerie carnival masks and centuries of cold-hearted business savvy on the high seas is no fair Verona when it comes to love – and hardly the place that Rosalba, housewife of Pescara, expected to find romance. Ignoring the throngs along the Grand Canal and the social cafés of St. Mark's Square, director Silvio Soldini tells the story of two soul mates who find one another in the quiet alleys, empty *campi,* and uncelebrated waterways of what approving critics term "the real Venice." The effort of filming in the narrow, labyrinthine streets usually jam-packed with tourists paid off handsomely: Soldini and his two leading actors each took home a David di Donatello, the Italian Oscar, and the gratitude of an international audience charmed by the story's disarming sincerity.

No midnight gondola ride, but a chance meeting in a simple restaurant brings Rosalba (Licia Maglietta) and Fernando (Bruno Ganz) together. She, a forty-something mother of two, is wedded to a boorish plumbing supplies salesman named Mimmo (Antonio Catania), who characteristically fails to notice when their bus tour leaves her behind at a gas station. Rosalba hitchhikes to Venice and almost immediately encounters her unlikely suitor. Fernando is a native of Iceland, a grandfather, and a former cruise-line crooner who gave up music when his wife passed away. Both lead characters battle a loneliness that borders on despair, Rosalba in the lap of her ungrateful family and Fernando with no companion at all.

The love affair unfolds slowly. After thumbing a ride to Venice, Rosalba spends her first day in town on a walking tour of the great sights of the city, taking snapshots of **St. Mark's Square** and writing postcards to her family. The next day she makes the acquaintance of a blustery anarchist, Fermo (Felice Andreasi), who offers her a job in his **flower shop** on the square named

Even the tulips hang their heads in sorrow: Fernando (Bruno Ganz) lives a solitary life, but love comes his way when Rosalba moves into his house on Campazzo San Sebastian in the modest Santa Croce quarter (below).

for its church, the famous **Chiesa dei Miracoli** in the Cannaregio district. Fernando puts her up in a spare room in his apartment, and while settling in she meets a new best friend, new-age masseuse Grazia (Marina Massironi). It's as though a new family has assembled itself for Rosalba out of thin air.

She periodically phones home to "extend" her vacation, and yet no one seems to miss her. Hubby Mimmo only really becomes nervous when he runs out of pressed shirts and his mistress refuses to iron them. He sends an enthusiastic job applicant to Venice as a private dick to find his wife. The corpulent would-be detective takes a room on a houseboat, tapes up photos of Rosalba around town, and finally makes contact. Rosalba is lured to the meeting with promises of important news from home, but after a brief encounter on the **Campo Due Pozzi**, a typical residential square between **S. Giorgio degli Schiavoni church** and the gates of the **Arsenale,** she flees, only to be tailed all the way to the flower shop where she works.

The chase continues, leading next to her **apartment building** on **Campazzo San Sebastian** in the working-class quarter of Santa Croce, a neighborhood that had rarely seen tourists

Rosalba (Licia Maglietta) blossoms in Venice.

reality." Not even Rosalba knows for certain what she will do next. As the story draws to a close, the viewer feels certain that whatever she does, she'll never again fail to follow her heart.

Rosalba builds a new life between tiny Campo due Pozzi (left) **and the flower shop next to the Chiesa dei Miracoli, or "church of miracles"** (below).

before the movie's debut. Requests to purchase apartments in the building poured in after the film was released, and it immediately got a much-needed renovation. Hours of walking – and clever film editing – lie between the three points, but for a non-Venetian the sequence appears seamless and perfectly plausible. In her heart of hearts, Rosalba knows that she has been purposefully assembling a new family in Venice to replace her dysfunctional life back home in Pescara. But what about her sons? Torn between concern for her children and affection for Fernando, Rosalba's sudden break with the world she knows seems perfectly underscored by the unlikely backdrop of Venice, a place Soldini called "an ideal set to create distance from

THE THIRD MAN

Director	Carol Reed
Starring	Joseph Cotten, Orson Welles, Alida Valli, Trevor Howard
UK, 1949	

Orson Welles as the ruthless con man Harry Lime.

Vienna as a film location may bring to mind Milos Forman's *Amadeus* (1984), a movie actually filmed in Prague, or the sweet nothings whispered between Ethan Hawke and Julie Delpy in the sugary sweet romance *Before Sunrise* (1995). But no film takes on Vienna quite like *The Third Man* (1949).

Zither master Anton Karas in front of the Ferris wheel where Holly Martins confronts his enigmatic pal Harry Lime.

London Film Productions boss Alexander Korda and his friend at Wien-Film, Karl Hartl, chose Vienna over London for their thriller, filming almost entirely on location under director Carol Reed in the rubble-filled aftermath of World War II. The result is Cold War film noir at its finest, even more iconic now than in 1949 when it won the Golden Palm at the Cannes Film Festival, or the year following when it took an Oscar for cinematography.

Harry Lime (Orson Welles), a kingpin in the postwar penicillin racket, invites an old school friend from the States to work for him in Vienna. Unsuspecting pulp fiction writer Holly Martins (Joseph Cotten) doesn't know that Lime is up to no good. The first thing Martins learns, on the day he arrives, is that his pal has been killed in a car accident and is being lowered into a grave at the **Zentralfriedhof** cemetery. British liaison Major Calloway (Trevor Howard) insists that Harry was a criminal, but Martins won't have it. He starts his own bumbling investigation to clear his friend's name. In the process he naively falls for Lime's girlfriend, Anna Schmidt (Alida Valli), who helps him

The Third Man

1. Zentralfriedhof cemetery on Simmeringer Hauptstrasse, southeast of the old city
2. Harry's apartment, Palais Pallavicini, Josephsplatz 5
3. Doorway at Schreyvogelgasse 8
4. Ferris wheel in the Prater amusement park
5. Mariensäule, Platz am Hof
6. Hotel Sacher, Philharmonikerstrasse 4

Map labels:

VIENNA
0   100 m

Universität · Schottenstift · Maria am Gestade · Salzgries · Schottengasse · Schreyvogelgasse · Scottish Church · Wipplinger Strasse · Old Town Hall · Church of St. Salvator · Fleischmarkt · Dr.-Karl-Lueger-Ring · Teinfaltstrasse · Freyung · Tiefer Graben · Färbergasse · Platz am Hof · Hoher Markt · Burgtheater · Herrengasse · Naglergasse · Tuchlauben · Brandstätte · Bauernmarkt · Rotenturmstrasse · Bankgasse · Wallnerstrasse · St. Peter's Church · Archbishop's Palace · Church of the Minorites · Kohlmarkt · Graben · Pestsäule (Plague Column) · St. Stephan's Cathedral · Stephansplatz · Austrian Federal Chancellery · St. Michael's Church · Stock-im-Eisen-Platz · Lowelstr. · Schauflergasse · Spanish Riding School · Dorotheergasse · Church of the Teutonic Order · Singerstrasse · Volksgarten · Ballhausplatz · In der Burg · Plankengasse · Alte Hofburg Palace · Josephsplatz · Dorotheum · Helden-platz · National Library · Augustinerstr. · Kapuziner Church · Himmelpfortgasse · Neue Burg · Augustinerbastei · Burgring · Dorotheum · Johannesgasse · Maria-Theresien-Platz · Burggarten · Albertina · Kärntner Strasse · St. Anna's Church · Schellinggasse · Kunsthistorisches Museum (Museum of Fine Arts) · Goethegasse · Opernring · Albertinaplatz · Philharm.str.

An unexpected appearance in the doorway at Schreyvogelgasse 8.

look for clues at Harry's flat in the **Palais Pallavicini** at **Josephsplatz 5.** It is there that Martins learns that eyewitnesses spotted an enigmatic "third man" at the scene of the accident. The mysterious number three turns out to be Lime himself, a suspicious character whose actions are accompanied by the haunting zither music of Anton Karas. He's alive, and makes one of cinema's greatest appearances when he suddenly turns up in the doorway at **Schreyvogelgasse 8.** The reunion turns sour at the **Ferris wheel** in the **Prater amusement park** when the two finally meet, and Lime, unable to win Martins to the dark side, threatens his friend's life. Not until the film's climactic end, after a chase that leads to a fictitious secret doorway by the **Mariensäule** on **Platz am Hof** and down through the **sewers** beneath the city, does Martins realize that, alas, there's no saving Harry. Fans of the film can accompany specialist Brigitte Timmermann on tours of the subterranean system, just one aspect of the film covered in her comprehensive book on *The Third Man.*

British novelist Graham Greene had already developed the idea for his screenplay with director Carol Reed when he arrived at the luxurious **Hotel Sacher** at **Philharmonikerstrasse 4** in 1948. The auberge doubled as the British army headquarters, and Greene, known for low-level intelligence gathering, sat at the information nexus of the occupation by the four Allied powers. The French, Americans, British, and Russians ran separate sectors and conducted bureaucratic turf wars over the bombed-out city, more than a third of it reduced to rubble in air raids. Greene had heard stories of criminals going underground, using the sewers, storm drains, and canals of the city for their sordid business: Penicillin pilfered from hospitals was watered down and sold on the black market, a practice that killed many who needed the drug to battle infection. This scandalous practice gave Greene his plot, and he modeled his main character Harry Lime on an intelligence agent he had known. *The Third Man* distills the dilemma of survival into a showdown between good and evil.

INDEX OF NAMES

Abbott, Diahnne 106
Abraham, F. Murray 130-131
Adjani, Isabelle 115
Affleck, Ben 74-75
Aimée, Anouk 140
Alberini, Filoteo 135
Albert, Eddie 138-139
Alea, Tomás Gutiérrez 36, 42-43
Alekan, Henri 18
Allen, Corey 84
Allen, Woody 6, 68, 82, 93, 99, 108-109, 111, 112, 166, 175
Altman, Robert 82
Ambrosio, Arturo 135
Andreasi, Felice 186
Andresen, Björn 180-181
Anschütz, Ottomar 12
Askin, Leon 16
Attenborough, Richard 68
Austen, Jane 76
Autiero, Gaetano 178-179
Avery, Brian 87
Axelrod, George 103
Aykroyd, Dan 26-27, 64

Backus, Jim 84
Bacon, Kevin 156
Badalamenti, Angelo 96
Bancroft, Anne 86
Barkin, Ellen 64
Basinger, Kim 81, 94-95
Battiston, Giuseppe 186
Bay, Michael 156
Béart, Emmanuelle 132
Beatles, The 66, 67
Beatty, Warren 58
Beckinsale, Kate 36-37
Bel Geddes, Barbara 148
Belmondo, Jean-Paul 118-119
Belushi, John 26-27, 64
Bening, Annette 122
Beresford, Bruce 160
Bergman, Ingrid 68, 114, 179
Berridge, Elizabeth 130
Bertolucci, Bernardo 8, 28, 115, 134
Binoche, Juliette 120-121
Bishop, Joey 60
Bisset, Jacqueline 150
Blades, Rubén 54
Blanchett, Cate 142-143
Bleibtreu, Moritz 20
Blessed, Brian 37
Bogarde, Dirk 180-181
Bogart, Humphrey 81, 90, 114, 118, 145
Bois, Curt 18
Bonham Carter, Helena 34, 184
Bonneville, Hugh 72
Boulanger, Daniel 118
Boyle, Peter 106
Bozzuffi, Marcel 104-105
Branagh, Kenneth 30, 36-37, 66
Brando, Marlon 85, 115
Brazzi, Rossano 175, 178
Brecht, Bertolt 13
Briers, Richard 36-37
Broadbent, Jim 76
Brosnan, Pierce 67, 154-155
Brown, James 26-27
Bruckheimer, Jerry 156
Buain, Daniel 120
Buchholz, Horst 16-17

Burgess, Anthony 70
Burnham, Daniel 23
Burns, Mark 180
Burton, Richard 86

Cage, Nicolas 57, 156
Cagney, James 16
Caine, Michael 66
Callow, Simon 34, 130
Calloway, Cab 26
Campion, Jane 31, 160
Cancelier, Urbain 124
Candy, John 26-27
Capellani, Albert 114
Capote, Truman 103
Capri, Ahna 50
Carax, Leos 116, 120-121
Carlini, Paolo 138
Carlos, Walter "Wendy" 70
Carradine, David 50
Cartier-Bresson, Henri 142
Castro, Fidel 39, 42
Catania, Antonio 186
Chaka Khan 26
Chambers, Emma 72
Chan, Jackie 47
Chandler, Raymond 88
Chaplin, Charlie 22, 23
Charles, Ray 26
Chase, Chevy 893
Cheadle, Don 82
Chen, Joan 8-9
Cheung, Maggie 48, 52, 54
Chevalier, Maurice 114
Chow, Stephen 47
Christie, Julie 182
Clarke, Warren 70
Clift, Montgomery 13
Clooney, George 60-61
Close, Glenn 122-123
Clouse, Robert 50
Coen, Joel 93
Collette, Toni 162
Coltrane, Robbie 22, 78-79
Columbus, Chris 78, 154
Connery, Sean 28-29, 67, 77, 156
Cooder, Joachim 44
Cooder, Ry 44
Coppola, Sofia 172-173
Corri, Adrienne 70
Corrieri, Sergio 40
Costner, Kevin 22, 28-29
Cotten, Joseph 32, 188
Coward, Noel 39
Cox, Brian 112-113
Cromwell, James 94-95
Crosby, Bing 86
Crowe, Russell 81, 94-95
Cruise, Tom 95, 132-133, 159
Cruz, Vladimir 42
Crystal, Billy 100, 110, 115
Culkin, Macaulay 22
Cuny, Alain 140-141
Curtis, Richard 72, 76
Czerny, Henry 132-133

Damon, Matt 6, 61, 142, 176
Daniels, William 86
David, Liliane 118
Davidtz, Embeth 76-77
Davis Jr., Sammy 58, 60-61
Dawson, Rosario 112-113

Day-Lewis, Daniel 34-35, 66, 99
De Mille, Cecil B. 99
De Niro, Robert 28-29, 58, 62-63, 98, 99, 106-107
De Palma, Brian 28, 32, 132
De Sica, Vittorio 134, 136
Dean, James 6, 81, 84-85
Debbouze, Jamel 124
Del Rio, Rebekah 96-97
Del Toro, Benicio 64
Delon, Alain 115, 142
Delpy, Julie 188
Dench, Judi 34-35, 74
Depp, Johnny 57, 64
DeVito, Danny 80, 94-95
Diaz, Cameron 24
DiCaprio, Leonardo 94
Dick, Philip K. 90
Dickinson, Angie 60
Dietrich, Marlene 13, 16
Dillon, Matt 82
Dommartin, Solveig 18
Doran, Ann 84
Dotrice, Roy 130
Drago, Billy 29
Dreyfus, James 72
Du Maurier, Daphne 175, 182
Dun, Dennis 8
Dunaway, Faye 88
Duvall, Robert 150

Eastwood, Clint 152-153, 156
Ebert, Roger 28
Ebsen, Buddy 102-103
Edison, Thomas 12, 22, 66, 99, 114
Edwards, Blake 102
Ekberg, Anita 136, 140-141
Elliott, Stephan 160
Elliott, Denholm 34
Elliott, Alison 184
Ellroy, James 94
Ephron, Nora 110-111

Falk, Peter 18-19
Faris, Anna 172
Fat, Chow Yun 48
Fell, Norman 150
Fellini, Federico 92, 116, 134, 136, 140-141, 142, 175
Ferrer, Ibrahim 44
Field, Sally 154
Fielding, Helen 76
Fiennes, Joseph 74, 175
Fierstein, Harvey 154-155
Firth, Colin 74-75, 76, 122
Fishburne, Laurence 164
Fisher, Carrie 26-27, 110
Fontaine, Joan 32
Ford, Harrison 90-91, 116
Forman, Milos 122, 127, 128, 130-131
Forristal, Susan 92
Forster, E.M. 30, 34
Foster, Jodie 31, 106-107
Foster, Gloria 164
Fox, William 99
Frankenheimer, John 105
Franklin, Aretha 26
Frears, Stephen 122
Freeman, Kathleen 26
Friedkin, William 104

Fuji, Takashi 172
Furneaux, Yvonne 140

Gabor, Zsa Zsa 115
Ganz, Bruno 18, 186
Garbo, Greta 13
Garcia, Andy 28-29
Gattorno, Francisco 42
George, Heinrich 13
Gere, Richard 82
Gershwin, George 108-109, 111
Gibson, Mel 160
Gielgud, John 66
Gilliam, Terry 58, 59, 64-65
Gish, Lilian and Dorothy 32
Go, Jade 9
Godard, Jean-Luc 115, 116, 118-119, 120
Goldwyn, Samuel 99
Gong, Li 54
González, Rubén 44-45
González, Juan de Marcos 44
Gordon, Don 150
Grandison, Pippa 162
Grant, Cary 68, 100
Grant, Hugh 66, 68, 72, 76
Grant, Richard E. 92-93
Greene, Graham 39, 189
Griffiths, Rachel 162-163
Grint, Rupert 78-79
Grüber, Klaus-Michael 120-121
Guardino, Harry 152
Guinness, Alec 39, 66

Hackman, Gene 104-105
Hallström, Lasse 175
Hamilton, Murray 86
Hammond, Rosalind 162
Hampton, Christopher 122-123
Han, Maggie 8
Hanks, Tom 100, 110, 116
Hannah, Daryl 90-91
Hannam, Ken 160
Hanson, Curtis 94-95
Harrelson, Woody 57
Harring, Laura Elena 96-97
Harris, Richard 78
Harris, Ed 156
Hart, Ian 78
Hartl, Karl 188
Hauer, Rutger 90-91
Havel, Milos 127
Hawke, Ethan 188
Hawks, Howard 145
Hedaya, Dan 96
Helmore, Tom 148
Hemingway, Ernest 39, 40
Hemingway, Mariel 108-109
Henner, Marilu 92
Hepburn, Audrey 98, 102-103, 114, 136, 138-139
Hepburn, Katharine 175, 178-179
Hepworth, Cecil 66
Hertz, Carl 160
Highsmith, Patricia 142
Hirata, Akihiko 170-171
Hitchcock, Alfred 22, 66, 67, 148
Hoffman, Dustin 81, 86
Hoffman, Philip Seymour 103, 112-113, 142-143
Hogan, P.J. 22, 160, 162
Holliday, Polly 154

Honda, Ishiro 170
Hopkins, Anthony 31
Hopper, Dennis 84-85
Hoskins, Bob 66
Howard, Ron 97
Howard, Trevor 188
Hughes, Howard 80
Hui, Ann 48
Hui, Michael 47, 54
Hulce, Tom 130-131
Hunter, Bill 162
Hurt, William 115
Huston, John 88-89, 115

Ibarra, Mirta 42-43
Ifans, Rhys 72
Imamura, Shohei 168
Irons, Jeremy 46, 54-55, 66, 127, 128, 175
Itami, Juzo 168
Ito, Daisuke 167
Ivory, James 30, 34-35

Jackson, Mick 92
Jackson, Peter 97
James, Steve 22
James, Henry 175, 184-185
Jarrett, Belinda 162
Jennings, Alex 184
Jeunet, Jean-Pierre 124-125
Johansson, Scarlett 68, 167, 172-173
Jolson, Al 24, 80
Jones, Gemma 76
Jones, Jeffrey 130-131

Kadár, Ján 128
Kaneshiro, Takeshi 52
Karas, Anton 188-189
Karlin, Miriam 71
Kassovitz, Mathieu 124
Keaton, Michael 36-37
Keaton, Diane 82, 108-109, 111
Keitel, Harvey 99, 106-107
Kelly, Jim 50
Kelly, Gene 70, 100, 114, 115
Kerr, Deborah 100
Kidman, Nicole 115, 159
Kingsley, Ben 66
Kirby, Bruno 66
Kitano, Takeshi 168
Knaup, Herbert 20
Kochi, Momoko 170-171
Korda, Alexander 67, 188
Król, Joachim 20
Kubrick, Stanley 68, 70
Kurosawa, Akira 168, 170, 171
Kurtz, Swoosie 122-123

Laclos, Choderlos de 122
Ladd, Diane 88
Lamarr (Kiesler), Hedy 127
Lambert, Christopher 115
Lancaster, Burt 156
Landis, John 26
Lang, Fritz 13, 91
Lapaine, Daniel 163
Larch, John 152
Laurents, Arthur 179
Lavant, Denis 120-121
Law, Jude 6, 142
Lawford, Peter 60
Lawless, Peter 164

Leach, Rosemary 34
Lean, David 178-179
Lee, Brandon 51
Lee, Bruce 47, 50-51
Lee, Spike 100, 112-113
Lee, Sophie 162
Leigh, Vivien 67
Leonard, Robert Sean 36-37
Leone, Sergio 100
Le Roy, Mervyn 135
Leung Chiu Wai, Tony 52-53
Leyva, Pio 44
Li, Jet 47
Lin, Brigitte 52
Lo Bianco, Tony 104
Lollobrigida, Gina 134
Lone, John 8-10
Lopez, Perry 88-89
Loren, Sophia 134, 141
Lorre, Peter 13
Lucas, George 144
Luhrmann, Baz 160
Lumière, L.-J. and Auguste 12, 66, 114-115, 159
Lynch, David 81, 96-97

Machatý, Gustav 127
MacLaine, Shirley 61
Madden, John 74-75
Magee, Patrick 70
Maglietta, Licia 186-187
Maguire, Tobey 64, 95
Maguire, Sharon 66, 76
Malkovich, John 122-123
Mamet, David 28
Mancini, Henry 103
Mangano, Silvana 180
Mann, Thomas 175, 180-181
Marcus, James 70
Marini, Lou 26
Martin, Dean 60-61
Martin, Steve 82, 92-93
Marx, Frederick 22
Mason, Hilary 182
Massironi, Marina 186-187
Mastroianni, Marcello 134, 140-141
Matania, Clelia 182
McCabe, Richard 72
McDowell, Malcolm 70
McEwan, Ian 175
McGovern, Elizabeth 184
McInnerny, Tim 72
McKee, Gina 72
McKellen, Ian 116
McQueen, Steve 150-151
Mead, Syd 91
Menzel, Jiří 128
Merchant, Ismail 30, 34-35
Merlin, Serge 124-125
Messter, Oskar 12
Michell, Roger 72
Milestone, Lewis 60
Miller, Ann 96
Miller, Bennett 103
Miller, George 160
Mineo, Sal 84
Minghella, Anthony 136, 142-143
Minnelli, Vincente 114
Miranda, Isa 178
Mirren, Helen 66
Mitchum, John 152

Miyazaki, Hayao 168
Mizoguchi, Kenji 168
Monroe, Marilyn 81, 86, 98, 103, 136
Montgomery, Monty 96
Moore, Demi 57
Moore, Julianne 31
Moore, Robin 104
Moore, Roger 115
Moorhouse, Jocelyn 160
Morricone, Ennio 28
Morse, David 156
Moss, Carrie-Anne 164
Mulholland, William 88
Murata, Takeo 170
Murnau, Friedrich Wilhelm 13
Murphy, Eddie 82
Murphy, Matt "Guitar" 26
Murphy, Michael 108
Murray, Bill 172-173
Mussolini, Benito 135
Mussolini, Vittorio 135

Neal, Patricia 102
Newman, Paul 22
Newton, Thandie 158, 159
Nichols, Mike 86
Nicholson, Jack 64, 81, 88
Nielsen, Asta 13
Ninchi, Annibale 140
Noël, Magali 140
Noir, Thierry 19
Norton, Edward 112-113
Novak, Kim 148-149
Noyce, Phillip 159, 160

O'Toole, Peter 8-9, 66
Oakland, Simon 150
Oberon, Merle 66
Ochoa, Eliades 44
Olivier, Laurence 66, 67
Olmos, Edward James 90
Oshima, Nagisa 168
Ozu, Yasujiro 168

Pacino, Al 32, 175
Paltrow, Gwyneth 74-75, 142-143
Pantoliano, Joe 164-165
Paquin, Anna 112-113
Parke, MacDonald 178
Parker, Sarah Jessica 57, 92-93
Pasolini, Pier Paolo 136
Pasquale, Frédéric de 104
Pathé, Charles 114
Paul, Robert W. 66
Paull, Lawrence 91
Pearce, Guy 94
Peck, Gregory 136, 138-139
Penn, Sean 172
Peppard, George 102-103
Pepper, Barry 112-113
Pérez, Fernando 40
Perry, Joseph 160
Perugorría, Jorge 42-43
Pesci, Joe 58, 62-63
Petri, Nina 20
Pfeiffer, Michelle 99, 122-123
Philippe, Ryan 82
Pileggi, Nicholas 62
Pitt, Brad 61-62
Polanski, Roman 88-89, 100, 116

Polgar, Alfred 13
Pollack, Sydney 32, 40
Portuondo, Omara 44-45
Potente, Franka 20
Power, Hartley 138
Prawer Jhabvala, Ruth 35
Presley, Elvis 58, 60
Prieto, Rodrigo 112
Prowse, David 71
Proyas, Alex 160
Pulver, Liselotte 16

Radcliffe, Daniel 78
Rampling, Charlotte 184
Ray, Nicholas 84
Redford, Robert 22, 57, 58
Redgrave, Vanessa 132-133
Reed, Carol 13, 39, 66, 188-189
Reeves, Keanu 36-37, 122-123, 164
Reiner, Rob 110-111
Renella, Pat 150
Reno, Jean 132
Rey, Fernando 104-105
Rhames, Ving 132
Ribisi, Giovanni 172
Ricci, Christina 64
Rickles, Don 62
Riefenstahl, Leni 13
Roache, Linus 184
Roberts, Julia 22, 24, 59, 61, 68, 72, 82, 162, 175
Robertson, Cliff 32
Robinson, Andrew 152
Roeg, Nicolas 182
Rohde, Armin 20
Roncoroni, Carlo 135
Rooney, Mickey 102
Root, John W. 23
Rose, Jane 178
Ross, Katharine 86-87
Rossellini, Roberto 12, 13, 32, 134, 179
Rowling, Joanne 78
Rufus 124
Rush, Geoffrey 74
Russell, Theresa 127
Ryan, Meg 100, 110
Ryder, Winona 125

Sakamoto, Ryuichi 8
Sander, Otto 5, 18
Sanderson, William 90-91
Sands, Julian 34
Santesso, Walter 136, 140
Santoni, Reni 152
Saxon, John 50
Scheider, Roy 104
Schepisi, Fred 160
Schwarzenegger, Arnold 82
Scorsese, Martin 57, 62-64, 80, 99, 106-107, 112-113, 136
Scott, Ridley 31, 81, 90-91, 136
Scott Thomas, Kristin 132-133
Seberg, Jean 118
Secchiaroli, Tazio 141
Segundo, Compay 44-45
Selig, William 23, 24
Sellers, Peter 66
Serato, Massimo 182-183
Shaffer, Peter 131
Shakespeare, William 36-37, 74-75, 175

Sharp, Anthony 71
Shaw, Fiona 78
Shepherd, Cybill 106-107
Shih, Kien 50
Shimura, Takashi 170
Shue, Elisabeth 57
Siegel, Don 152
Sinatra, Frank 58, 60-61, 100
Siragusa, Tony 112
Sitch, Rob 160
Skelton, Red 61
Skladanowsky, Max 12
Slater, Christian 156
Smith, Charles Martin 28-29
Smith, Maggie 34, 66, 78
Soderbergh, Steven 61, 127, 128
Softley, Iain 184-185
Soldini, Silvio 186
Spacey, Kevin 94-95
Spencer, John 156
Spielberg, Steven 27, 40, 90, 175
Stalens, Marion 120
Stewart, James 148
Stone, Sharon 62-63
Strathairn, David 95
Streep, Meryl 125
Sutherland, Donald 182
Suzuki, Kensaku 167
Sverák, Jan 128

Tabío, Juan Carlos 40
Takarada, Akira 170-171
Tanaka, Eizo 167
Tanaka, Tomoyuki 170
Tarantino, Quentin 61, 82, 118
Tarn, Michael 70
Tate, Sharon 89
Tautou, Audrey 116, 124
Taylor, Elizabeth 73, 86
Tennant, Victoria 92
Theroux, Justin 96
Thompson, Hunter S. 57, 64-65
Thompson, Emma 36-37, 66
Thurman, Uma 122-123
Tiffin, Pamela 16
Towne, Robert 88
Travolta, John 100
Truffaut, François 118
Turkel, Joe 90-91
Turner, Kathleen 86
Tykwer, Tom 14, 20-21

Ustinov, Peter 66

Valli, Romolo 180
Valli, Alida 188
Vangelis 90
Vaughn, Robert 150-151
Vernon, John 152-153
Villalonga, José Luis de 102
Visconti, Luchino 134, 180-181
Voight, Jon 132

Wachowski, Andy and Larry 164-165
Wall, Robert 50-51
Walsh, M. Emmet 90-91
Wang, Wayne 54-55
Warhol, Andy 80
Warner, Jack 60
Washington, Denzel 36, 82
Watson, Emma 78-79
Watts, Naomi 80, 96-97, 115
Weaver, Sigourney 125
Weaving, Hugo 164-165
Webb, Charles 86
Wegener, Paul 127
Weintraub, Jerry 60
Weir, Peter 160
Welles, Orson 188
Wenders, Wim 4, 5, 13, 18-19, 40, 44-45
Widmer, Jörg 44
Wilder, Billy 13, 16-17, 103, 138
Williams, Robin 154-155
Willis, Bruce 82
Wilson, Elizabeth 86
Winger, Debra 115
Winslet, Kate 94
Wong, Faye 48, 52-53
Wong, Kar-Wai 48, 52-53
Wong, Victor 8
Wood, Natalie 84
Woods, James 62
Wright, Frank Lloyd 81, 91, 98
Wright, Geoffrey 160
Wright Penn, Robin 22
Wu, Vivian 10
Wyler, William 136, 138

Yates, Peter 150
Yeoh, Michelle 48
Ying, Ruocheng 8
Young, Sean 90-91

Zecca, Ferdinand 114
Zeffirelli, Franco 31
Zellweger, Renée 76
Zwerling, Darrell 88

CREDITS

THE AUTHORS

Claudia Hellmann is an American Studies specialist and freelance journalist who works for various travel and cultural publications. She discovered her passion for film in L.A. and New York.

Claudine Weber-Hof is an architectural historian who specialized in city history during her studies at Georgetown University and the University of Virginia. She is a freelance editor and journalist.

THE PHOTOGRAPHER

Cornwall native David John Weber chose city portraits as his focus during his studies with the New York Institute of Photography. His great love is shooting photo essays of the Alps, just south of his adopted home of Münsing, Germany.

TEXT CREDITS

The Urban Landscape: First published in the USA by Farrar, Straus and Giroux, LLC, 19 Union Square West, New York, NY 10003. First published in the UK by Faber and Faber Limited, 3 Queen Square, London WC1N 3AU.
Hong Kong & San Francisco chapters: Daniela Yew

PHOTO CREDITS

Front cover, top: David John Weber; center: Volkmar Janicke; bottom: David John Weber; back cover, top and center: David John Weber; spine: Birgit Koch/IFA; film stills on the cover: Cinetext Bild- und Textarchiv GmbH, Frankfurt am Main.

Film stills and posters in this volume provided with few exceptions by Cinetext Bild- und Textarchiv GmbH, Frankfurt am Main. Also from Cinetext: 32 t., 57 t. and c., 59 b.l., 65 t.r., 81 t., 82 t., 85 c., 180 b.r., 185 b.l., 188 b.l.

David John Weber: 7, 12 l., 13 b., 14 b., 16 b.r., 17 t.r. and b., 19 b., 21 all, 30, 31 b., 31 c., 32 c. and b., 34 b.r., 35 t.l. and b.r., 56 b., 61 t., 63 b.r., 67 top 3, 68 t. and b., 73 t. (all 3), 74 b.l., 75 b.l., 76 b., 77 c. and b., 78 b.r., 79 (all 3), 82 b., 85 t.l. and b., 87 t. and r., 89 t.l. and b., 90 b., 91 b., 92 b.l., 93 t. and b.l., 95 t.r. and b.l., 96 b.l., 97 (both), 98 t.l. and b., 99 b., 100 (all 3), 102 b.r., 105 b.l., 106 b., 108 t.l., 109 t.l., b.l. and b.r., 110 b., 111 t. and b., 113 c.r., 115 t. and c.r., 116 t., 119 t.l. and t.r., 120 b., 122 b., 123 t.l. and b., 124 t.l., 125 t.r. and b.l., 128 (all 3), 130 b.l. and b.r., 131 b., 132 b., 133 b.l., 134, 135 t. and b., 136 (all 3), 138 b.l., 139 b., 143 t.l., 144, 145 b., 146 t., 151 t.l. and b.l., 152 t.l., 155 t. and b., 157 c.r., 171 c.l., 175 t., 176 t., 178 b., 179 t.r. and b., 182 b., 183 t.r., 186 b.l., 187 c. and b., 189 c.

Darren Baker: 36 b.; Alex Bramwell: 40 c.; Luke Brighty: 162 b., 163 b., 165 b.l., b.c. and b.r.; Martin Bunzendahl: 23 c. and b., 26 b., 27 b., 28 t.l., 29 c.; Richard Ammon, www.GlobalGayz.com: 42 b.; Arthur Duncan: 9 c.r., 10 t.; Hans Engels: 38, 39 c., 43 t., 44 b.l. and b.r., 45 b.; Fairmont Hotels and Resorts: 157 c.l.; Dan Falcon, private collection: 24 b.r., 40 t., 51 b., 60 b.r., 61 b.l., 65 b.l., 86 c.; Julia Fuchshuber: 37 c.r.; Herbert Hartmann: 121 r.; Jerry Harpur/Hatfield House: 75 b.r.; Claudia Hellmann: 40 b., 103 t.r., 104 b., 107 b.; Dieter Hellmann: 31 t., 174; Hong Kong Tourism Board: 46 b., 47 all, 48 t. and b.l., 53 t., 55 b.l. and b.r.; Illinois Department of Commerce and Community Affairs: 22 c. (Marc Lansky), 23 t., 24 t. (Vito Palmisano) and b.l., 27 t.l., 28 b.;

Interfoto Pressebildagentur & Bildarchiv: 5; ISIFA/IFA: 131 t.l.; Volkmar Janicke: 8 b., 9 t., 10 b., 11 b., 13 t., 14 t., 18 b., 39 t., 50 b., 126, 127 b., 158, 159 c., 160 b.l. and b.r., 166, 167 t. and b.r., 168 c., 170 b., 172 l.; Andrew F. Kazmierski: 99 t.; Birgit Koch/IFA: 81 c.; Las Vegas News Bureau/LVCVA: 56 t., 58 b.r.; Renee Lee: 145 t.; Leonardo: 58 b.l., 63 l., 141 b.l., 181 l.; David Liu: 80; Los Angeles Convention & Visitors Bureau: 81 b. (Glenn Cormier), 91 t.r. (Michele & Tom Grimm), 95 b.r. (Tom & Michele Grimm); Celia Martinez: 133 b.r.; Linda & Colin McKie: 160 t.; Stacy Munn: 127 t.; Christian Noval: 140 b.; Park Hyatt Tokyo: 171 t., 173 t.r.; Reverse Angle Library GmbH, Argos Films S.A., 1987: 18 t., 19 t. and c.; Reverse Angle Library GmbH, 1999: 44 t., 45 t.; Bradley Rex: 58 t., 59 b.r.; Jennifer Rolwes: 153 b.; Juergen Sack: 167 b.l.; San Francisco Convention & Visitors Bureau: 146 b., 148 b., 156 b. (Lewis Sommer); David Schultz: 168 t.; Harris Shiffman: 149 t.; Franky Sze: 113 b.; Tourism New South Wales: 159 t. (Hamilton Land); Sally Trussler: 71 c. and b.; Claudine Weber-Hof: 116 b.; The Westin Sydney: 160 c.; Daniela Yew: 146 c., 152 b.

See our full listing of illustrated books at www.bucher-publishing.com

CONCEPT

Claudia Hellmann and Claudine Weber-Hof with support from Gerhard Grubbe, Grubbe Media GmbH, Munich, Germany

EDITORIAL COORDINATION Dr. Birgit Kneip
MANUSCRIPT EDITED BY Peter Meredith, Severna Park, Maryland
TRANSLATION OF PARTS OF THE MANUSCRIPT FROM GERMAN TO ENGLISH Claudia Hellmann and Claudine Weber-Hof

GRAPHIC DESIGN, CONCEPT & LAYOUT

VOR-ZEICHEN, Munich, Germany, Marion Sauer and Johannes Reiner, www.vor-zeichen.de

CARTOGRAPHY Astrid Fischer-Leitl, Munich, Germany
PRODUCTION Bettina Schippel
LITHOGRAPHY Repro Ludwig, Zell am See, Austria
PRINTING AND BINDING Printer Trento, Trento, Italy

This volume has been carefully researched and checked for accuracy by the authors and by the publisher. The publishing house cannot accept any liability for the correctness of the information in this book. We are grateful for any corrections or suggestions. Please send submissions to: C.J. Bucher Publishing, Product Management, P.O. Box 80 02 40, 81602 Munich, Germany, e-mail: info@bucher-publishing.com

Most of the film locations in this volume are open to the public, either for visitation or viewing. Others are private property. Please do not disturb the owners or residents of private property. By no means should private property be trespassed upon.